THE PENGUIN CLASSICS

FOUNDER EDITOR (1944–64): E. V. RIEU

MARIE DE RABUTIN CHANTAL, Marquise de Sévigné (1626–1696), one of the world's greatest letter-writers, was born in Paris, in what is now the Place des Vosges, married at eighteen to the Marquis de Sévigné and was left a widow at twenty-five with two children, a daughter, who was to become Mme de Grignan, and a son. For over forty years, during the period of Mazarin and the Fronde and then the brilliant first thirty years of the personal reign of Louis XIV, she moved in literary and society circles, knew personally almost everybody who counted – her close friends were Mme de La Fayette and La Rochefoucauld – went to the plays of Corneille, Molière and Racine, heard the orations of Bossuet and Bourdaloue and followed closely all the political and military events. She narrated in her letters all the news and scandal of the Court, from the behaviour of the King's mistresses and the emergence of Mme de Maintenon (another personal friend) and the goings-on of the homosexual Monsieur, the King's brother, to the Revocation of the Edict of Nantes and the ensuing persecutions, the arrival in France of the deposed James II and the beginning of the reign of William and Mary. The letters, especially from 1671, when her daughter left for Provence to join her husband, are a continuous chronicle and commentary of events, told with a rare descriptive gift, a bubbling sense of humour tempered with introspective melancholy and a love of nature quite unusual at that period.

More than anyone else she typifies the average educated person whose tastes, attitudes, likes and dislikes, beliefs and prejudices form and explain the great Age of Louis XIV.

LEONARD TANCOCK has spent most of his life in or near London, apart from a year as a student in Paris, most of the Second World War in Wales, and three periods in American universities as visiting professor. He is a Fellow of University College, London, and was formerly Reader in French at the University. Since preparing his first Penguin Classic in 1949, he has been intensely interested in the problems of translation, about which he has written, lectured and broadcast, and which he believes is an art rather than a science. His numerous translations for the Penguin Classics include Zola's *Germinal*, *Thérèse Raquin*, *The Debacle*, *L'Assommoir* and *La Bête Humaine*; Diderot's *The Nun*, *Rameau's Nephew* and *D'Alembert's Dream*; Maupassant's *Pierre and Jean*; Marivaux's *Up from the Country*; Constant's *Adolphe*; Prévost's *Manon Lescaut*; La Rochefoucauld's *Maxims*; and Voltaire's *Letters on England*.

Madame de Sévigné

*

SELECTED LETTERS

*

TRANSLATED

WITH AN INTRODUCTION BY

LEONARD TANCOCK

Penguin Books

Penguin Books Ltd, Harmondsworth, Middlesex, England
Penguin Books, 625 Madison Avenue, New York 10022, New York, U.S.A.
Penguin Books Australia Ltd, Ringwood, Victoria, Australia
Penguin Books Canada Ltd, 2801 John Street, Markham, Ontario, Canada L3R 1B4
Penguin Books (N.Z.) Ltd, 182–190 Wairau Road, Auckland 10, New Zealand

–

First published 1982

–

Made and printed in Great Britain by
Richard Clay (The Chaucer Press) Ltd, Bungay, Suffolk
Filmset in Monophoto Ehrhardt by
Northumberland Press Ltd, Gateshead, Tyne and Wear

CONTENTS

INTRODUCTION

With the possible exception of Voltaire, Mme de Sévigné is the greatest letter-writer in French literature. She is certainly among the three or four greatest the world has known. But whereas Voltaire's correspondence is cosmopolitan, addressed to everybody of distinction in Europe, including scientists, politicians and even crowned heads, and his subjects, literary, political and what the eighteenth century called philosophical, were part of the development of thought in the eighteenth century, Mme de Sévigné wrote to a limited number of family and friends. Yet paradoxically that very fact makes her letters not only deeper but much wider in their range than those of Voltaire. For in addition to the accounts of public and political events, wars, literary and artistic matters (and she knew personally almost everybody, from the highest in the Court downwards), the letters are full of family preoccupations, concern for people's health, a bubbling sense of humour and, as so often happens in people with a strong sense of the comical, a vein of melancholy, almost morbid introspection, a love of nature, solitude and meditation very rare indeed for her time and a genuine, if somewhat conventional, religious faith. As a narrator, describer of people, dress, places, details of all kinds, she is unsurpassed, and some of her portraits bear comparison with those of La Bruyère.

Yet with all these gifts she might best be characterized as a writer of supremely articulate 'averageness', and that is what makes her letters so illuminating. She is the average educated person for whom the great artists of the classical age produced their work. Her opinions, tastes, prejudices, attitudes, hopes and fears are those which, so to speak, form and explain the great Age of Louis XIV.

Marie de Rabutin Chantal was born in February 1626 in the Place Royale, today the Place des Vosges and still one of the architectural gems of Paris. It was then one of the most fashionable residential parts of Paris; Richelieu lived there and it was the scene of one of Corneille's early comedies, *La Place Royale*. In the nineteenth century Victor Hugo lived there, and his house is now a museum. Her father came of old Burgundian nobility and her grandmother, Jeanne de Chantal, was to be canonized in the eighteenth century. Her mother, Marie de Coulanges, belonged to a wealthy financial family. The child lost her father in 1627 and her mother in 1633, and she was brought up, still in the Place Royale, in the Coulanges family. Her official guardians were her uncle Philippe de Coulanges and his wife. Another uncle, Christophe de Coulanges, whom she later called *le Bien Bon* and who was one of those worldly abbés of the time and also a skilful financier, managed her affairs all his life and she loved him as a father. Her cousin Philippe Emmanuel ('le petit Coulanges') she thought of as a young brother, and he and his wife (a cousin of Louvois) were close friends all through her life.

Her cousin on her father's side, Roger, known as Bussy-Rabutin, was a brilliant, spiteful man, who in his scandalous *Histoire Amoureuse des Gaules* (1660) drew a wicked portrait of her under the name of Mme de Cheneville. They had been the best of friends, but his nastiness caused an estrangement for some years. Ultimately she forgave him. Many of their letters to each other survive, including a very amusing exchange when she forgave him, and some of these are given in this selection.

The girl's education was remarkable even by modern standards, partly thanks to her mentors, Ménage and Chapelain, friends of the Coulanges family. She reached a high standard in Italian and knew some Spanish. Her Latin was on more of a schoolgirl level – she confessed later in life that she preferred reading the Latin classics with an Italian version at her elbow. Her reading all through her life was surprisingly deep and wide for a society woman: French history, including medieval, works of philosophy, religion and theology, above all what the French call *moralistes* – writers who delve into human character and behaviour – and that in her case included Montaigne and Rabelais. Not that she neglected her great contemporaries, Corneille, Molière, La Fontaine and the Pascal of the *Lettres Provinciales*. She had a slight mistrust of Racine and thought he wrote some of his great, passionate roles with an actress in view (usually La Champmeslé) rather than eternity. Her loyalty to Corneille is characteristic of her loyalty to all her old friends. Later in life she knew Boileau personally, and indeed he read his *Art Poétique* to her and a select band well before it was published. Nor were novels and romances neglected, such as *L'Astrée* and the interminable novels of her friend Mlle de Scudéry, while she rhapsodized about the *Cléopâtre* of La Calprenède. In addition to all that, she knew her Italian poets, *Don Quixote* and all sorts of foreign books.

In 1644, at eighteen, she married Henri de Sévigné, of old Breton nobility. The marriage was thoroughly unsatisfactory. Charming, no doubt, Sévigné was a spendthrift and at once began exercising his charm on other women. Fortunately a separation of their money was soon arranged, for he was killed in 1651 in a duel over another woman, leaving her with two young children, Françoise Marguerite, the future Mme de Grignan, born in 1646, and Charles, born in 1648. Thanks to the ever watchful *Bien Bon*, most of her fortune was intact.

During the troubled years of the Fronde Mme de Sévigné made several friendships that were to be lifelong. The most notable were with Mme de La Fayette and Mlle de Scudéry, both novelists, and with Mme Scarron, wife of the crippled and impotent burlesque poet Paul Scarron, who was destined as Mme de Maintenon to have one of the most astonishing careers in French history. Subsequent opinion has been divided; some have said that she enjoyed one of the most meteoric rises from nothing to the highest position in the land thanks merely to her great intellectual and moral qualities, others that she owed everything to devious calculation and was thoroughly evil and hypocritical. Chosen as a young and discreet widow to be governess to the King's children by Mme de Montespan, she finally replaced Montespan and other mistresses in the King's favour, converted him from his evil ways (in early middle age he was sated with women anyway), and after the death of the Queen married the King morganatically and was Queen in all but name for the last thirty years of the reign. She remained one of Mme de Sévigné's friends. Others in the circle were La Rochefoucauld, who shared his invalid later life with the equally ailing Mme de La Fayette, Cardinal de Retz, the Marquis de Pomponne and Nicolas Foucquet, the great financier who was impeached for corruption and whose trial, in 1664, was one of the *causes célèbres* of the century. Mme de Sévigné reported this trial in a series of letters to Pomponne so graphic that they read as though she had sat through the trial herself and taken shorthand notes.

In January 1669 came the event which altered the course of her life and to which we owe the great majority of the letters. Her daughter married the Comte de Grignan, then aged thirty-seven and twice widowed, who was shortly afterwards to be appointed Lieutenant-General (equivalent of Governor) of Provence and leave for the south of France and live either in his ancestral château of Grignan or in Aix. For a time Mme de Grignan remained in Paris, where her first child, a girl, was born in 1670. She left in February 1671 to rejoin her husband. Mme de Sévigné was prostrated with grief, and one might say that from that moment separation from her daughter was the central fact in her life. She tried to fill the aching void of loneliness by writing endless letters and holding, so to speak, a non-stop conversation with her loved one. 'Are you not mistaken, my child,' she writes on 20 January 1672, 'in the opinion you have of my letters? The other day some horrible man, seeing my immense letter, asked me whether I thought anyone could read it. I trembled, but with no intention of mending my ways, so abiding by what you say about them I shan't spare you a single trifle, small or large, that might amuse you. My life and sole pleasure is the correspondence I keep up with you; other things are far behind.'

It must be said that by any normal standard Mme de Sévigné's devotion to her daughter was morbidly, unreasonably possessive. Not only did she take separation from a married daughter as an unmitigated tragedy, but she lectured and nagged her continuously and to the point of interference about her health which, it is true, was delicate, about her behaviour, her extravagance and gambling. Nor was Grignan forgotten, for she continually blamed him also for his extravagant way of life, his gambling and debts. She must have been a formidable mother-in-law, and it says much for her other qualities that Grignan seems, in spite of all, to have looked upon her with affection and respect. She even deplores her daughter's frequent pregnancies (commonplace in those days of terrible infant mortality), and harps on their sleeping in separate beds, as though that were the answer.

But the idolatry in which she held her daughter did not apply to her son Charles. To him she was always a good, affectionate mother, but with none of the unhealthy love she had for Mme de Grignan. Charles had his father's charm and was easy-going, but with little vice in him. He experimented with many women, including actresses and the famous courtesan Ninon de Lenclos, before he made a good marriage, financially, at the then advanced age of thirty-four. The relationships between the members of the family were unusual, to put it mildly. On 8 April 1671, she writes to her daughter that she is glad that there has been a break with Ninon and that she has praised her son for coming back to the good life, but then she goes on to say that unfortunately Charles is still carrying on with the Champmeslé, the famous actress who created some of Racine's greatest roles and had been his mistress. Mme de Sévigné was no prude, and she describes with relish and in crude terms how poor Charles, having got the lady to the point, had had an attack of impotence, to his extreme discomfiture. That any man could have told his mother about this intimate humiliation is surprising, that the mother should recount this as a good joke to his sister is astonishing, but that the son should then say to his mother that he must have inherited her frigidity is astounding. How did he know? In the end they all seem to have had a good laugh about it.

The last twenty-five years of her life were spent between Paris, where for many years she lived in the Hôtel (now Museum) Carnavalet, in what is now the rue de Sévigné, only a few yards from her birthplace, at the Sévigné ancestral home, Les Rochers, near Vitré, and at her daughter's home, the château de Grignan, in Provence, with many short stays at the home of Le Bien Bon at Livry, about ten miles east of Paris, now swallowed up in greater Paris. There are therefore long gaps in the correspondence, either when she was visiting her daughter at Grignan or when Mme de Grignan was in or near Paris. Sometimes these visits lasted for several months.

Mme de Sévigné spent much time at Les Rochers for financial reasons, both because it was cheaper and because she could keep an eye on the profitable running of the estate. Although she should have been comfortably off, there was the constant drain of helping the debt-ridden Grignans or coming to the rescue of Charles during his many years of sowing wild oats. She also took her Breton responsibilities fairly seriously, in spite of frequent digs at the provincial conceit and funny ways of the French Celtic fringe.

It has been suggested above that Mme de Sévigné is a perfect specimen of the average educated person who explains and forms the Age of Louis XIV. That statement must be qualified slightly. In one or two ways she is not representative at all, but what is very significant is that when she does not quite conform to the accepted stereotype she nearly always apologizes for it or laughs it off as an oddity or funny quirk in herself.

The first commandment for the decent average citizen was: *Thou shalt conform to the practice of the majority, thou shalt not be different.* It was held by all right-minded people that the man who tries to be different, who thinks himself unique or original is either a conceited ass, a dangerous and anti-social person, comic or mad. At the very least he is a tiresome bore. It is noteworthy that in French to this day a secondary meaning of the adjective *original* is odd, eccentric, and that the noun *un original* means an odd fish, a crank, a 'character'. Most of Molière's greatest characters are *originaux* in this sense, or unbalanced people who try to impose their views upon others. And the same applies to those of La Bruyère.

So Mme de Sévigné respects the hierarchy, never questions the political situation or appalling social inequalities of the time, worships the King as the embodiment of the glory of France and fears any anti-social opinion or behaviour. This is also true in the matter of religion. Her own beliefs are orthodox but none the less sincere. But although her sympathies and many friends might be called Jansenist (her great friend Pomponne belonged to the Arnauld family), she greatly admires the orthodox Bossuet, while her favourite preacher is the Jesuit Bourdaloue. So it is not surprising that in common with the majority she hails the Revocation of the Edict of Nantes, with the ensuing persecutions and enforced 'conversions', as a masterly stroke of King and Church to rid the country of Protestants, those dangerous and treacherous pests. Which raises the question of cruelty. She lived of course in a brutal age, for all its polish, and to modern eyes she appears hard and lacking in compassion, except when the sufferings of family or friends are concerned. But here again she is of her time. You had to accept the world as it is, and there is no point in sentimental gush and pity for people whose suffering and pain is the result of their own foolishness or evildoing; so she describes with relish the dreadful tortures inflicted upon the Brinvilliers woman, the notorious poisoner, for they were a just punishment for the agonies she had inflicted upon others. In our own day the pendulum has swung in the opposite direction, and it is fashionable to pity the criminal and forget all about his victim.

The second commandment might be expressed as: *Thou shalt not talk about thyself*. In all the great classical artists *le moi est haïssable*, and human truth is presented in generalized form, but with so much psychological penetration that the truth strikes home to all of us. This is not just a matter of good manners; it is based on the profound, if regrettable, truth about human nature that each one of us is so exclusively concerned with himself that he resents being distracted from his eternal self-regard by having other people's selves thrust upon his attention. It might at first sight be thought that this cannot apply to a writer of personal letters, and that surely a mother can talk to her daughter about herself and her daily doings. That is true, but even then it is noteworthy that she frequently becomes uneasy about this, and apologizes, even to her own daughter, for rambling on about herself. Moreover she is unusual for her age in the obvious joy she finds in the beauty of nature and the countryside for its own sake, and for the opportunity it affords for solitude and sweet melancholy, whereas most of her contemporaries regarded being alone in the country, without a soul to talk to, as the ultimate horror. Nature for them was simply emptiness, absence of the human and social life which alone should interest intelligent people. The unreasonable Alceste, it will be remembered, wanted to take Célimène away to *le désert*, meaning away from Paris. Yet here again Mme de Sévigné feels she is becoming a bore by dwelling on the beauty of the country and apologizes to her own daughter: 'Alas, my dear,' she writes from Les Rochers on 31 May 1671, after a passage about her trees there, 'how dreary my letters are! Where is the time when I talked about Paris like everybody else? You will have nothing but news of me, and such is my conceit that I am persuaded you prefer that to any other.'

The letters of Mme de Sévigné that have been preserved (and it is possible that others may still be found) span a period of nearly fifty years, and in the latest and most complete scholarly edition, edited by Roger Duchesne, Bibliothèque de la Pléiade, 3 vols., Gallimard, 1972–8, from which this selection is taken, there are 1,372 letters, of which a few are from others to her. In this Penguin edition clearly there is space for barely 10 per cent of the letters, so that the choice is inevitably influenced by personal factors, and another would have chosen differently. But I have tried to give what might be called the 'canon' of obvious ones which are important for subject-matter, form and style, whether the subject be great historical, political or military events, artistic or literary matters, gossip or more intimate personal revelations. It is not always remembered that in the seventeenth century one of the functions of the letter was simply to convey news, for the only periodicals in existence were the *Gazette*, with official information, or such things as the *Mercure Galant* which, as its name suggests, was not concerned with mere news. So letters were not necessarily regarded as private and confidential, but were read or passed round within a group of friends, no doubt with the more intimate and personal parts withheld by the addressee. Indeed some people enjoyed a reputation as letter-writers, and their letters were eagerly awaited by a circle. These semi-public letters, or letters addressed to highly intelligent or literary persons, were usually written with great attention to style and dramatic effects. Mme de Sévigné's letters to Coulanges, M. de Pomponne or Bussy-Rabutin often came into this category, but for obvious reasons those to her daughter contain intimate and often highly emotional passages, interspersed with set-pieces which presumably were for more general consumption. So the letters vary between emotional effusions, some nagging, some purely business or legal matters, some melancholy self-revelation and religious meditation and pieces of brilliant journalism.

This is why I have adopted the policy of always giving complete letters. With such a huge volume of material to choose from and space for relatively few, the temptation to give a selection of snippets and purple passages is very strong, and indeed that is what other selections have done. It is so easy to cut out the bits which might seem tedious or obscure or esoteric. But that is to sacrifice the true picture and fail to show the character of the woman herself, warts and all, fun and mischief and all, sorrow and all. So many of her letters dart from one topic or mood to another as she tries to get everything in before Wednesday or Friday, when the post departs from Paris. In any regular correspondence between intimate friends or members of a family there are bound to be incomprehensible allusions along the lines of: 'I spoke to X about that little business of yours, and he said . . .' And in this case there is no clue because the other half of the correspondence is missing. In most of these cases the *French* is perfectly clear, but even the Pléiade edition in a note says '*allusion très obscure*'.

Here is a good example of the mixed type of letter, suppression of any part of which would be a betrayal: on 9 August, 1675 she sends her daughter a letter which begins with general news from the war front, including how the Chevalier de Grignan had distinguished himself. From that she passes to Cardinal de Retz, then to a noble passage about the death of Turenne on the battlefield. Thence, with no transition except 'but here is a bit of news', she embarks on a scurrilous story of a tiff between the homosexual Monsieur and his lover the Chevalier de Lorraine. The Chevalier rushed after Monsieur to Versailles and, in the King's presence, complained about how nasty his dear one had been. The King, to conceal his mirth, and unwilling to adjudicate in such a delicate matter, excused himself and withdrew. Many other examples are equally assorted or contain gems, sublime or ridiculous, embedded in what might seem ordinary routine news, as when at a grand Court ceremony two noble lords in elaborate robes got inextricably hooked up with each other, while another had his shirt outside his breeches and nothing would make it stay inside.

A NOTE ON THE HISTORICAL BACKGROUND

In general (politics, wars, government, provincial affairs, etc.) see the many books of reference. There are three very helpful books for this period: John Lough, *An Introduction to Seventeenth Century France*, Longmans, Green; F. C. Green, *The Ancien Régime*, Edinburgh University Press; Harvey and Heseltine, *The Oxford Companion to French Literature*, Clarendon Press.

A note here might be useful on two circumstances of great importance in the reign of Louis XIV:

The Fronde (from *la fronde*, sling or catapult, used as a symbol of schoolboy impudence, 'cocking a snook' against authority). Name given to civil wars between 1648 and 1653. This extremely confused period was primarily a double revolt of oppressed taxpaying people and also great nobles against the monarchy, which during the minority of Louis XIV meant the Queen Mother and Cardinal Mazarin. But also it was an unscrupulous scramble for power in which people changed sides for purely personal ends. Notable figures were Condé, Mademoiselle, the King's cousin, Retz and La Rochefoucauld, the two last close friends of Mme de Sévigné. The unpleasant experiences and humiliations suffered by the young King resulted in his withdrawing to Versailles, where he centralized government and made the monarchy stronger than ever before or since.

Religious sects. The Jansenists might be described as Puritans within the Catholic Church. Named after Jansenius, Bishop of Ypres (1585–1638), whose posthumously published *Augustinus*, drawn from St Augustine, expounded a doctrine resembling Calvinism, in which the stress is on predestination, fatality from which only those chosen by grace can be saved. This austere doctrine was centred in the Abbey of Port-Royal, near Paris, leading figures in which were the Arnauld family, very well known to Mme de Sévigné. Jansenism was condemned as a heresy by more than one Pope, and the sect was violently attacked by the Jesuits. It was to repel some of these attacks that Pascal wrote the *Lettres Provinciales* (1656–7), a brilliant satire which branded the Jesuits as hypocrites and casuists, a reputation that has clung to them until modern times. It was because he felt that he had gone too far and undermined the credibility of Christianity itself that Pascal began writing notes for a great apologia for Christianity. He did not live to complete the work, but these notes, the *Pensées*, contain some of the most profound, eloquent and beautiful prose in French literature.

Later in the century, and cutting across both Jansenism and Jesuit orthodoxy, arose a form of mysticism known as Quietism, based on writings of a Spanish priest, Molinos, developed in France by Mme Guyon. This consisted of passive contemplation and unbroken communion with God. The logical, and to the orthodox Christian horrifying, implications of this could be that since the sacraments of the Church simply have as object to establish communion with God, they can be dispensed with if we already are in a state of permanent communion. Moreover one's body can be free to go about its business, even commit sins, provided that this spiritual communion is unbroken. The terrible danger, in the eyes of the orthodox, such as Bossuet, developed when the writings of Mme Guyon, which might otherwise have been dismissed as those of a crank, won the sympathy of Fénelon, Archbishop of Cambrai, one of the foremost ecclesiastics of the day.

Apart from the King and Queen and some special cases to be mentioned later, everybody was referred to as Monsieur, Madame or Mademoiselle, always abbreviated to M., Mme or Mlle, apart, of course, from direct address in speech or letters. This applied even to dukes (M. de La Rochefoucauld, M. de Chaulnes) and Mme de Sévigné uses the full spelling only for members of the royal house or prelates (bishops and archbishops): Monsieur le Dauphin, Madame la Dauphine, Monsieur de Reims, de Paris, de Marseille, etc. In addition, some members of the royal house, including the collateral family of Condé, were almost always referred to by certain conventions: Monseigneur for the Dauphin; Monsieur and Madame for the brother of the King and his wife, in this case Philippe d'Orléans and his two wives; Mademoiselle, known to history as la Grande Mademoiselle, for the daughter of the previous Monsieur, Gaston d'Orléans, brother of Louis XIII, and consequently first cousin to Louis XIV and Charles II of England; Monsieur le Prince for the Prince de Condé, known as 'le grand Condé'; Monsieur le Duc for the duc d'Enghien, son and heir of Condé.

Another convention which might catch the unwary is that the title *Prince* is not necessarily as exalted as in England, as it was used for the son and heir of a duke. The heir of the duc de La Rochefoucauld was le Prince de Marsillac. Comte corresponds to Earl, and the title Marquis is not as distinguished as an Englishman might suppose, corresponding roughly to the courtesy title Lord. Molière mocks at *les petits marquis* as one might at petty lordlings. And Mme de Sévigné, writing to her daughter who is pregnant, hopes that this time the baby will be *un petit marquis*. The title Chevalier is used for younger sons or brothers of nobility, a usage corresponding to The Hon. in English.

*

More than with any other work I have done, my wife has been a continual help by advising, checking and correcting, to say nothing of putting my Gallicisms into English. It says something for the charm of Mme de Sévigné that in spite of all this drudgery she has come to like her.

April 1981   L.W.T.

LIST OF PRINCIPAL PERSONS

This list contains only persons frequently named and some for whom Mme de Sévigné uses a different name from the one generally known. Well-known historical characters are omitted.

ADHÉMAR. Family name of many of the Grignans. *See* Grignan.

ANTIN, Duc d'. Legitimate son of Mme de Montespan.

ARLES, Bishop of, *see* Grignan.

ARNAULD. Great Jansenist family:

    1. Antoine (1612–94), Jansenist theologian, known as le grand Arnauld. Collaborated with Nicole (q.v.).

    2. Robert Arnauld d'Andilly (1589–1674), his elder brother. Theologian. Mme de Sévigné often refers to him as '*notre cher solitaire*'.

    3. Angélique (1591–1661), sister of the above. Abbess of Port-Royal.

    4. Agnès (1593–1671), another sister, also Abbess of Port-Royal.

    5. Simon Arnauld d'Andilly (1618–99), son of Robert Arnauld d'Andilly. Marquis de Pomponne. Great friend of Mme de Sévigné. After various embassies became Foreign Minister in 1671, disgraced in 1679, later back in favour. Recipient of the letters describing the Foucquet trial.

BOILEAU. In his *Art Poétique*, the great formulator of classical art. His full name was Nicolas Boileau-Despréaux. Almost always referred to by contemporaries, including Mme de Sévigné, as Despréaux.

BOSSUET. The greatest religious orator of the seventeeth century. Referred to usually as Monsieur de Meaux, his bishopric.

BOURDALOUE. Famous Jesuit preacher, greatly admired by Mme de S.

BRANCAS, Comte de. Notable for his absent-mindedness, said to be the original of Ménalque in La Bruyère.

BRINVILLIERS, Marquise de (1630–76). Poisoner, murdered her husband and attempted to kill her father. Fled to England, then Liège, whence brought back to France. Death recounted by Mme de S.

CHAMPMESLÉ, Marie (1642–98). Actress. Interpreter of Racine heroines, including Phèdre. Mistress of Racine, also, for a time, of Charles de Sévigné.

CHAPELAIN, Jean (1595–1674). Writer and critic. An early theorist of classicism and founder member of the Académie Française. Important in intellectual formation of Mme de S.

CHAULNES, Duc and Duchesse de. Governor of Brittany and later Ambassador to Rome. Great friends of Mme de S.

COLIGNY, Louise Françoise de Bussy-Rabutin, Marquise de. Widowed daughter of Bussy-Rabutin.

CORBINELLI, Jean. Intimate friend of Bussy-Rabutin and of Mme de S. A distinguished scholar, he frequented Mme de S.'s home and helped and advised in many ways.

COULANGES. Family related to Mme de S., whose mother was a Coulanges:

1. Philippe (1572–1636), father of:

2. Marie (1603–33), married Celse-Bénigne de Rabutin, mother of Mme de S.

3. Christophe (1607–87), Abbé of Livry. Beloved uncle of Mme de S., whom she named *le Bien Bon*.

4. Philippe-Emmanuel (1633–1716). Cousin and lifelong friend of Mme de S., whom she called 'le petit Coulanges'. His wife, a Du Gué Bagnols, was a cousin of Louvois.

DANGEAU, Philippe, Marquis de (1638–1720). Courtier, whose *Journal* from 1684 onwards gives accurate details of the Court of Louis XIV. Saint-Simon affected to despise him, but freely plundered him for his *Mémoires*. A brilliant card-player whose concentration won him much money, according to Mme de S.

DESPRÉAUX, *see* Boileau.

DU PLESSIS. A huge family, ramified by marriage into Créquy, Guénégaud, Choiseul, Clérambault families. La Rochefoucauld's wife was a Du Plessis.

FONTANGES, Marie-Angélique. The last mistress of Louis XIV before the reign of Mme de Maintenon.

FORBIN. Family in Provence. Toussaint de Forbin-Janson was Bishop of Digne and later Marseilles.

GONDI, Paul de. Family name of Cardinal de Retz.

GOURVILLE, Jean Hérault de. Began life as a servant in the La Rochefoucauld family, became steward and then secretary to La Rochefoucauld, then financier. Involved in Foucquet scandals, condemned to death, fled and after eight years returned to France and enriched himself further by attaching himself to Condé. Always helpful to La Rochefoucauld in the latter's needy days. A rare example of loyalty and kindness to a former employer.

GRIGNAN family:

1. François, Comte de (1632–1714), married, as his third wife:

2. Françoise Marguerite de Sévigné (1646–1705), daughter of Mme de S., to whom most of the letters were addressed.

3. Jacques Adhémar de Monteil de (d. 1674), Bishop of Uzès.

4. Jean-Baptiste de (1639), Coadjutor and later Archbishop of Arles. Brother of (1).

5. Joseph (1641–1713), Brother (le Chevalier). Also referred to as Adhémar.

6. Louis (1650–1722), Abbé de Grignan, later Bishop of Carcassonne. Brother.

7. Louise-Catherine (b. 1660) and Julie-Françoise (b. 1663). Daughters of (1) by first wife, often referred to as Mlles de Grignan.

Children of M. and Mme de Grignan:

8. Marie-Blanche (1670–1735), became a nun.

9. Louis Provence (1671–1704), Marquis de Grignan, predeceased his father.

10. Jean-Baptiste (1676–7). Died in infancy.

11. Pauline (1674–1737), married the Marquis de Simiane. The end of the direct line.

GUITAUT, Comte and Comtesse de. Friends and neighbours, whose château d'Époisse was near Mme de S.'s family estate of Bourbilly in Burgundy. They feature in the story of the fire in Paris.

D'HACQUEVILLE, M. Obliging friend, so helpful to so many people that Mme de S. called him *les* d'Hacqueville.

HUXELLES, Marie Le Bailleul (1626–1712). Friend, same age as Mme de S., twice widowed, one of her 'Bonnes veuves'.

LA FAYETTE, Marie Madeleine Pioche de la Vergne, Comtesse de (1634–93). Novelist, whose *La Princesse de Clèves* is one of the masterpieces of the seventeenth century. Perhaps the friend Mme de S. loved most. With La Rochefoucauld they formed a devoted trio.

LA GARDE, Antoine Escalin Adhémar, Marquis de. Cousin of François de Grignan whose property adjoined Grignan. A link between the Sévigné and Grignan families.

LAMOIGNON, Guillaume de (1617–77). First President of the Parlement of Paris. Presided with impartiality over the Foucquet trial. Had a famous brush with Molière over *Tartuffe*. Chrétien-François, son of the above and Advocate-General, was a frequent host of Mme de S. at his home, Bâville, near Versailles.

LA ROCHEFOUCAULD, François, Duc de (1613–80). Author of the *Maximes*. Intimate friend of Mme de S. and Mme de La Fayette.

LA TROCHE, Mme de. Wife of Marquis de La Troche, Conseiller at the Parlement of Rennes. Kind friend of Mme de S., but given to jealous fits, which gave rise to the nickname *la Trochanire*.

LA TROUSSE, Mme de. Wife of the Marquis de La Trousse. Born Henriette de Coulanges, aunt of Mme de S. Looked after the baby Marie-Blanche de Grignan when Mme de S. was away in 1671. In 1672 her illness delayed Mme de S.'s departure for Provence.

LAUZUN, Antoine Nompar de Caumont, Duc de (1633–1723). Gascon soldier and adventurer, one of the most colourful careers in the century. In high favour in spite of a scandal in 1665, he inspired a passionate and short-lived romance with Mademoiselle, and was disgraced and imprisoned at Pignerol in 1671 (where Foucquet had been sent). Pardoned in 1681, possibly thanks to large payments of money by Mademoiselle who, it was said, secretly married him. Sent to London in 1688, he escorted to France James II's queen, Mary of Modena, and the infant Prince of Wales (James Edward, the Old Pretender). Married daughter of Maréchal de Lorges in 1695, aged sixty-two, and lived to be ninety.

LA VALLIÈRE, Louise, Duchesse de (1644–1700). First noteworthy mistress of Louis XIV, supplanted by Mme de Montespan. Mother of Mlle de Blois. Retired to a convent.

LAVARDIN, Mme de. One of Mme de S.'s close friends, whom she relied on for news. She described sessions with her as *en Bavardin* or *Bavardinage* (*bavarder*, to gossip).

LENCLOS, Ninon de (1620–1705). Combined life as a *demi-mondaine* with great wit and intelligence. All the great writers of the age frequented her salon. Had a short-lived affair with Charles de Sévigné. In her old age met the young Voltaire and discerned his intelligence.

LORRAINE. Great family. In particular in these letters Philippe de Lorraine-Armagnac, Chevalier de Lorraine, lover of Monsieur, the King's brother, which however did not prevent his having affairs with women.

LOUVOIS, Michel Le Tellier, Marquis de (1641–91). Great War Minister of Louis XIV, flattered all the King's warlike sentiments. At odds with Colbert.

LULLY, Jean-Baptiste (1633–87). The most popular composer of the age. Wrote music for some of Molière's entertainments and operas with libretti by Benserade and Quinault. The favour of Louis XIV earned him quasi-monopoly of Paris theatre. In self-defence companies of actors combined to form the Comédie Française in 1680.

MAINE, Louis-Auguste de Bourbon, Duc du (1670–1736). Son of Louis XIV and Mme de Montespan, brought up and worshipped by Mme de Maintenon. Later legitimized by the King. He and his wife, granddaughter of Condé, in their home at Sceaux, held a brilliant literary and political salon during the Regency and early reign of Louis XV.

MAINTENON, Marquise de (1635–1719), earlier Mme Scarron, *see* Introduction.

MARANS, Mme de. Acquaintance of Mme de S. and her circle, much laughed at for her eccentricities. Nicknamed *Mélusine*.

MARSILLAC, Prince de. Title of son and heir of La Rochefoucauld.

MARTILLAC, Mlle de. Governess in the Grignan household. Mme de S. calls her Martille.

MASCARON, Jules (1634–1703). Bishop of Tulle. Famous preacher, popular at Court.

MEAUX, Bishop of, *see* Bossuet.

MÉNAGE, Gilles (1613–92). Scholar and philologist. Responsible for much of the education of Mme de S.

MÉRI, Suzanne de La Trousse, known as Mlle de Méri. Daughter of Mme de La Trousse (q. v.). Sickly and querulous cousin who abused Mme de S.'s hospitality.

MONTAUSIER, Duc and Duchesse de. She was Julie d'Angennes, daughter of the great *précieuse* hostess, Mme de Rambouillet. Their daughter Angélique was the first wife of François de Grignan.

MONTGOBERT, Elisabeth de. Companion and secretary to Mme de Grignan, in the confidence of Mme de S. Often wrote to her if Mme de Grignan was indisposed.

MOULCEAU, Philippe d.: President of the Chambre des Comptes at Montpellier, where Mme de S. met him on a trip from Grignan. Friend and correspondent.

NICOLE, Pierre (1625–95). Moralist and theologian. Author of *Essais de Morale* (1671). Friend and collaborator of Arnauld. The *Essais* greatly admired and frequently quoted by Mme de S.

ORMESSON, Olivier Lefèvre d'. Brother of Marie Lefèvre d'Ormesson, wife of Philippe de Coulanges, guardian of the young Marie de Rabutin Chantal and so a kind of uncle whom Mme de S. had known since childhood. Her main source of information about the Foucquet trial.

POMPONNE, *see* Arnauld.

QUINAULT, Philippe (1635–88). Poet and dramatist, wrote libretti of many of Lully's operas.

RETZ, Paul de Gondi, Cardinal de (1614–79). With no religious vocation, but love of politics and intrigue, active in the Fronde (in which he changed sides). His *Mémoires* are a brilliant, if unreliable, account of the period, with some remarkable portraits. Mme de S. was devoted to him.

SANZEI, Anne Marie de Coulanges, Comtesse de. Aunt of Mme de S.

SCHOMBERG, Frederic Armand de, Marshal; also known as Frederick Hermann, Duke of (1615–90). Born at Heidelberg of German father and English mother. Captain in French army (Scottish Guards), became marshal in French army 1675. A Protestant, he left France after the Revocation of the Edict of Nantes, and commanded under William of Orange. Conducted the Ulster campaign and was killed at the battle of the Boyne.

SÉGUIER, Pierre (Monsieur le Chancelier, b. 1588). Chancellor of France from 1635. Openly hostile to Foucquet, at whose trial he presided.

SIMIANE, Pauline, Marquise de, *see* Grignan.

TARENTE, Amélie de Hesse-Cassel, Princesse de. Aunt of the second Madame, the Princess Palatine. She lived near Les Rochers and was a very kind friend to the lonely Mme de S.

TÊTU, Abbé. An Academician and literary worthy much admired by a circle including Mme de Coulanges and Mme Scarron (de Maintenon).

VARDES, François René, Marquis de. Notorious seducer in his young days, banished from Court for a time owing to scandals. Finally recalled, and died in an odour of sanctity.

VINS, Mme de. Sister-in-law of Pomponne, married Jean de La Garde, a cousin of the Comte de Grignan. Spent much of her time at Pomponne, where Mme de S. frequently saw her. They became great friends. She lost her only son at the battle of Steenkerke in 1692 and was inconsolable. Mme de S. refers to this tragedy in her very last letter.

NICKNAMES

Mme de Sévigné invents nicknames for many of the people she writes about. The following short-list omits persons who do not appear in this selection and a few for whom no research so far has found the originals.

ALCINE, Mme d'Oppède

AMALTHÉE, Mme Du Plessis-Guénégaud

BEAUTÉ, LA, a daughter of the Guitauts

CHIMÈNE, Duchesse de Brissac

DAGUE, LA, Montgobert

DÉGEL, LE, Mme de Maintenon

DEW, Comtesse de Louvigny, later Duchesse de Gramont

DIVINES, LES, Mlles Du Plessis-d'Argentré et D'Outrelaise

DON QUIXOTE, M. de Béthune

DORIMÈNE, wife of Louis Du Plessis

FOG, Brancas?

GRANDE FEMME, LA, Mme d'Heudicourt

HAIL, Toussaint de Forbin-Janson

IO, Mme de Ludres

IRIS, Mme de Montglas

LEAF, Mme de Coulanges?

LIGHTNING, Mme de Monaco

MANIEROSA, Duchesse de Sully

SELECTED LETTERS OF
MADAME DE SÉVIGNÉ

To Bussy-Rabutin

[Les Rochers, Sunday 15 March 1648]

I think you're a nice one not to have written to me for two months. Have you forgotten who I am, and the position I occupy in the family? Well, really, young man, I shall make you remember it, and if you annoy me I shall reduce you to the label.[1] You know that I am at the end of a pregnancy, and I can't see in you any more sign of anxiety than if I were still a virgin. Very well then, I am informing you, even though it may infuriate you, that I have brought forth a boy, whom I shall make suck hatred of you in with his milk, and that I shall have lots more simply to make more enemies for you. You haven't had the wit to do so yourself, you fine maker of daughters.

But that is quite enough of concealing my love, dear cousin – nature wins over what is politic. I had meant to scold you for your laziness from the beginning of my letter to the end, but it is too much of an effort, and I must come back to telling you that M. de Sévigné and I love you dearly and often talk of the pleasure of being with you.

Part of Bussy-Rabutin's reply

[Valence, Sunday 12 April 1648]

In reply to your letter of 15 March, I will say, Madame, that I perceive that you are getting into a certain habit of scolding me more suitable to a mistress than a friend. Mind what you are letting yourself in for, for once I have made up my mind to suffer I shall want the rewards of lovers as well as their sufferings. I know that you are the head of the family, and that I owe respect to that quality, but you are taking too much advantage of my submissiveness. It is true that you are as quick to cool down as to fly into a temper, and that if your letters begin with: *I think you're a nice one*, they end up with: *M. de Sévigné and I love you dearly* ...

... So, if you take my advice, keep to the one boy you have just had;

1. *label*: a term of heraldry indicating cadet branch.

it is a very praiseworthy act. I admit that I have not had the wit to do as much myself. So I envy M. de Sévigné's good fortune more than anything in the world ...

To Madame de La Fayette

[Paris, Tuesday 24 July 1657]

You know, my dear, that one cannot take baths every day, so during the three days when I haven't been able to dip in the river I have been to Livry, whence I came back yesterday, intending to return there when I have finished my baths and our Abbé has completed one or two little bits of business he still has here.

The day before leaving for Livry I went to see Mademoiselle, who was kindness itself. I paid her your compliments, which she acknowledged very nicely, at any rate it did not seem to me that she had any reservations. I had gone with Mlle de Rambouillet, Mme de Valençay and Mme de Lavardin. She is now going off to Court, and this winter she will be so content that she will be on the best of terms with everybody.

I don't know of any news to send you today, for I have not seen the *Gazette* for three days. But you must know that Mme des N— is dead, and that Trévigny, her lover, nearly died of grief. For my part I would have preferred him really to die of it for the honour of the ladies.

I have still got blotches, my dear, and am still taking remedies. But as I am in the hands of Bourdelot, who is purging me with melons and ice, and as everybody comes and tells me it will kill me, this thought throws me into such a state of uncertainty that although I feel that what he prescribes is doing me good, I only do it in fear and trembling. Good-bye, my dearest, you know that nobody can love you more tenderly than I do.

To Pomponne

[Paris, Monday 17 November 1664]

Today, Monday 17 November, M. Foucquet was cross-examined for the second time. He sat down without ceremony, as on the other occasion. M. le Chancelier began once again to instruct him to raise his hand; he replied that he had already stated the reasons preventing his taking the oath, and it was not necessary to do so again. Thereupon the Chancellor embarked on long speeches to show the legitimate powers of the chamber that the King had established and that the commissions had been confirmed by the sovereign companies. M. Foucquet answered that often things were done by authority which were found to be unjust when they had been thought over. The Chancellor interrupted, 'What! So you are saying that the King abuses his power?' M. Foucquet answered, 'It is you who are saying that, Monsieur, not I. That is not what I have in mind, and I am amazed that in the state I am in you should want to make trouble between the King and me. But Sir, you know full well that one can be overtaken by events. When you sign an order you think that it is right. The following day you quash it; you see that it is possible to change one's mind and opinion.' 'But yet,' said the Chancellor, 'although you don't recognize the court you are answering, you are submitting requests and you are being examined.' 'True, Sir,' he replied, 'here I am. But I am not here of my own volition, I have been brought here. There is a power one must obey, and it is a mortification God inflicts upon me and which I receive from His hand. Perhaps I might have been spared it after the services I have rendered and the offices I have had the honour of holding.' After that the Chancellor continued the interrogation about the commission on the salt-tax, which M. Foucquet answered very well.

The interrogations will go on and I shall go on faithfully reporting them to you. I would only like to know whether my letters are safely delivered to you.

Madame your sister, who is with our Sisters near here, has signed; she is seeing the community at this moment and appears to be quite happy. Madame your aunt doesn't seem angry with her. I don't think she would be the one to take the plunge; there is still another.

You probably know about our defeat at Gigeri, and how those who gave the advice now seek to throw the blame on those who carried it out. They mean to impeach Gadagne for not defending himself properly; there are people thirsting for his blood. But all the general public is sure that he could not have done otherwise.

There is much talk here about Monsieur d'Aleth, who has excommunicated the minor officials of the King who wanted to compel

31

priests to sign. That will put him on bad terms with your father, as it will improve his relations with Père Annat.

Good-bye, I can feel a desire to gossip coming over me. I don't want to give in to it; narrative style should be brief.

To Pomponne

[Paris, Tuesday evening, 18 November 1664]

I have had your letter which shows me that I am not merely doing a kindness to an ungrateful person; never have I seen anything so charming and kind. One would have to be remarkably free from vanity not to be affected by praises like yours. So I confess I am delighted at your good opinion of my sensitivity, and moreover I assure you, without seeking to bandy compliment for compliment, that my esteem for you is infinitely greater than the words usually used to express what one feels, and that I find great joy and consolation in being able to tell you about an affair in which we both take so much interest. I am very glad that our beloved solitary[1] has a share in it. I also believed that you were informing your incomparable neighbour. It is a pleasant piece of news you pass on by telling me that I am making a little progress in her affection; there is nobody's affection in which I am more pleased to be progressing. When I want a moment's joy I think of her and her enchanted palace. But to return to our affairs; unconsciously I was amusing myself by talking about my feelings for you and your charming friend.

Today our dear friend's cross-examination has been resumed. The Abbé d'Effiat bowed to him as he passed by. He returned the salute and said, 'Monsieur, I am your very humble servant,' with that laughing and acute expression we know so well. The Abbé d'Effiat was so overcome with emotion that he could say no more.

As soon as M. Foucquet entered the chamber the Chancellor told him to be seated. He replied, 'Sir, you took advantage yesterday of my having sat and thought it meant recognizing the court. Since that is the case I beg you to be so good as to permit me not to sit in that seat.' Thereupon the Chancellor said that in that case he could retire. M.

1. Robert Arnauld d'Andilly, Pomponne's father.

Foucquet replied, 'Sir, I do not intend to provoke a fresh incident. I merely wish, with your permission, to register my usual protest and make a token gesture, after which I shall answer.' Things were carried out as he wanted, he sat down and the interrogation on the commission on the salt-tax was continued, and his answers were perfectly correct. If he continues in that way the interrogation will go in his favour. There is much talk in Paris about his admirable intelligence and strength of mind. He asked for one thing which makes me shudder. He calls upon a lady friend of his to let him know his sentence by a certain magic means, whether it be good or bad as God wills, and without any preamble so that he may have time to prepare himself to receive the news from those who come to tell him, adding that so long as he has half an hour to prepare himself he is capable of hearing without emotion the worst that can be told. This brings tears to my eyes, and I am sure it will rend your heart.

[Wednesday 19 November]

There has been no sitting in the chamber today owing to the illness of the Queen, which has been extremely grave; but now she is a little better. Yesterday evening she received Our Lord as a viaticum. It was the most impressive and sad thing in the world to see the King and the whole Court, with candles and countless torches, going to get the Blessed Sacrament and bringing it back. It was received with countless more lights. The Queen made an effort to raise herself and received it with a devoutness that moved everybody to tears. It was not without difficulty that she had been brought to this frame of mind. Only the King had been able to make her see reason. To everyone else she had said that she was willing to take communion, but not as a preparation for death. It had taken two hours to persuade her.

The extreme approval expressed about all M. Foucquet's replies is most annoying to *Petit*, who fears he will gain people's hearts. It is even thought that *Petit* will make *Puis* feign illness so as to interrupt the flow of admiration and gain time to recover a bit of breath after other failures. I am the most humble servant of the dear solitary, of Madame your wife and of the adorable *Amalthée*.

To Pomponne

M. Foucquet was questioned this morning on the gold mark, and he answered very well. Several judges bowed in approval. The Chancellor disapproved of this, saying that it was not customary, and said to the Breton councillor, 'It is because you come from Brittany that you bow so low to M. Foucquet.' Passing the Arsenal on his way back on foot for the exercise, he asked who were the workmen he saw and was told that they were men working on the basin of a fountain. He went over to them and said what he thought about the job, then turned to Artagnan and said laughingly, 'Don't you wonder what I am up to? It's because long ago I used to be quite good at that sort of thing.' Those who are fond of M. Foucquet admire this calmness, and I am of their number. The others say it is an affectation. That is the way of the world.

Mme Foucquet senior has given the Queen a plaster which has cured her of her convulsions, which were really the vapours. Most people, because that is what they wish for, imagine that the Queen will use this occasion to ask the King's pardon for this poor prisoner; but for my part I hear little about tenderness in that quarter, and I don't believe a word of it. What is remarkable is the fuss everybody is making about this plaster, saying that Mme Foucquet is a saint and can work miracles.

[Friday 21 November 1664]

Today, Friday 21st, M. Foucquet has been questioned about wax and sugar. He lost patience with certain objections brought up, which seemed ridiculous to him, and he showed it a little too much and replied in a haughty tone which made an unfavourable impression. He will put this right, for that attitude is not good. But it really is irritating, and I think I should act exactly like him.

I have been to Sainte-Marie, where I saw your aunt who seemed lost in God; at Mass she was in a sort of trance. Your sister looked pretty, with fine eyes and a lively expression. The poor child fainted this morning; she is far from well. Her aunt is still just as kind to her.

Monsieur de Paris has given her a sort of exemption which has touched her heart, and that is what has made her sign this infernal formula. I did not speak to either, Monsieur de Paris had forbidden it. Here is yet another illustration of prejudice. Our Sisters of Sainte-Marie said to me, 'Well, God be praised! He has touched the heart of this poor child and she has taken the path of obedience and salvation.' From there I went to Port-Royal, where I found a certain distinguished solitary whom you know, who began by saying to me, 'Well, that poor goose has signed. So God has abandoned her and she has taken the plunge.' For my part I nearly died of laughing as I reflected on what prejudice can do. That is humanity in its natural state. I think that the middle way between these extremes is always the best.

[Saturday evening, 22 November 1664]

M. Foucquet entered the chamber this morning and was interrogated about tolls. He was attacked very clumsily and defended himself very well. Between ourselves it is not one of the most precarious parts of his affair. Some good angel has warned him that he has been too haughty, but he has corrected himself today just as people have refrained from bowing to him. There will be no sitting until Wednesday, so I will not write until that day.

Furthermore, if you persist in pitying me for the trouble I am taking to write to you, and in begging me not to go on, I shall think that you are the one who is bored with reading my letters and tired of answering them, but then I shall promise again to shorten my letters if I can; and I release you from the bother of replying, although I enjoy your letters very much indeed. After these declarations I don't think that you can stop the flow of my gazettes. The thought that I give you a little pleasure gives me a great deal. There are so few opportunities of expressing one's esteem and friendship that we must not miss them when they present themselves. Please give my compliments to all at home and in your neighbourhood.

The Queen is much better.

To Pomponne

If I go by what I feel, I am the one to be really obliged to you for taking so well my efforts to instruct you. Do you think I don't find consolation in writing to you? I assure you that I do find a great deal and that I find no less pleasure in holding these conversations with you than you have in reading my letters. All the feelings you have about what I am telling you are very natural. That of hope is common to everybody, nobody can say why, but anyhow it keeps up our spirits.

I went to dinner at Sainte-Marie de Saint-Antoine two days ago. The Mother Superior told me in detail about four visits that *Puis* paid her in the past three months, which astonished me very much indeed. He came to tell her that the Blessed Bishop of Geneva[1] had obtained for him such special grace during his illness last summer that he could not doubt the obligation he owed him, and begged her to ask all the community to pray for him. He gave her a thousand écus to accomplish his vow. He asked her to let him see the heart of the Blessed One. When he was in front of the grille he fell on his knees and for more than a quarter of an hour he was in tears, addressing this heart and asking it for a spark from the fire with which the love of God had consumed it. The Mother Superior also wept and gave him a reliquary containing relics of the Blessed One. He wears it always, and during these four visits appeared to be so touched with desire for salvation, so repelled by the Court, so transported by the longing for conversion that a subtler woman than the Superior would have been taken in. She adroitly brought up the case of M. Foucquet, and he replied like a man concerned with God alone, that he did not know him, that it would depend, and that he would do justice according to God's will, considering nothing but Him. I was never more surprised than on hearing all this talk. If you ask me now what I think about it all, I will say that I know nothing, understand nothing and that on the other hand I cannot imagine what the point of this play-acting can be. And if it is not play-acting how has he reconciled all the steps he has taken since then with such fine words? These are things that time alone must

1. Saint François de Sales.

36

explain, for in themselves they are obscure. However, don't say anything about it, for the Mother Superior has asked me not to spread this little story.

I have seen M. Foucquet's mother. She told me how she had sent this plaster to the Queen through Mme de Charost. It certainly had a prodigious effect. In less than an hour her head felt clear, and she had such an extraordinary evacuation of such poisonous matter, which would probably have caused her death the following night, that she herself said aloud that it was Mme Foucquet who had saved her, that it was what she had just passed that had caused the convulsions from which she had nearly died the night before. The Queen Mother was convinced of it and said so to the King, but he would not listen. The doctors, without whose knowledge they had applied the plaster, did not say what they thought, but paid their court at the expense of the truth. That same day the King would not look at these poor women who went to throw themselves at his feet. Yet everybody knows in his heart that this is true. This is yet another of those things the sequel of which we must wait for.

[Wednesday 26 November]

This morning the Chancellor questioned M. Foucquet, but in quite a different manner. It seems he is ashamed of being taught every day by Berrier.[2] He told the reporter[3] to read out the article on which it was proposed to interrogate the accused. The reporter read, and this reading lasted so long that it was half past ten by the time it was over. He said, 'Let Foucquet be brought in,' and then corrected himself, 'Monsieur Foucquet.' But it turned out that he had not said that he was to be summoned, so that he was still in the Bastille. So somebody went to find him, and he arrived at eleven. He was interrogated on the tolls and he answered very well. But he did get muddled about certain dates, about which they might have made things very awkward for him if they had been clever and awake. But instead of being alert the Chancellor was gently dozing. People looked at each other, and I think our poor friend would have laughed had he dared. Anyway, he re-

2. Louis Berrier was in league with Colbert, and falsified the evidence.
3. D'Ormesson.

covered and went on with the questioning. And M. Foucquet, although he insisted too much on this point on which he could be shaken, will, as it turns out, have spoken well, for in his misfortune he has certain little bits of good luck which happen to him alone. If every day's proceedings go as uneventfully as today's, the case will go on for ever.

I shall write every evening, but I shall not send my letter off until Saturday evening or Sunday, which will give you an account of Thursday, Friday and Saturday, and we might get another to you on Thursday which would inform you about Monday, Tuesday and Wednesday. Thus letters would not wait a long time at your end. Do please pass on my compliments to our dear solitary and your dear other half. I make no reference to your neighbour; it will soon be my turn to send you news of her.

To Pomponne

[Paris, Thursday 27 November 1664]

The interrogation about the tolls was continued today. The Chancellor had every intention of pushing M. Foucquet to extremes and embarrassing him, but he did not succeed. M. Foucquet got himself out of it very well indeed. He did not enter until eleven because the Chancellor made the reporter read as I have told you, and despite all that fine display of devotion he always said the very worst about our poor friend. The reporter always took his side because the Chancellor was so biased. Finally he said, 'Here is a matter on which the accused cannot reply.' The reporter said, 'Ah, Sir, as to that matter, here is that plaster that heals him,' and gave a very good reason, and then added, 'Sir, in the situation I am in, I shall always speak the truth, whatever it turns out to be.' The word *plaster* raised a smile because it recalled the one that has made such a stir. Thereupon the accused was brought in and was less than an hour in the chamber, and as they left several people complimented T— on his firmness.

I must tell you what I have done. Just imagine, some ladies suggested that I should go into a house that looks straight at the Arsenal, so as to see our poor friend return. I saw him coming from quite a distance. M. d'Artagnan was by his side and fifty musketeers behind, at thirty or forty paces. He looked very preoccupied. When I saw him my legs trembled and my heart beat so fast that I felt quite faint. As he drew near to us on the way back to his cell, M. d'Artagnan nudged him and pointed out that we were there. So he bowed to us and took on that gay expression you know so well. I don't think he recognized me, but I confess I felt strangely moved when I saw him disappear through that little door. If you knew how wretched you feel when you have a tender heart like mine I am sure you would take pity on me, but I doubt whether you get off any more lightly, knowing you as I do.

I have been to see your dear neighbour; I am just as sorry for you for not having her as we are happy to have her. Of course we talked of our dear friend; she has seen *Sapho*, who gave her fresh courage. I shall go and see her tomorrow to renew my own courage, for now and again I feel I need comfort. Of course we all say a thousand things calculated to give hope, but there! my imagination is so lively that any uncertainty is the death of me.

[Friday 28 November 1664]

The sitting began first thing in the morning. The Chancellor said they must discuss the four loans.[1] Thereupon T— said that it was a quite insignificant matter about which there was nothing to reproach M. Foucquet, and that he had declared it at the outset of the case. An attempt was made to contradict him, so he asked if he could explain the affair as he saw it, and begged his colleague to listen. This was done and he persuaded the assembly that this article was not important. Thereupon the order was given to admit the accused; it was eleven o'clock. You observe that he was not more than an hour under examination. The Chancellor wanted to speak about these four loans. M. Foucquet asked for permission to say what he had been unable to say the day before about the tolls. He was listened to; he said some brilliant things. When the Chancellor said, 'Have you had your receipt for the use of this sum?' he said, 'Yes, Sir, but it was jointly with other matters,' which he detailed and which will come up in their turn. 'But,' said the Chancellor, 'when you had your receipts you had not yet spent the monies?' 'That is true,' he said, 'but the sums were earmarked.'

1. *four loans*: Foucquet had lent to the State four times, using four men of straw.

39

'That is not good enough,' said the Chancellor. 'But, Sir, for example,' said M. Foucquet, 'when I paid you your emoluments, sometimes I had the receipt a month earlier, and as this sum was earmarked it was just as if it had been paid.' The Chancellor said, 'That is true, and I was much obliged to you.' M. Foucquet said that this was not to reproach him for it, that he was happy to be in a position to serve him at that time, but that these examples came back to him as he needed them.

The next hearing will not be until Monday. It is certain that they want to drag the thing out. *Puis* has promised to call the accused as little as possible. They think he is speaking too well, so they seek to question him perfunctorily and not go into all the articles. But he wants to speak on everything, and will not have his case judged on matters on which he has not stated his reasons. *Puis* is always scared of displeasing *Petit*. The other day he apologized to him because M. Foucquet had gone on speaking for too long and he had not been able to interrupt him. Chamillart is behind the screen during the interrogations; he listens to what is said and offers to go and see the judges and explain his reasons for coming to such extreme conclusions. This whole process is out of order and shows great vindictiveness against the poor man. I confess I have lost all peace of mind. Good-bye, my poor friend, until Monday. I wish you could realize the extent of my feelings for you. You would then be sure of the friendship you say you value a little.

To Pomponne

[Paris, Monday 1 December 1664]

Two days ago everyone believed that the authorities wanted to drag M. Foucquet's affair out; now it is not the same at all, quite the opposite. The interrogations are being rushed through in an extraordinary way. This morning the Chancellor took up his paper and read out, like a list, ten charges to which he gave no time for reply. M. Foucquet said, 'Sir, I do not propose to drag matters on, but I beg you to give me time to reply. You question me, but it seems that you don't want to hear my answers. It is important for me that I should speak.

There are several articles I must explain, and it is only fair that I should reply to all those that are in my case.' So they had to listen to him against the wishes of the ill-intentioned, for it is certain that they cannot abide his defending himself so well. He answered extremely well on all counts. They are going on at once and the matter will go through so quickly that I think the interrogations will be over this week.

I have been to supper at the Hôtel de Nevers, and the hostess and I had a good talk about all this. We are in a state of worry that you alone can understand, for in the whole of the unfortunate man's family tranquillity and hope reign supreme. It is reported that M. de Nesmond said on his deathbed that his keenest regret was that he had not agreed with these two judges, and that had he seen the end of the case he would have righted that wrong, and that he prayed God to forgive him for what he had done.

I have just had your letter; it is better than anything I can ever write. You subject my modesty to too great a strain when you tell me how I stand with you and our dear solitary. I feel I can see him and hear him saying all you write. I am very sorry it was not I who said *the metamorphosis of Pierrot into Tartuffe*. That is put so naturally that had I as much wit as you credit me with I would have found it on the tip of my pen.

I must tell you a nice little story which is quite true and will amuse you. The King has taken lately to writing verse. Messieurs de Saint-Aignan and Dangeau are teaching him how to set about it. The other day he wrote a little madrigal, which he himself did not think much of. One morning he said to Maréchal de Gramont, 'Monsieur le Maréchal, will you kindly read this little madrigal and see whether you have ever seen anything so pointless. Just because it is known that I have recently taken to liking verses, people bring me all kinds.' Having read it the Marshal said, 'Sire, your Majesty is an inspired judge of everything, and it is true that this is the silliest and most ridiculous madrigal I have ever read.' The King burst out laughing and said, 'Isn't it true that whoever wrote this is a conceited puppy?' 'Sire, he cannot be called anything else.' 'That's excellent,' said the King. 'I am delighted that you have spoken so candidly; I wrote it myself.' 'Oh, Sire, what treachery! Will your Majesty please give it back to me, I only glanced through it rapidly.' 'No, Monsieur le Maréchal, first impressions are always the most natural.' The King laughed very much at this trick, but everyone thinks it is the most cruel thing one can do to an old courtier. Personally I always like reflecting about things, and I wish the King would think about this example and conclude how far he is from ever learning the truth.

We are on the point of seeing a very cruel truth – the redemption of our annuities at a rate that will send us straight to the poorhouse. The emotion is considerable, but the harshness is much worse. Don't you think that this is undertaking a lot of things at once? The one that touches me most is not the one that deprives me of part of my money.

[Tuesday 2 December]

M. Foucquet spoke today for two whole hours on the six million, and he compelled them to listen. He spoke wonderfully, everybody was touched, each according to his own point of view. Pussort made faces expressing disapproval and negation which scandalized right-thinking people. When M. Foucquet had finished speaking Pussort leaped up impetuously and said, 'Thank God there will be no complaint that he hasn't been allowed to talk his fill.' What do you think of those fine words? Don't they come from an excellent judge?

It is said that the Chancellor is very scared by M. de Nesmond's erysipelas, which caused his death; he is afraid there might be a repetition for him. If that were capable of giving him the sentiments of a man about to appear before God, it would be something, but we must fear that it will be said of him as of Argante, *E mori come visse*.*

[Wednesday 3 December]

Our dear unhappy friend spoke for two hours this morning, and so admirably that many present could not help admiring him. M. Renard, among others, said, 'It must be admitted that this man is incomparable. He never spoke so well in Parlement; he is more self-possessed than he has ever been.' It was once more on the six million and his expenses. Nothing is so admirable as everything he has said on that subject. I will write on Thursday and Friday, which will be the final days of the interrogation, and I shall go on further to the end.

* 'He died as he lived.' (Adaptation of a line from Tasso, *Gerusalemme Liberata*.)

42

God grant that my last letter will tell you the thing I most ardently wish for in the world. Good-bye, dear Sir, ask our solitary to pray for our poor friend. I embrace you both with all my heart – out of modesty I add Madame your wife.

To Pomponne

[Paris, Thursday 4 December 1664]

At last the interrogations are over. This morning M. Foucquet entered the chamber. The Chancellor had the project read out in full. M. Foucquet began speaking first and said, 'Monsieur, I don't think you can deduce anything from that document apart from the effect it has just made, namely to cause me a great deal of embarrassment.' The Chancellor said, 'Yet you have just heard, and thus been able to see, that this great passion for the State that you have talked about so many times, has not been of such importance but what you have nearly wrecked it from one end to the other.' 'Monsieur,' said M. Foucquet, 'those are thoughts that came to me in the depths of despair I was thrown into sometimes by the Cardinal, principally when, after I had done more than anyone in the world to help him return to France, I saw myself rewarded by such base ingratitude. I have a letter from him and one from the Queen Mother which bear out what I say, but they have been removed from my papers, together with many others. My misfortune is that I did not burn that miserable document, which was so out of my memory and mind that I went for more than two years without thinking about it or believing I had it. In any case I repudiate it most willingly, and beg you to believe, Monsieur, that my passion for the person and service of the King has by no means been lessened.' The Chancellor said, 'It is very difficult to believe this when one sees an opinion obstinately expressed at different times.' M. Foucquet answered, 'Monsieur, never at any time, even at the risk of my life, have I abandoned the King's person, and in those days, Monsieur, you were chief adviser to his enemies and your associates were giving free passage to the army fighting against him.' The Chancellor felt this thrust, but our poor friend was excited and not quite master of his emotions.

Next he was asked about his expenditure, and he said, 'Monsieur, I undertake to demonstrate that I have incurred none that I could not have paid either from my own income, known to the Cardinal, or from my official salary or from my wife's money. And if I should not be able to prove what I am saying, I consent to be treated as harshly as can be imagined.' In the end this cross-questioning went on for two hours, during which M. Foucquet spoke extremely well, but hotly and in anger, because the reading of this project had annoyed him intensely.

After he had gone the Chancellor said, 'This is the last time we shall question him.' M. Poncet came up and said to him, 'Monsieur, you haven't made any mention to him of the proofs that exist that he has begun to carry out the project.' The Chancellor replied, 'Monsieur, these proofs are not convincing enough, he would have refuted them too easily.' After which Sainte-Hélène and Pussort said, 'Not everyone shares that opinion.' Which gives food for thought and reflection. The rest tomorrow.

[Friday 5 December]

This morning they discussed appeals, which are relatively unimportant except in so far as right-minded people will want to bear them in mind when judging. So that is that. M. d'Ormesson has to speak on Tuesday, when he recapitulates the whole affair. That will last all the coming week, which means that between now and then the life we shall be living will not be life at all. I am hardly fit to know and doubt if I can carry on until then. M. d'Ormesson has asked me not to see him again until the case is judged. He is in conclave, and doesn't want to have any dealings with the outer world. He is putting on a great show of reserve, he never says a word, but listens. As I took my leave of him I had the pleasure of telling him all I think. I will let you know anything I learn, and God grant that my final news will be what I want it to be! I assure you we are all to be pitied – I mean you and me and those who take a personal interest as we do. Good-bye, dear Sir, I am so sad and weighed down tonight that I cannot go on.

To Pomponne

I assure you that these days drag on very slowly and that uncertainty is a dreadful thing. It is an affliction that the poor prisoner's whole family is unaware of; I have seen them and admired them. It looks as though they have never seen or read what has been happening in the recent past. What surprises me even more is that *Sapho*, whose intelligence and penetration are boundless, is just the same. When I think it over I flatter myself and am convinced, or at least try to convince myself, that they know more about it than I do. On the other hand, when I discuss it with others less biased, but whose discernment is admirable, I find the proceedings so fair that it will be a real miracle if the affair goes off as we wish. You only ever lose by one vote and that vote settles everything. I remember those impugnments, which these poor women thought they were sure of; it is true that we lost them by only five to seventeen. Since then their confidence has caused some misgivings. And yet in the depths of my heart I have a tiny wisp of confidence. I don't know where it comes from or where it is going, and it isn't even big enough to let me sleep in peace.

Yesterday I was talking about the whole business with Mme du Plessis – I cannot see or abide anyone except people with whom I can discuss it and who share my sentiments. She hopes as I do without knowing why. 'But why do you hope?' 'Because I hope.' Those are our answers; aren't they perfectly reasonable? I said to her with the utmost truthfulness that if we had a decision such as we wish for, my greatest joy would be to think that I could dispatch a man on horseback to ride at full speed and tell you this happy news, and that the pleasure of imagining the pleasure I should give you would make my own quite complete. Like me, she understood that and our imaginations gave us more than a quarter of an hour off.

However, I want to revise that last day of the cross-questioning on the crime of high treason. I wrote to you what I had been told, but the same person has now remembered more clearly and has told me the story again. Everybody has heard it explained by several judges. After M. Foucquet had said that the only conclusion that could be drawn from the project was to have subjected him to the embarrassment of hearing it, the Chancellor said to him, 'You cannot deny that that is high treason.' He countered, 'I admit, Monsieur, that it is silly and extravagant, but it is not high treason. I beg these gentlemen,' he said, turning towards the judges, 'to permit me to explain what high treason is – not that they are not cleverer than I, but I have had more leisure to examine it. High treason is when a man in a responsible position is in the confidence of the Prince and then suddenly puts himself at the head of his enemies, brings all his family to the same side, has the gates of the cities of which he is governor opened to the enemy army and shuts them against the real master, and divulges to his party all the state secrets. That, gentlemen, is what is called high treason.' The Chancellor didn't know where to hide himself, and all the judges felt like laughing. That is the true version of how things happened. You will admit that nothing could be wittier, more delicate and even funnier. The whole of France has heard and admired this answer. Then he defended himself in detail and said what I have told you. I would have felt miserable had you not known this part of it as it is. Our dear friend would have lost a great deal.

This morning M. d'Ormesson began to recapitulate the whole case; he spoke very well and very clearly. He will state his conclusions on Thursday. His colleague will speak for two days. They want a few more days for the other opinions. Some of the judges mean to spread themselves, so that we still have to languish until the coming week. Really the state we are in isn't living at all.

[Wednesday 10 December]

M. d'Ormesson has continued his recapitulation of the case. He has done wonders, that is to say he has spoken with extraordinary clarity, intelligence and ability. Pussort interrupted him five or six times with no other aim than to prevent his speaking so well. On one point which seemed to him very much in favour of M. Foucquet he said, 'Monsieur, we shall speak after you, we shall speak after you.'

To Pomponne

M. d'Ormesson has still gone on. When he reached a certain article about the gold mark, Pussort said, 'That is against the accused.' 'True,' said M. d'Ormesson, 'but there is no proof.' 'What!' said Pussort, 'those two officers were not interrogated?' 'No,' said d'Ormesson. 'Oh, that's not possible,' replied Pussort. 'I find nothing about it in the case,' said d'Ormesson. Thereupon Pussort exclaimed in a fury, 'Oh, Monsieur, you should have said that earlier, that is a grave oversight.' M. d'Ormesson made no reply. But if Pussort had said another word he would have answered, 'Sir, I am a judge and not an accuser.' Don't you remember what I told you once at Fresnes? That's how it is. M. d'Ormesson has only discovered this when there is no remedy left.

The Chancellor interrupted M. d'Ormesson several times more. He told him he must not talk about the project, and that is out of malice, for many will think it is a serious crime, and the Chancellor would rather M. d'Ormesson did not show the proofs, which are ludicrous, so as not to weaken the idea that has been given of them. But M. d'Ormesson will refer to them because this is one of the articles that make up the case. He will wind up tomorrow. Sainte-Hélène will speak on Saturday. On Monday the two reporters will give their views and on Tuesday they will all meet in the morning and not separate until they have given a verdict. I am petrified when I think of that day. Yet the family still has great hopes.

Foucault goes about soliciting everywhere, showing a document from the King in which he is made to say that he would deem it very wrong that judges should base their opinion on the purloining of papers, that he himself had them taken, that not one of them would be useful for the defence of the accused, that they are documents concerning his realm and that he is declaring this so that they should not think of basing any judgement on them. What do you think of this nice way of going on? Aren't you appalled that people can put things in this way to a prince who would love truth and justice if he met them? He said the other day at his levée that Foucquet was a dangerous man and now this is what is being put into his head. In fact our enemies know no restraint. They are riding hell for leather now – threats, promises, anything is called into play. *If God is for us we shall overcome.* You will still have, perhaps, another letter from me, and if we have good news I will send it by a special man at full speed. I don't know what I shall do if it is not so. I can't imagine myself what will become of me. Countless greetings to our solitary and to your dear other half. Get everyone to pray.

[Saturday 13 December]

After much chopping and changing they decided that M. d'Ormesson should give his opinion today, so that Sunday should come in between and Sainte-Hélène, beginning on Monday, should start afresh and make sure of an impression. So M. d'Ormesson suggested permanent banishment and confiscation of all possessions by the King. M. d'Ormesson has thereby crowned his reputation. The sentence is somewhat severe, but let us pray that it will be followed. It is always good to assume the offensive.

To Pomponne

[Paris, Wednesday 17 December 1664]

You are wilting, poor Monsieur, but so are we. I have been sorry that I told you that there would be a verdict on Tuesday, for with no news from me you will have taken it that all is lost. However, we still have all our hopes.

I told you on Saturday how M. d'Ormesson had reported on the affair and given his opinion, but I did not tell you enough about the extraordinarily good opinion he has won for himself by this action. I have heard it said among people of his profession that what he has done was a masterpiece in the way he explained himself so clearly and supported his opinions by such solid, strong arguments, and he added eloquence and even embellishments. In short, never has a man in his profession had a finer opportunity to show himself to advantage, nor availed himself of it better. If he had been willing to open his door to praises, his house would never have been empty. But he wanted to appear modest, and concealed himself carefully.

His odious colleague Sainte-Hélène spoke on Monday and Tuesday. He went over the whole business again, but feebly and wretchedly, reading his speech, neither adding anything nor giving any new twist to it. He gave as his opinion, without supporting it in any way, that M. Foucquet should have his head cut off for treason. And to win more people over to his side and do a real Norman trick, he said that no doubt the King would grant a pardon and that he alone could do so. It was yesterday that he did this noble deed which upset everybody, just as they had been pleased by the opinion of M. d'Ormesson.

This morning Pussort spoke for four hours, but with so much vehemence, heat, passion and rage that several of the judges were outraged, and it is thought that this fury may do more good than harm to our poor friend. He redoubled his frenzy towards the end of his diatribe, and said of this high treason that a certain Spaniard should put us to shame, for he had felt such horror at a traitor that he had burned his house down because Charles de Bourbon had passed that way; that even more we should hold in abomination M. Foucquet's crime; that for his punishment the only suitable things were the rope and the gibbet, but that because of the offices he had held and his many important connections, he would show mercy to the extent of sharing the opinion of M. de Sainte-Hélène. What do you think of such moderation? It is because he is the uncle of M. Colbert and has been challenged that he wanted to conduct himself so well. The very thought of this infamy makes me leap to the skies.

I don't know whether the judgement will be tomorrow or whether they will drag the thing on all the week. We still have grand salvoes to face, but perhaps somebody will take up the opinion of poor M. d'Ormesson, who up to now has been so ignored. But do listen to three or four little things that are perfectly true and rather extraordinary.

First, a comet has been appearing for four days. At first it was only pointed out by some women, and they were laughed at, but now everybody has seen it. M. d'Artagnan sat up last night and saw it very well. M. de Neuré, a great astrologer, says it is a very large one. I have seen M. de Foix, who has seen it with three or four scientists. I myself will sit up tonight to see it too. It appears at about three – I am warning you so that you can have the pleasure or displeasure.

Berrier has gone mad, literally, that is to say that having been copiously bled he is still in a frenzy. He talks of gallows and the wheel, chooses trees specially and says they are trying to hang him. He makes such an appalling noise that he has to be tied down. There you have a punishment from God that is really visible and apt.

One Lamothe has stated, on the point of being sentenced, that MM. de Besmaus, Chamillart and Berrier (Poncet is added, but I am not so sure of that) had pressed him several times to speak against M. Foucquet and against Delorme, that in consideration of that they would set him free, that he refused and now declares it before being judged. He was condemned to the galleys. Mesdames Foucquet have got a copy of this deposition which they will present tomorrow in the chamber. Perhaps they won't accept it because they are at the voting stage, but the ladies are free to say it, and as the rumour has gone round it must make a great effect on the judges' minds. Isn't it true that all this is pretty extraordinary?

I must tell you yet another heroic act by Masnau. A week ago he was at death's door with a nephritic colic, he took various medicines and at midnight had himself bled. The next day, at seven in the morning, he had himself dragged to the chamber, where he suffered inconceivable pain. The Chancellor saw him turn pale and said to him, 'Monsieur, you can't go on, do withdraw.' But he replied, 'Sir, that is true, but I must die here.' The Chancellor, seeing him half fainting but also adamant, said, 'Very well, then, we will wait for you.' Thereupon Masnau went out for a quarter of an hour, and during that time he passed two stones so large that really it could be called a miracle, if men deserved that God should perform one. The old chap came back jolly and perky, and everyone was truly amazed.

That is all I know. Everybody is interested in this grand affair. Nobody talks of anything else, people argue, draw inferences, count on their fingers, they wax emotional, hope, fear, curse, wish, hate, admire, grow sad, are overwhelmed – in fact, my dear Sir, the state we are in at present is most extraordinary. But the resignation and stead-fastness of our poor dear friend is an inspiring thing. Every day he knows what is happening, and every day one should write volumes in his praise.

I beg you to thank your father very much for his kind little note and the nice things he said. Alas, I have read them, although my head is splitting. Tell him I am delighted that he is a bit fond of me, that is to say quite a lot, and that I am even fonder of him. I have had your last letter. Oh dear, you pay me in excess of what I do for you, so I am in your debt.

To Pomponne

[Paris, Friday 19 December 1664]

This is a day that gives us great hopes, but I must begin further back. I told you how on Wednesday M. Pussort was for the death sentence. On Thursday Noguez, Gisaucourt, Ferriol, Hérault were also for death. Roquesante finished the morning, and having spoken admirably for an hour, he came back to the opinion of M. d'Ormesson. This morning the wind has been in our favour, for two or three hoverers have made up their minds, and one after another we have had La Toison, Masnau, Verdier, La Baume and Catinat of M. d'Ormesson's opinion. It was Poncet's turn to speak, but deciding that the remainder are more or less all in favour of life, he didn't want to speak, although it was only eleven. It is thought that it is to consider what they would like him to say, and that he didn't want to lose favour by voting for death unnecessarily. That is the position, which is such an advantageous one that our joy is not unmixed, for you remember that M. Colbert is so furious that we expect something atrocious and unjust which will throw us back into despair. Were it not for that, my poor friend, we shall have the pleasure and joy of seeing our friend, unhappy though he be, at least with his life saved, which is a great thing. We shall see what happens tomorrow. We have seven, they have six. Here are the remaining ones: Le Féron, Moussy, Brillac, Besard, Renard, Voisin, Pontchartrain and the Chancellor. In that remainder there are more good ones than we need.

[Saturday 20 December]

Praise God, Monsieur, and thank Him. Our poor friend is saved. It went through by thirteen of the opinion of M. d'Ormesson and nine of that of Sainte-Hélène. I am so happy that I am beside myself.

To Pomponne

I was frightened to death that somebody else might have given you the pleasure of learning the good news. My messenger was not in a great hurry; he had said on leaving that he would only get to Livry that night. Anyway, he did get there first, by what he told me. Lord, what a delightful emotion this news was for you, and what an inconceivable joy one feels in the moments which suddenly relieve heart and mind from such a terrible anxiety! It will take me a long time to recover from the joy I felt yesterday. Seriously, it was too complete, I could hardly bear it. The poor man learned this news by some aerial means a few minutes later, and I don't doubt he felt it in all its significance.

This morning the King sent the captain of the watch to Mesdames Foucquet, to command them both to go to Montluçon in Auvergne, the Marquis and Marquise de Charost to Ancenis, and young Foucquet to Joinville in Champagne. The good woman wrote to the King that she was seventy-two and begged His Majesty to give her her last son to help her at the end of her life, which apparently would not be long. As for the prisoner, he has not yet heard his sentence. It is said that tomorrow he will be taken to Pignerol, for the King has changed exile to prison. He is not allowed to have his wife with him, which is against all the rules. But mind you don't let your joy be diminished by all this, mine has increased if possible and shows me even more the extent of our victory. I will faithfully recount to you the sequel to all this, it is curious:

> Non da vino in convito
> Tanto gioir, qual de'nemici il lutto.*

This is what has happened today. The rest tomorrow.

[Monday evening, 22 December]

This morning at ten o'clock M. Foucquet was taken to the chapel of the Bastille. Foucault held his sentence in his hand. He said to him,

---

* 'Wine at a feast gives less joy than the mourning of the enemy.'

'Monsieur, you must tell me your name, so that I know who I am talking to.' M. Foucquet answered, 'You know perfectly well who I am and I shall no more say my name here than I did in the chamber. And to follow the same procedure, I make my protest against the sentence you are going to read to me.' What he said was written down, and at the same time Foucault put on his hat and read the sentence. M. Foucquet listened to it bareheaded. Then Pecquet and Lavalée[1] were separated from him, and the cries and weeping of those poor men were enough to pierce the heart of any whose heart is not made of stone. They made such a strange noise that M. d'Artagnan was constrained to go and console them, for it seemed as though it were a sentence of death that had been read to their master. They were both put in a room at the Bastille, and it is not known what will be done with them.

Meanwhile M. Foucquet went to M. d'Artagnan's room. While he was there he saw M. d'Ormesson pass by the window, having recovered some papers that were in M. d'Artagnan's hands. M. Foucquet saw him and greeted him with an open face full of joy and gratitude. He even called out that he was his very humble servant. M. d'Ormesson returned his greeting with very great civility and came away very sad at heart to tell me what he had seen.

At eleven there was a coach ready, which M. Foucquet entered with four men; M. d'Artagnan was on horseback with fifty musketeers. He will escort him to Pignerol, where he will leave him in prison in the keeping of a certain Saint-Mars, a very decent man, who will have fifty soldiers to guard him. I don't know whether he has been given another manservant. If you only knew how this cruelty appears to everybody, to have taken away these two men, Pecquet and Lavalée. It is inconceivable, and people even draw nasty conclusions from it, from which God will preserve him as He has done hitherto. We must put our trust in Him and leave him under His protection, which has been very helpful. They still refuse to let him have his wife. Permission has been granted for his mother to go only as far as Le Parc, where her daughter is Abbess.[2] His younger brother[3] will follow his sister-in-law; he declared that he had not the wherewithal to live elsewhere. M. and Mme de Charost are still going to Ancenis. M. Bailly, the advocate-

1. *Pecquet and Lavalée*: Foucquet's doctor and personal valet, faithful into exile.
2. At Senlis.
3. Gilles Foucquet.

general, has been dismissed for saying to Gisaucourt, before the verdict, that he ought to restore the company of the Grand Council to honour, and that it would be thoroughly dishonoured if Chamillart, Pussort and he went the same way. That grieves me because of you; it is very hard. *Tantaene animis coelestibus irae?**

No, that doesn't come from so high a quarter. Such coarse and mean revenges could not come from a heart like that of our master. People use his name and take it in vain, as you see. I will tell you the upshot. A great deal could be said about all this, but it is impossible in a letter.

Good-bye, my friend. I am not as modest as you, and without taking refuge in the crowd I assure you that I am very fond of you and think very highly of you.

I saw the comet last night. Its tail is of a most impressive length; I pin some of my hopes on it.

I kiss the hands of your dear wife a thousand times.

To Pomponne

[Paris, Thursday evening, 25 December 1664]

At last mother, daughter-in-law and brother are permitted to be together; they are going off to Montluçon, in the depths of Auvergne. The mother had permission to go to the Parc-aux-Dames with her daughter, but her daughter-in-law is carrying her off with her. M. and Mme de Charost have left for Ancenis. Pecquet and Lavalée are still in the Bastille. Is there anything in the world so horrible as this injustice? Some other manservant has been allotted to the poor unfortunate. M. d'Artagnan is his sole consolation during the journey. It is said that the person who will have custody of him at Pignerol is a very good man. God grant it may be so or, better still, God protect him! He has so visibly protected him that we must believe He is taking particular care of him. La Forêt accosted him when he was leaving and he said, 'I am so glad to see you. I know your fidelity and affection. Tell our womenfolk not to be too cast down, that I am being brave and am well.' That is really admirable. Good-bye, dear Sir. Let us be brave

*'Can there be such violent anger in the hearts of the gods?' Virgil, *Aeneid* I.

like him and not let the joy of Saturday's admirable sentence become stale.

Mme de Grignan is dead.[1]

[Friday evening, 26 December]

Your handsome thanks suggest that you are giving me my dismissal, but I'm not accepting it yet. I mean to write to you when I like, and as soon as there are some verses from the Pont-Neuf[2] or elsewhere I will send them post-haste. Our dear friend in on the road. A rumour had spread here suggesting he was very ill. Everybody said, 'What! Already?' It was also rumoured that M. d'Artagnan had sent a request to Court asking what he should do with a sick prisoner, and that the harsh reply was that he should continue escorting him whatever his condition. That is all false. But you can see from that what we all have in our hearts and how dangerous it is to lay foundations upon which we magnify everything we see. Pecquet and Lavalée are still in the Bastille. This conduct is indeed astonishing. The sittings of the chamber will be resumed after Epiphany.

I think that the poor exiled women have now reached their resting-place. When our friend is at his I will let you know, for I must see him as far as Pignerol, and please God that from Pignerol we can bring him back where we would like him to be. And you, poor Sir, how long is your exile going on? I often wonder. Embrace your father a thousand times on my behalf. I have been told that Madame your wife is here; I will go and see her. I had supper yesterday with your friend and she and I spoke of going to see you.

To Bussy-Rabutin

[Paris, Tuesday 4 December 1668]

Didn't you get my letter in which I spared your life and refused to kill you when you were down? I expected a response after that noble action,

---

1. Mme de Grignan. First wife of the future son-in-law of Mme de S.
2. *verses from the Pont-Neuf*: lampoons and scurrilous attacks were publicly shown there.

but it never occurred to you; you were content to get to your feet and take up your sword again as I ordered. I hope it won't ever be to use it against me.

I must tell you a piece of news which will perhaps give you joy. It is that at last the prettiest girl in France is marrying, not the prettiest boy, but one of the finest gentlemen in the realm, M. de Grignan, whom you have known for a long time. All his wives have died to make room for your cousin, and even his father and his son, by extraordinary good fortune, so that being richer than he has ever been and, moreover, by birth and position as well as his good qualities just what we could wish, we are not haggling as one customarily does; we put our trust in the two families who have been connected with him before us. He seems very pleased to be connected with us, and as soon as we have news from the Archbishop of Arles his uncle, his other uncle the Bishop of Uzès being here, the business will be concluded before the end of the year. As I am a fairly punctilious lady, I did not want to fail to ask your opinion and approval. The general public seems pleased, which is a great deal, for one is so silly that to some extent one is influenced by that.

But here is one more item about which I want you to satisfy me if you have a shred of affection left for me. I know that you have put at the bottom of a portrait you have of me that I was married to a Breton gentleman honoured by connections with the Vassé and Rabutin families. That is not fair, dear cousin. I have recently become so knowledgeable about the house of Sévigné that it would be on my conscience to leave you in this error. We had to prove our nobility in Brittany, and those who have the most have taken the greatest pleasure in using this chance to display their wares. Here are ours:

Fourteen marriage contracts from father to son, three hundred and fifty years of knighthood, the fathers sometimes important in the Breton wars and noted in history, sometimes in retirement at home like real Bretons; sometimes plenty of money, sometimes not much, but always good and great marriages. Those dating back three hundred and fifty years, before which there are only Christian names, are du Quelnec, Montmorency, Baraton and Châteaugiron. These names are distinguished: the women were married to Rohans and Clissons. Since these four there have been Guesclins, Coëtquens, Rosmadecs, Clindons, Sévignés of the same family, du Bellays, Rieux, Bodégats,

Plessis-Tréals and others I cannot recall at the moment, down to Vassé and Rabutin. All that is true, believe me. So I beg you, dear cousin, if you want to oblige me, to alter your nameplate, and if you don't want to put anything good on it not to put anything disparaging. I expect this proof of your sense of justice and the remains of your friendship for me.

Good-bye, my dear cousin. Let me have your news soon and let our friendship be henceforth unclouded.

From Bussy-Rabutin

[Chaseu, Saturday 8 December 1668]

I received your letter in which you told me you didn't wish to kill me when I was down, my dear cousin, and I did answer it and, moreover, I know that my letter was given to one of your servants. So please find out what has become of it.

You are quite right to believe that the news of the marriage of Mlle de Sévigné will give me joy; loving and admiring her as I do, few things can give me more, especially as M. de Grignan is a man of quality and merit and has a fine position. There is only one thing that makes me nervous for the prettiest girl in France, and that is that Grignan, who is not yet old, has already reached his third wife – he wears them out nearly as fast as his clothes, or at any rate his carriages. Apart from that I think my cousin is very fortunate, but on his side nothing could be added to his good fortune. For the rest, Madame, I am only too grateful for the deference you pay me in this matter. Mlle de Sévigné could not marry anyone to whom I would more wholeheartedly give my approval.

As to the other matter in your letter, in which you say that you know I have put at the bottom of the portrait I possess of you that you were *married to a Breton gentleman who was honoured by the connection with the Vassé and Rabutin families*, I will say that I don't doubt that that is what you have been told, but you must not doubt on your side that you have been told lies. If you still have a spark of friendship for me, my dear cousin, you will show those who have misinformed you what I am saying about them. You owe them this return for their false information, for perhaps they are trying to prejudice you quite wrongly against me. Perhaps also they want to ascribe to me the insult they mean to do to the house of Sévigné. Here, word for word, is what there is beneath the portrait of you in my drawing-room:

Marie de Rabutin, daughter of Baron de Chantal, Marquise de Sévigné; a woman of extraordinary genius, whose virtue is compatible with gaiety and charm.

If I had put what you write, I would freely admit it and I would change the nameplate if I were sure, for so much jiggery-pokery goes on in contracts that I rely more on accepted annals and common knowledge than on makers of genealogies.

As for the families you inform me are better than ours, I don't agree. I grant it to Montmorency for honours, but not for antiquity. But the others I don't know. I don't understand them any more than I do Low Breton, and yet I am not without some knowledge in this matter. I rank the Guesclins, Rosmadecs, Coëtquens and Rieux higher than Quelnecs, Baratons and Châteaugirons. But we are not making comparisons, we are only concerned with assuring you once again that those who have so carefully told you about the inscription I have concerning you in my room at Bussy have told you a wicked lie, and that you must not trust such people.

I have yet another portrayal of you in my room, under which is written:

Marie de Rabutin, lively, pleasant and virtuous, daughter of Celse-Bénigne de Rabutin and Marie de Coulanges and wife of Henri de Sévigné.

In our genealogy that I have had put at the end of my gallery at Bussy, this is what is written about you:

Marie de Rabutin, one of the prettiest girls in France, married Henri de Sévigné, gentleman of Brittany, which was a piece of good fortune for him, because of the wealth and beauty of the young lady.

There is nothing in all these inscriptions which could give cause for complaint from the house of Sévigné. As for the one in which I say that you were a piece of good fortune for your husband, I don't know whether he would have had the sincerity to agree, but I do know that you would have been so for an even greater aristocrat than he and a man of greater merit, and that is so firmly fixed in my head that nothing could remove it.

I believed that after our last combat I should never have another brush with you, particularly over the portraits, but I see that either you must take my life or I yours. Good-bye, beautiful cousin, I really do love you with all my heart.

To Madame de Grignan

[Livry, Saturday 1 June 1669]

My dear, I must be persuaded of your real affection for me, since I am still alive. The tenderness I feel for you is a very strange thing; I don't know whether unintentionally I show it very much, but I do know that I hide still more of it. I won't say what emotion and joy your manservant and your letter gave me. I have even had the pleasure of not believing you were ill; I have even been fortunate enough to believe it was just love. For a long time I have said: when you want to be you are adorable, and everything you do is perfect.

I am writing in the middle of the garden as you supposed, and the nightingales and little birds have heard with great pleasure, but scant respect, what I have told them on your behalf; they are perched in a way which deprives them of any kind of humility. Yesterday I was alone with the Hamadryads for two hours. I talked to them about you and their answers pleased me very much. I don't know whether the countryside here as a whole is very pleased with me, for having enjoyed all these beautiful things I couldn't help saying:

> Mais quoi que vous ayez, vous n'avez pas Caliste,
> Et moi, je ne vois rien quand je ne la vois pas.*

And that is so true that I am setting off again after dinner with joy. Decorum plays no part whatever in anything I do, which is why the excessive liberty you ascribe to me wounds my heart. This heart of mine has resources that you can't understand.

I congratulate you on winning twenty pistoles. Your loss seemed slight as it was followed by such a great honour and a good supper. I have remembered you to your uncles, aunts and cousins, who worship you and are delighted with your account. That suits them, but it doesn't at all where I am going for dinner, and that is why I am sending

*'But whatever you have, you have not Caliste
And I can see nothing when I don't see her.'

it back to you. I had left a letter for Brancas with my doorkeeper, I see it has been forgotten.

Good-bye, dearest and most lovable child, you know I am yours.

To Monsieur de Grignan

[Paris, Wednesday 6 August 1670]

Haven't I really given you the prettiest wife in the world? Can anyone show more breeding, be more decorous in her conduct? Can anyone love you more tenderly? Can anyone have more Christian sentiments? Can anyone long more passionately to be with you? And can anyone be more devoted to all her duties? It is quite ridiculous for me to be saying so much good about my own daughter, but I admire her behaviour as much as other people do, and all the more for seeing her closer at hand; and indeed, however fine an opinion I had of her conduct in the main things, I had no idea she was as punctilious about everything else as she is. I assure you that the world at large does justice to her too, and that she misses none of the praises she deserves. Here is my old thesis, for which I shall be stoned one of these days: it is that public opinion is neither mad nor unfair. Mme de Grignan must be too satisfied with it to argue with me just now.

You cannot conceive what worries she has gone through about your health, and I am delighted that you are better, both for love of you and love of her. I beseech you, if you still have any squalls to expect from your inside, to ask it to wait until my daughter has had her baby. She still grumbles every day about being kept here, and says in all serious-ness that it is very cruel to have been separated from you. It is just as though we have kept you two hundred leagues from her for fun. I urge you to reassure her about this and let her know what joy you feel in hoping she will have a happy confinement here. Nothing was more out of the question than to move her in her condition, and nothing will be better for her health, and even for her reputation, than to have her confinement here, where the greatest skill is available, and to have stayed here, given her way of life. If she then wanted to go flighty and coquettish she would do so more than a year before one would expect, so high is the opinion she has won for her good sense. I call upon all the Grignans here present to witness the truth of all I am saying. The joy it gives me touches me very closely too, and I am delighted that the outcome has so perfectly justified your choice.

I am not giving you any other news; it would be encroaching upon my daughter's rights. I only beg you to believe that nobody can be more affectionately concerned about all your affairs than I am.

To Coulanges

[Paris, Monday 15 December 1670]

What I am about to communicate to you is the most astonishing thing, the most surprising, the most marvellous, the most miraculous, most triumphant, most baffling, most unheard of, most singular, most extra-ordinary, most unbelievable, most unforeseen, biggest, tiniest, rarest, commonest, the most talked about, the most secret up to this day, the most brilliant, the most enviable, in fact a thing of which only one example can be found in past ages, and, moreover, that example is a false one; a thing nobody can believe in Paris (how could anyone believe it in Lyons?), a thing that makes everybody cry 'mercy on us', a thing that fills Mme de Rohan and Mme de Hauterive with joy, in short a thing that will be done on Sunday and those who see it will think they are seeing visions – a thing that will be done on Sunday and perhaps not done by Monday. I can't make up my mind to say it. Guess, I give you three tries. You give up? Very well, I shall have to tell you. M. de Lauzun is marrying on Sunday, in the Louvre – guess who? I give you four guesses, ten, a hundred. Mme de Coulanges will be saying: That's not so very hard to guess, it's Mlle de La Vallière. Not at all, Madame. Mlle de Retz, then? Not at all, you're very provincial. Of course, how silly we are, you say: It's Mlle Colbert. You're still further away. Then it must be Mlle de Créquy? You're nowhere near. I shall have to tell you in the end: he is marrying, on Sunday, in the Louvre, with the King's permission, Mademoiselle, Mademoiselle de ... Mademoiselle ... guess the name. He's marrying Mademoiselle, of course! Honestly, on my honour, on my sworn oath! Mademoiselle, the great Mademoiselle, Mademoiselle, daughter of the late Monsieur, Mademoiselle, granddaughter of Henri IV, Mademoiselle d'Eu,

Mademoiselle de Dombes, Mademoiselle de Montpensier, Mademoiselle d'Orléans, Mademoiselle, first cousin of the King, Mademoiselle, destined for a throne, Mademoiselle, the only bride in France worthy of Monsieur. There's a fine subject for conversation. If you shout aloud, if you are beside yourself, if you say we have lied, that it is false, that you are being taken in, that this is a fine old tale and too feeble to be imagined, if, in fine, you should even abuse us, we shall say you are perfectly right. We did as much ourselves.

Good-bye, letters coming by this post will show you whether we are telling the truth or not.

To Coulanges

[Paris, Friday 19 December 1670]

What you might call a bolt from the blue occurred yesterday evening at the Tuileries, but I must start the story further back. You have heard as far as the joy, transports, ecstasies of the Princess and her fortunate lover. Well, the matter was announced on Monday, as you were told. Tuesday was spent in talk, astonishment, compliments. On Wednesday Mademoiselle made a settlement on M. de Lauzun, with the object of bestowing on him the titles, names and honours needed for mention in the marriage contract, and that was enacted on the same day. So, to go on with, she bestowed on him four duchies: first the earldom of Eu, which is the highest peerage in France and gives him first precedence, the duchy of Montpensier, which name he bore all day yesterday, the duchy of Saint-Fargeau and that of Châtellerault, the whole estimated to be worth twenty-two millions. Then the contract was drawn up, in which he took the name of Montpensier. On Thursday morning, that is yesterday, Mademoiselle hoped that the King would sign the contract as he had promised, but by seven in the evening His Majesty, being persuaded by the Queen, Monsieur and divers greybeards that this business was harmful to his reputation, decided to break it off, and after summoning Mademoiselle and M. de Lauzun, declared to them, in the presence of Monsieur le Prince, that he forbade their thinking any more about this marriage. M. de Lauzun received this order with all the respect, all the submissiveness, all the stoicism and all the despair that such a great fall required. As for Mademoiselle, according to her mood she burst into tears, cries, violent outbursts of grief, exaggerated lamentations, and she remained in bed all day, taking nothing but broth. So much for a beautiful dream, a fine subject for a novel or a tragedy, but above all for arguing and talking for ever and ever. And that is what we are doing day and night, evening and morning, on and on without respite. We hope you will do the same. Upon which I most humbly kiss your hands.

To Coulanges

[Paris, Wednesday 24 December 1670]

You now know the romantic story of Mademoiselle and M. de Lauzun. It is a real subject of tragedy according to all the rules of the theatre. The other day we were plotting out the acts and scenes, giving it four days instead of twenty-four hours, and it made a perfect play. Never have such changes been seen in so short a time, never have you seen such general emotion, never have you heard such extraordinary news. M. de Lauzun has played his part as to the manner born; he has endured this misfortune with a self-control, courage and yet grief mingled with profound respect which have earned him universal admiration. What he has lost is of inestimable value, but the goodwill of the King, which he has kept, is also beyond price, and his fortune seems by no means in a parlous state. Mademoiselle has behaved very well too. She has wept a lot, but today she has returned her duty calls at the Louvre, whence she had been receiving all the visitors. So that is that. Good-bye.

To Coulanges

[Paris, Wednesday 31 December 1670]

I have received your replies to my letters. I can understand how astonished you have been about all that has gone on between the 15th and 20th of this month, astonishment well justified by the subject. I also admire your good sense and correctness of judgement in believing that this great enterprise could not keep going from Monday until Sunday. Modesty forbids my praising you unreservedly for this, as I said and thought exactly the same as you. I said to my daughter on Monday, 'This will never steer a safe course until Sunday,' and I was willing to bet, although everybody was full of the wedding, that it would not come off. And indeed on Thursday the weather clouded over and the storm broke at ten o'clock that night, as I told you.

That same Thursday I was at Mademoiselle's by nine in the morning, having heard that she was going off to be married in the country and that the Coadjutor of Reims was to officiate. That was decided on Wednesday evening, for the idea of the Louvre had been given up by Tuesday. Mademoiselle was writing, but she let me enter, finished her letter and then bade me kneel down beside her bed. She told me who she was writing to and why, and about the handsome presents she had given the day before and the name she had bestowed; that there was no suitable match for her in Europe, but that she wanted to be married. She told me word for word the conversation she had had with the King, and she seemed to be transported with joy at making a man so happy. She spoke tenderly about the qualities and the gratitude of M. de Lauzun. In view of all this I said, 'Well, Mademoiselle, you are very happy, but why didn't you finish the business at once, on Monday? Don't you see that such a long delay gives the whole kingdom time to talk and that it is tempting God and the King to want to pursue such an extraordinary affair for so long?' She said I was right; but she was so full of confidence that what I said hardly made any impression. She came back to the pedigree and great qualities of M. de Lauzun. I quoted these lines of Sévère in *Polyeucte*:

> Du moins ne la peut-on blâmer d'un mauvais choix:
> Polyeucte a du nom, et sort du sang des rois.*

She embraced me affectionately. This conversation lasted an hour, and it is impossible to repeat it all, but I had certainly made myself very pleasant throughout this time and I can say without vanity that she was very glad to have someone to talk to, for her heart was overflowing. At ten o'clock she received the rest of France who came to congratulate

---

* 'At least she cannot be blamed for choosing badly:
    Polyeucte has a name, and is of royal blood.'
                                            Corneille, *Polyeucte*.

her. She expected news all the morning, but none came. After dinner she amused herself by putting the finishing touches herself to M. de Montpensier's apartment. You know what happened in the evening.

The next day, Friday, I went to see her and found her in bed. When she saw me she cried all the more, and I was all wet with her tears. 'Alas,' she said, 'do you remember what you said yesterday? Oh what fatal prudence, oh, what prudence can do!' Her weeping made me shed tears too. I have been back there twice. She is very distressed, and has always treated me as someone who felt her grief, and she was not mistaken. On this occasion I have been through emotions one does not often feel for people of such rank. This only between the two of us and Mme de Coulanges, for you can well imagine that this gossip would seem quite silly to other people. Good-bye.

To Monsieur de Grignan

[Paris, Friday 16 January 1671]

Alas, I still have the poor child here, and in spite of all her endeavours it was not in her power to leave on the 10th of this month as she had planned. The rains have been and still are so terrible that it would have been madness to venture. All the rivers have burst their banks, all main roads are under water, the ruts cannot be seen and it is very likely that there would be a spill at every ford. In fact things are such that Mme de Rochefort, who is at her country home, desperately anxious to return to Paris, where her husband wants her and her mother is waiting for her with incredible impatience, cannot set out because there is no guarantee of safety, and certainly this winter is appalling. It has never frozen for a moment, but rained every day like cloudbursts. No boat can now pass under the bridges and the arches of the Pont-Neuf are almost submerged. Really it is most strange. I confess that the excessive amount of such awful weather set me against her departure for several days. I don't expect that she will avoid the cold, mud or exhaustion of the journey, but I don't want her to be drowned.

This reason, however valid, would not keep her here at present were it not for the Coadjutor,[1] who is to travel with her but has undertaken

---

1. *Coadjutor*: see Grignan, no. 4, in List of Persons.

to officiate at the wedding of his Harcourt cousin. This ceremony takes place at the Louvre. M. de Lyonne is the notary. The King has spoken to him (I mean the Coadjutor) on the subject. This affair has been postponed from day to day and may not come off for another week. Meanwhile I see my daughter in such a state of impatience to set off that life isn't worth living for her at present, and unless the Coadjutor drops the wedding I can see her tempted to do something silly, namely set off without him. It would be so strange to go alone and so fortunate for her to go with her brother-in-law that I shall do everything in my power to prevent their separating. Meanwhile the floods will abate a little.

Moreover I must point out that it gives me no pleasure to have her at present. I know she must go, and all she does here consists of duties and business. We are not interested in meeting anybody, we enjoy no pleasures, we always feel sad at heart, all the time we talk about the roads, the rains, tragic tales of people who have ventured. In a word, although you know how I love her, the state we are in at present is boring and wearisome. There has been no pleasure in these last few days.

I am most grateful, my dear Comte, for all your kindness to me and for all your sympathy. You understand what I am going through, and shall go through, better than anybody else. But I am sorry that the joy you will have when you see her may be marred by this thought. These are the ups and downs that life is made up of. Good-bye, my very dear Comte, the length of my letters is killing you, but I hope you will see what is making me write them.

To Madame de Grignan

[Paris, Monday 2 February 1671]

As you are quite determined to have your little box back, here it is. I do urge you to keep and receive, as lovingly as I am giving it to you, a little present I have destined for you. I have gladly had the diamond recut, with the idea that you will keep it all your life. I do beg you to, my dearest, and may I never see it in other hands than yours. May it remind you of me and of the overwhelming love I have for you, and in how many ways I would like to prove it to you on all occasions, whatever you may think about it.

To Madame de Grignan

[Paris, Friday 6 February 1671]

My affliction would be very ordinary if I could describe it to you, so I won't undertake it. I look in vain for my dear daughter, but can no longer find her, and her every step takes her further from me. So I went off to Sainte-Marie, still weeping, still lifeless. It seemed as if my heart and soul were being torn out of me, and truly, what a brutal separation! I asked to be free to be alone. I was taken into Mme du Housset's room, where they lit a fire for me. Agnes looked at me but didn't speak; such was our understanding. I stayed there until five and never stopped sobbing; all my thoughts were killing me. I wrote to M. de Grignan, in what tone you can well imagine. I went on to Mme de La Fayette's, and she intensified my grief by the sympathy she showed. She was alone and ill, and depressed about the death of one of her sisters who was a nun – in fact she was just as I would have wished her. M. de La Rochefoucauld came. We talked of nothing but you, of the justification I had for being upset and of his intention to speak severely to *Mélusine*. I can tell you that she will be harried. D'Hacqueville will give you a good account of this affair. I came home eventually from Mme de La Fayette's at eight, but coming in here, oh God! Can you imagine what I felt as I came up the stairs? That room where I always used to go – alas, I found the doors open but everything empty and in a muddle, and your poor little girl to remind me of my own. Can you understand all I went through? Black awakenings during the night, and in the morning I was not a step nearer finding rest for my soul. The time after dinner I spent with Mme de La Troche at the Arsenal. In the evening I had your letter, which threw me back into my first grief, and tonight I shall finish this at Mme de Coulanges's, where I shall hear some news. For my part this is all I know about, together with the regrets of all those you have left here. If I felt like it the whole of my letter could be full of people's good wishes.

I have learned at Mme de Lavardin's the news I am sending now, and I have heard from Mme de La Fayette that yesterday they had a conversation with *Mélusine*, the details of which are not easy to write, but in the end she was confounded and shattered by the enormity of her behaviour, which was condemned with no mitigation at all. She is very happy about the line suggested to her, which is to hold her tongue very devoutly, and on that condition she will not be shattered. You have friends who have your interests very much at heart. I see nothing but people who are fond of you and value you and so readily share my grief. So far I have only felt like going to see Mme de La Fayette. People are very eager to look me up and take me out, and that frightens me to death.

I do urge you, my dear child, to look after your health. Look after it for my sake, and don't give yourself up to that cruel self-neglect from which it seems to me one cannot recover. I embrace you with a love that can have no possible equal, with due respect to everybody else's.

The marriage contract between Mlle d'Houdancourt and M. de Ventadour was signed this morning, and also the Abbé de Chambonnais was appointed to the see of Lodève. Madame la Princesse will leave on Ash Wednesday for Châteauroux, where Monsieur le Prince wants her to stay for a time. M. de a Marguerie takes the place in the Council of M. d'Étampes, who has died. Mme de Mazarin arrives in Paris this evening; the King has extended his protection to her and has dispatched a carriage and team of horses to meet her at Le Lys with an officer and eight guards.

Here is a piece of ingratitude which won't fail to appeal to you, and which I mean to turn to good account when I write my book on great ingratitudes. Maréchal d'Albret has convicted Mme d'Heudicourt not only of an affair with M. de Béthune, which he had always been prepared to doubt, but of having said all the evil imaginable about him and Mme Scarron. There is no unkind thing, according to him, she has not tried to do to both of them, and it is so widely known that Mme Scarron won't see her any more, nor will the whole Hôtel de Richelieu. There is a woman with her reputation gone, but she has the consolation of not having contributed to it!

To Madame de Grignan

I do urge you, dear heart, to look after your eyes – as to mine, you know they must be used up in your service. You must realize, my love, that because of the way you write to me I have to cry when I read your letters. To understand something of the state I am in over you, add to the tenderness and natural feeling I have for you this little circumstance that I am quite sure you love me, and then consider my overwhelming emotion. Naughty girl! Why do you sometimes hide such precious treasures from me? Are you afraid I might die of joy? But aren't you also afraid that I should die of sorrow at believing I see the opposite? I call d'Hacqueville as witness to the state he saw me in once before. But let's leave these gloomy memories and let me enjoy a blessing without which life is hard and unpleasant; and these are not mere words, they are truths. Mme de Guénégaud has told me of the state she saw you in on my account. Do please keep the reason, but let us have no more tears, I beg you – they are not so healthy for you as for me. At the moment I am fairly reasonable. I can control myself if need be, and sometimes I go for four or five hours just like anyone else, but the slightest thing throws me back into my first condition. A memory, a place, a word, a thought if a little too clear, above all your letters (and even my own as I am writing them), someone talking about you, these things are rocks on which my constancy founders, and these breakers are often met with.

I have seen Raymond[1] at the Comtesse du Lude's. She sang me a new solo from the ballet – quite admirable. But if you want someone to sing it, do it yourself. I see Mme de Villars and enjoy seeing her because she enters into my sentiments. She sends you her kindest regards. Mme de La Fayette also appreciates fully the affection I feel for you and is touched by the affection you show me. I am most often in my family circle, sometimes here in the evening out of weariness, though not often.

I have seen poor Mme Amelot. She weeps a lot; I understand all about that. Refer to certain people in our letters, so that I can say so

---

1. *Raymond*: a famous singer.

to them. I have only seen the Verneuils and the Arpajons once. I go to the sermons of Mascaron, Bourdaloue and Company; they vie with each other.

Those are my bits of news. I very much want to know yours, and how you got on at Lyons, whether you looked beautiful there, what route you took, if you said a prayer for Monsieur le Marquis[2] and whether your prayers will have been answered for your embarkation. To tell you the truth, I think of nothing else. I know your route and where you have put up each night. On Sunday you were in Lyons, and you would have done well to rest there for a few days.

You have made me want to ask you about the Shrove Tuesday masquerade. I found out that a great man, three inches taller than anybody else, had had a wonderful suit made. He didn't want to wear it, and it happened quite fortuitously that a lady he doesn't know at all, and to whom he has never spoken, was not present at the assembly.[3] Furthermore, I must say like Voiture: *nobody has died so far because of your absence except myself*. Not but what the Carnival has been extremely dull – you can take credit to yourself for that; for my part I thought it was because of you, though not enough for an absence like yours.

This time I am sending this letter to Provence. My love to M. de Grignan, and I am dying to have news of you. As soon as I get a letter I want another at once, and only breathe again when one comes.

You tell me wonders about the tomb of M. de Montmorency and the beauty of the Mesdemoiselles de Valençay. You write extremely well, nobody writes better. Never abandon what is natural, your turn of phrase is formed upon it and it makes for perfect style. I have given your compliments to M. de La Rochefoucauld and to Mme de La Fayette and Langlade – they all esteem and love you and will do anything for you. As for D'Hacqueville, we never talk of anything but you.

I laughed at your madcap behaviour over divulging confidential matter, and understand it. But what an unfortunate chance that it should turn out that everything you wanted to find out from the Coadjutor and he from you should be precisely about things out of

2. Monsieur le Marquis, i.e. a son. Later Mme de S. will refer to the Grignan son as M. le Marquis.
3. The great man means the King, the lady either La Vallière or Montespan.

your control! Your songs seemed pretty to me, I recognized the various styles.

Ah, my dear, how I would love to see a bit of you, hear you, embrace you, watch you go by, even if the rest is too much to hope for. Well, well, these are thoughts I cannot resist. I feel I suffer at having lost you, and this separation pains my heart and soul just like a bodily illness. I can't thank you enough for all the letters you have written on the journey. These attentions are too kind and have an effect also, for nothing is lost on me. You have written from everywhere. I have marvelled at your kindness. It cannot be done without a great deal of love, for without that one would find it much pleasanter to rest and go to bed. It has been a great consolation to me. The impatience I feel to have more, from Roanne and Lyons and your point of embarkation, is anything but ordinary; whether you disembarked at the bridge, and your arrival at Arles, what you thought of that raging Rhône compared with our gentle Loire to which you have said so many polite things. How good of you to remember it like an old friend! Alas, what don't I remember? The tiniest things are dear to me, I have a thousand imaginary worries. What a difference! I always used to come back here with impatience and pleasure, but at present look where I will I can't find you. How can one live in the knowledge that whatever one does one will never find such a dear child again? I will prove whether I long for her by the journey I shall undertake to find her again. I have had a letter from M. de Grignan. There are none for you. He tells me that he will be back here next winter. Will he leave you there or will you be following? But in this uncertainty shall I let your apartment? Every day I am on the point of settling it. Let me know.

The Dauphin was ill, but he is better now. The Court will be at Versailles until Monday. Mme de La Vallière is quite back in favour. The King welcomed her with tears of joy, and likewise Mme de Montespan, with much affectionate talk. It is all difficult to understand, and we must keep our own counsel. This year's news doesn't last from one post to the next.

Mme de Verneuil, Mme d'Arpajon, Mmes de Villars, de Saint-Géran, M. de Guitaut, his wife, the Comtesse, M. de La Roche-foucauld, M. de Langlade, Mme de La Fayette, my aunt, my cousin, my uncles, my other cousins, male and female, Mme de Vauvineux, all kiss your hands thousands and thousands of times.

I see your daughter every day in front of the fire, as you might say. I want her to be fine and upstanding, that is my chief care. It would be a fine thing to be your daughter and M. de Grignan's and not be beautifully formed. I am clever, I even take unnecessary precautions.

Yesterday I saw Mme du Puy-du-Fou, who sends greetings. Also Mme de Janson and one Mme Le Blanc. Anything to do with you even a hundred leagues away is more pleasant to me than anything else. Oh Lord, that Rhône! You are on it now! I can think of nothing else. I kiss your poor girls.

To Madame de Grignan

[Paris, Friday 20 February 1671]

I confess I am extraordinarily anxious to have news of you. Remember, my dear love, that I have had none at all since La Palisse. I don't know anything, therefore, about the rest of your journey as far as Lyons, nor your route down to Provence. In a word, I am eating my heart out, and my impatience is upsetting my sleep. I am quite sure there will be some letters (I don't doubt you have written), but I am waiting for them and haven't got them. So I have to find consolation and enjoyment in writing to you.

Know then, my child, that the day before yesterday, Wednesday, after returning from M. de Coulanges's, where we make up our letters for post-day, I returned home to bed – nothing extraordinary about that. But what is most extraordinary is that at three in the morning I heard people shouting 'Burglars', 'Fire', and these shouts were so near me and so persistent that I was sure it was here. I even thought I heard my granddaughter's name, and felt sure she had been burnt alive. I got up with this fear in the dark and shaking so much that I could hardly stand. I rushed to her room – that is, yours – and found everything perfectly quiet. But I saw Guitaut's house well alight, and the flames were blowing over Mme de Vauvineux's house. In our courtyards, and especially M. de Guitaut's, there was a horrible glare. And cries, confusion, terrifying noises, beams and joists coming down. I had my doors opened and sent my servants to help. M. de Guitaut sent me a cashbox containing his most precious valuables. I stored it in my room and then was anxious to go out into the street to gape like everybody else. There I found M. and Mme de Guitaut half naked, Mme de Vauvineux, the Venetian Ambassador and all his staff, the little Vauvineux girl who was being carried still asleep into the Ambassador's house, and various pieces of furniture and silver also being taken there. Mme de Vauvineux was having her furniture moved out. I myself was in a sort of island, but I felt very sorry indeed for my poor neighbours. Mme Guéton and her brother were handing out good advice. We were all in a state of consternation, the fire had now such a hold that nobody dared go near it, and we could only hope that the blaze would come to an end with the end of poor Guitaut's house. He was pitiful to behold. He wanted to go and rescue his mother, in danger of being burnt to death on the third floor, but his wife clung to him and held him back by force. He was torn between the agony of not helping his mother and fear of hurting his wife, who was five months pregnant. He was pitiful to behold. Finally he begged me to look after his wife, which I did. He found that his mother had got through the flames and was safe. He wanted to go and recover some papers, but could not get near where they were. At length he came back to us in the street, where I had made his wife sit down.

Some Capuchins, full of charity and skill, worked so well that they isolated the fire. Water was then thrown on the rest of the blaze and at last *Le combat finit faute de combattants*,* that is to say after the first and second floors of the antechamber and the small room and study to the right of the drawing-room had been completely destroyed. They were thankful for what remained of the house, although poor Guitaut will have suffered a loss of at least ten thousand écus, for they intend to have this apartment rebuilt, and it was painted and gilded. There were also several fine pictures belonging to M. Le Blanc, who owns the building, as well as lots of tables, mirrors, miniatures, pieces of furniture and tapestries. They are very upset about some letters; I have taken it into my head that they were from Monsieur le Prince. However, by about five in the morning we had to think about Mme Guitaut. I offered her my bed, but Mme Guéton put her in her own because she has several furnished rooms. We had her bled and sent for Boucher, who is very afraid that the great shock will bring on a miscarriage in

*'The fight ended for want of fighters.' Corneille, *Le Cid*.

a matter of days (there is every chance of it). So she is at poor Mme Guéton's; everyone goes in to see them and I go on with my attentions because I began too well not to carry on to the end.

You will ask how the fire started in that building; we had no idea. There was no fire burning in the apartment where it began. But if one could have seen the funny side on such a terrible occasion, what portraits could not have been painted of the state we were all in? Guitaut was in his nightshirt, with some breeches on. Mme de Guitaut was bare-legged and had lost one of her bedroom slippers. Mme de Vauvineux was in her petticoat with no dressing-gown. All the servants and neighbours had nightcaps on. The Ambassador, in dressing-gown and wig, maintained perfectly the dignity of a Serene Highness. But his secretary was wonderful to behold. Talk about the chest of Hercules! This was a very different affair. The whole of it was on view, white, fat and dimpled, particularly as he was without a shirt, for the string that should keep it on had been lost in the scrimmage. That is the sad news from our neighbourhood. I beg M. Deville[1] to go the rounds every night to see that all fires are out; one cannot take too many precautions against a disaster like this. I trust, my dear, that the passage on the water was good. In a word, I wish you every good thing and pray God to shield you from all the bad.

M. de Ventadour was to have been married on Thursday, that is yesterday, but he has a temperature. The Maréchale de La Mothe has lost five hundred écus' worth of fish.

Mérinville is marrying the daughter of the late Launay Gravé and Mme de Piennes. She has 200,000 francs. Monsieur d'Albi assured us he deserved 500,000, but it is true he will have the support of M. and Mme de Piennes, who certainly won't be out of favour at Court.

I recently saw Monsieur d'Uzès at Mme de Lavardin's; we talked all the time about you. He told me that that matter of yours at the States should go through without difficulty; if that is so, Monsieur de Marseille won't be awkward. You must see the thing through, my dearest. Do your utmost, be nice to Monsieur de Marseille, let the Coadjutor play his part properly and let me know how it goes off. You can easily imagine the interest I take in it.

The other day at table at the home of Monsieur du Mans, Courcelles

---

1. M. Deville, steward to the Grignans.

said he had two bumps on his head that prevented his putting on a wig. This ridiculous tale drove us all away from the table before the fruit was finished for fear of bursting out laughing in his face. Shortly afterwards d'Olonne arrived. M. de La Rochefoucauld said to me, 'Madame, they can't both stay together in this room,' and in fact Courcelles left.

For the rest, that illusion they wanted to give the Coadjutor that there would be a present for whoever married off his cousin was a very hollow one; he didn't get any more than the person who brought about the engagement. I was very pleased about it. D'Hacqueville had forgotten to put this in his letter.

I cannot cope with those who send you their love. They are numberless – Paris, the Court, the universe. But La Troche wants special mention, and so does Lavardin.

There's a lot of odds and ends for you, my poor dear. But to keep on saying I love you, think only of you, am only concerned with what concerns you, that you are the delight of my life, that nobody has ever been loved as dearly as you, such repetition would bore you. A kiss for my dear Grignan and my Coadjutor.

I have not yet had my letters. M. de Coulanges has his, and I know, dearest, that you reached Lyons in good health and more beautiful than an angel, according to M. du Gué.

To Madame de Grignan

[Wednesday 4 March 1671]

Oh, my dear, what a letter! What a picture of the state you have been in, and how little I should have kept my word had I promised not to be terrified by so great a peril! I know perfectly well that it is over, but it is impossible to envisage your life so near its end without shuddering with horror. And M. de Grignan lets you steer the boat! And when you are foolhardy he thinks it funny to be even more so! Instead of making you wait until the storm was over he was willing to expose you to danger without caring a bit! Oh Lord, how much better it would have been to be nervous and tell you that if you weren't frightened yourself he was, and that he wouldn't let you cross the Rhône in such weather! How hard I find it to understand his love at a time like that! That Rhône terrifies everybody! That bridge at Avignon under which it would be wrong to pass even after taking precautions in advance! A whirlwind that blew you violently under an arch! What a miracle that you weren't smashed and drowned in a moment! My dear, I can't bear to think of it, it makes me shudder, and it has awakened me with a start quite out of my control. Do you still think the Rhône is just some water? Honestly, weren't you terrified of such an imminent and inevitable death? Did you find this peril to your taste? Another time won't you be a little less daring? Won't an adventure like this make you see the dangers in their full horror? Do please confess to me how you feel about it now. I think at least that you have thanked God for saving you. I at any rate am persuaded that the Masses I have had said for you every day have worked this miracle.

It is M. de Grignan whom I blame. The Coadjutor is all right, he has only been scolded for the mountain of Tarare, which looks to me now like the slopes of Nemours. M. Busche came to see me recently to bring back some plates. I nearly kissed him as I thought how well he had conducted you. I talked a lot with him about your doings and then gave him something to drink my health. This letter will seem very silly to you; you will receive it at a time when you won't be thinking any more about the bridge at Avignon. But I am thinking of it now! The trouble about correspondence over such long distances is that all the answers seem to be dealing the wrong cards. We must put up with it and not even rebel against this custom. It is natural and it would be too much of a constraint to stifle all one's thoughts. We must submit to our nature and respond to anything that touches our heart. So make up your mind to excuse me often.

I am expecting accounts of your stay in Arles. I know you will have found many people there; unless honours (as you threaten me) change customs, I want more details. Aren't you grateful to me for teaching you Italian? Look how well you got on with that Vice-Legate – what you say about that scene is excellent. But how little I enjoyed the rest of your letter! I spare you my everlasting returns to the bridge at Avignon. I shall never forget it in my life, and I am more grateful to God for having preserved you then than for having brought me into the world; there is no comparison.

To Madame de Grignan

Here comes a terrible lot of chatter, my poor dear. I have been here three hours, having left Paris with the Abbé, Hélène, Hébert and *Marphise*, with the object of retreating here until Thursday evening from the world and its noise. I intend to live in solitude. I am turning this into a little Trappist house; I mean to pray to God and give myself up to a thousand meditations. I intend to fast for all sorts of reasons, walk for as long as I have been in my room and altogether be bored to death for the love of God. But, poor dear, what I shall do far better than all that is think about you. I haven't stopped doing so since I arrived, and being unable to contain all my feelings I have set myself to writing to you at the end of that little dark avenue that you love, sitting on that mossy seat where I sometimes saw you lie. But oh dear, where haven't I seen you here? And how all these thoughts pass through my heart! There is no single nook or cranny in the house or in the church, in the neighbourhood, in the garden, where I haven't seen you. There are none which don't bring to mind something, somehow. And in one way or another it pierces my heart. I see you, you are present, I think of everything and then think again. I rack my brains, but wherever I turn or look that dear child I love so passionately is two hundred leagues away; I have lost her. Then I cry, unable to prevent it; I give up, dear child. It's all very feeble, but I can't be strong against so right and natural a love. I don't know what sort of state you will be in when you read this letter. It may well be that it comes at a bad time and won't perhaps be read in the spirit in which it is being written. I don't know any cure for that. Anyway, it helps to relieve me at the moment, and that is all I ask of it. The condition this place has put me into is incredible. Please don't talk about my weaknesses, but you must love them and respect my tears, which come from a heart that is all yours.

[Livry, Maundy Thursday, 26 March]

If I had wept for my sins as I have wept for you since I have been here I should be well prepared to make my Easter communion and gain indulgence. I have spent the time I had intended here in the way I had imagined, apart from my memories of you, which have plagued me more than I had foreseen. A lively imagination which conjures up everything as though it were still happening is a strange thing, and so one thinks about the present, and when one's heart is like mine that is killing. I don't know where to escape from you; our Paris house still drives me mad every day and Livry finishes me off. In your case you think of me by an act of memory; Provence is not obliged to give me back to you as these places here must give you back to me. I have found some pleasure in the melancholy I have felt here. Deep solitude, deep silence, a sad church service, Tenebrae, sung with devotion (I had never been to Livry in Holy Week), a canonical fast and beauty in these gardens which would delight you, I have enjoyed all these things. Alas, I have wished you were here! However awkward you might be about solitudes you would have loved this one. But I am going back to Paris of necessity. I shall find letters from you, and tomorrow I want to go to the Passion sermon of Fr Bourdaloue or Fr Mascaron. I have always had a great respect for fine Passions. Good-bye, dear Comtesse. This is as much as you will get from Livry, I shall finish this letter in Paris. If I had had the strength not to write to you from here and to make a sacrifice to God of all I have felt, it would have been worth more than all the penitences in the world. But instead of putting it to good account I have looked for consolation in talking about it to you. Oh, my dear, how weak and wretched this is!

[Continued in Paris, Good Friday, 27 March]

I have found a large packet of your letters here. I will answer them when I am much less devout. Meanwhile embrace your dear husband for my sake; I am touched by his affection and his letter.

I am very glad to know that the bridge of Avignon is still the Coadjutor's responsibility. So it was he who made you go under it, for poor Grignan would let himself be drowned just out of annoyance with you, preferring death to being with such unreasonable creatures. It's all up with the Coadjutor for this crime on top of so many others.

I am very obliged to Bandol for having let me have such a charming account. But how comes it, my dear, that you fear another letter might eclipse yours? You haven't re-read it, for to me, who read with great attention, it has given notable pleasure, a pleasure not to be effaced by anything else, too delightful a pleasure for a day like today. You satisfy my curiosity about many things I wanted to know. I strongly suspected that prophecies about Vardes would be quite false. I also suspected that you would not have committed any incivility. Furthermore I had suspicions about the boredom of the life you lead, and what will surprise you is that however averse to narrations I have always seen you to be I have thought you were too intelligent not to see that they are sometimes pleasant and necessary. I think too that nothing should be banished altogether from conversation and that judgement and the way events occur should introduce in turn what is most appropriate. I don't know why you say that you are no good at telling stories, for I know nobody who holds listeners better than you. It would not be the kind of thing to wish for exclusively, but when it has to do with the mind and the necessity of saying only pleasant things, I think one must be very glad to carry it off as you do.

I tremble at the thought that your business may not be successful. Ah, my dear, the First President must do the impossible. I don't know how I stand now with Monsieur de Marseille. You have done quite right to maintain a footing of friendship, we must see if he is worthy of it. A pun occurs to me on the word worthy,[1] but I am being pious today.

If at this moment I had a glass of water on my head I wouldn't spill a drop. If you had seen our man at Livry on Maundy Thursday, it was worse than all through the year. Yesterday he held his head more stiffly than a church candle, and his steps were so tiny that he didn't appear to be walking at all.

I have heard Mascaron's Passion sermon, which really was most beautiful and moving. I had been very anxious to go to the Bourdaloue, but as that was impossible I lost the desire to do so. Lackeys were there from Wednesday, and the crush was intolerable. I knew that he was to repeat the one that M. de Grignan and I heard last year at the Jesuit Church, and that was why I wanted to go. That was perfectly lovely, and now I only recall it like a dream. How sorry I am that you had a bad preacher. But why does it make you laugh? I am tempted

1. Pun on the word worthy – Monsieur de Marseille was formerly bishop of Digne (*digne* – worthy).

to say what I told you once before: 'Just be bored, as it is so awful.'

I have never thought that you were not on the best of terms with M. de Grignan. I don't think I have shown that I ever had any doubts about it. At the most I wished I could hear a word either from him or from you, not by way of news but to confirm something I passionately wish for. Provence would not be bearable otherwise, and I very easily understand his fears about seeing you languish and die of boredom. He and I have the same symptoms. He writes that you love me, and I think you don't doubt that this is something more wonderful than anything else I can wish for in the world. And to return to you, imagine the interest I am taking in your affair. It is over now, and I tremble about the outcome.

Maréchal d'Albret has won a lawsuit involving 40,000 livres of income from land. He regains all the property of his grandfathers and ruins the whole of Béarn. A score of families had bought and resold, and it all has to be given back with its accretions for a hundred years. It is a frightful business because of its consequences.

You are naughty not to have sent me Mme de Vaudémont's reply – I had asked you to and written to her. What will she think?

Good-bye, my dearest. I should like to know when I shall not think so much about you and your affairs. The answer must be:

> Comment pourrais-je vous le dire?
> Rien n'est plus incertain que l'heure de la mort.*

I am annoyed with your daughter. She gave me a sour welcome yesterday, and wouldn't ever smile. Sometimes I feel I want to take her to Brittany to amuse me.

I am sending off my letters early today, but never mind. Didn't you send yours very late when you were writing to M. de Grignan? How did he receive them? It must be the same thing. Good-bye, you little demon who are leading me astray; I should have been at Tenebrae over an hour ago.

My dear Grignan, I embrace you. I will answer your nice letter.

Thank you for all the compliments you send to people. I distribute them suitably, and they always send a hundred thousand to you. You

---

* 'How could I tell you?
Nothing is more uncertain than the hour of death.'

are still very much alive everywhere. I am delighted to know you are beautiful, and would like to kiss you. But how silly always to wear that blue dress!

Don't fret about Adhémar. The Abbé will do what you want and doesn't need your help – far from it.

For Madame la Comtesse de Grignan

To Madame de Grignan

[Saint-Germain, Monday 30 March 1671]

I am sending you little news, my dear Comtesse; I am relying on M. d'Hacqueville, who will let you know everything. Besides, I don't know any, I should just be able to tell you that M. le Chancelier has used an enema.

I saw something yesterday at Mademoiselle's that rejoiced me very much. Gêvres arrived, beautiful, charming, elegant. Mme d'Arpajon was ahead of me. I thought Gêvres expected me to give her my place, but I owed her something from the other day, and I paid her back in full and didn't budge. Mademoiselle was on her bed. So she was compelled to take her place at the bottom, below the dais – very annoying. Mademoiselle's drink was served and the serviette had to be offered. I spied Mme de Gêvres slipping her glove off her skinny hand. I nudged Mme d'Arpajon, who understood, took off her own glove and advanced a step, cut out Gêvres and took and offered the serviette. Gêvres was covered with shame and looked very sheepish. She had stepped up on to the dais and taken off her gloves, all just to see the serviette offered from nearer at hand by Mme d'Arpajon. My dear, I'm spiteful – I was delighted. It was very well done, too; did you ever see anybody rush to take away from Mme d'Arpajon, already at the bedside, a little honour naturally hers? The Puisieux burst into laughter, Mademoiselle dared not raise her eyes and I went quite expressionless. After that they said thousands of nice things about you, and Mademoiselle commanded me to tell you that she was so glad you hadn't been drowned and were in good health.

We went from there to Mme Colbert's, and she asked about you. This letter is a lot of terrible nonsense, but I don't know anything else.

You see I have given up being pious. Alas, I could really do with the Matins and solitude of Livry. So I shall give you those two books of La Fontaine even if it makes you angry. There are some pretty, very pretty parts and others that are boring. People will never be content with doing well; thinking to do better they do badly.

To Madame de Grignan

[Paris, Wednesday 1 April 1671]

I came back from Saint-Germain yesterday and wrote the news I had heard there. I was with Mme d'Arpajon. The number of those who asked for news of you is as great as that of the whole Court. I think I must single out the Queen, who moved towards me and asked for news of my daughter and said she had heard that you had nearly been drowned. I thanked her for the honour she did you by remembering you. She went on, 'Tell me how she nearly died.' I embarked on telling her about your foolhardiness in wanting to cross the Rhône in a high wind, and how this wind had quickly blown you under an arch at no distance from a pier, where you would certainly have perished if you had run into it. She said, 'And was her husband with her?' 'Yes, Madame, and the Coadjutor as well.' 'Really, it was very wrong of them,' she went on, and sighed and said some very kind things about you.

After that lots of duchesses came up to me, including the young Ventadour, very beautiful and attractive. Some moments elapsed before they brought her the sacred *tabouret*. I turned towards M. le Grand Maître and said, 'Alas, let her have it, it has cost her a lot.' He shared my opinion.

In the midst of the silence of the circle the Queen turned to me and said, 'Who does your granddaughter take after?' 'Madame,' I said, 'she is like M. de Grignan.' She uttered a cry. 'I am so sorry,' she said softly to me, 'she would have done better to take after her mother or grandmother.' That's how you turn me into a courtier, my dear.

Maréchal de Bellefonds made me promise to distinguish him from the crowd, and Mme de Duras and her husband, to whom I gave your compliments, likewise MM. de Charost and de Montausier, and *tutti quanti*. I gave your letter to Monsieur de Condom. I nearly forgot Monsieur le Dauphin and Mademoiselle. I mentioned Segrais to her, quite boldly defending him, but she is not reasonable about anything within nine hundred leagues of the sight of a certain Cape from which can be descried the lands of Micomicon.[1]

I have seen Mme de Ludres. She came up to me with a superabundance of friendliness that surprised me. She spoke of you in the same tone and then suddenly, as I was by way of replying, I found she was no longer listening, and her lovely eyes were running round the room. I saw this at once, and those who saw that I saw were glad I had noticed it and began to laugh. She was plunged into the sea. The sea saw her nakedness and was much prouder because of it – I mean the sea, for the fair one was very humiliated.

The *hurlubrelu* hair styles have amused me very much. Some of them I would like to hit. According to Ninon, Choiseul looked exactly like a picture of springtime at a country inn. That is an excellent comparison.

But what a menace that Ninon is! If you knew how she dogmatizes about religion it would give you the horrors. Her zeal for perverting the young is like that of a certain M. de Saint-Germain we once met at Livry. She thinks your brother is as simple as a dove; he is like his mother. Mme de Grignan has all the brains of the family and isn't so silly as to fall into such docility. Somebody tried to take your side and reduce the esteem she has for you, but she shut him up, saying that she knew better than he did. How corrupt she is! Because she thinks you are beautiful and clever she wants to add to that this other quality, without which, according to her principles, one can't be perfect. I am very upset about the harm she has done my son in this way. Don't write to him to this effect. Mme de La Fayette and I are doing our best to get him out of such a dangerous entanglement. He also has a little actress, and all the Boileaus and Racines as well, for he is the one who pays for the suppers. In fact it is a real mess. He laughs at people like Mascaron, as you have seen. He really ought to have your Minim.[2]

I have never seen anything so funny as what you write about that. I read it to M. de La Rochefoucauld, who laughed heartily. He will have you know that there is a certain apostle who is running after his rib, and would very much like to annexe it as his own property, but

1. *Micomicon*: a land in *Don Quixote*.
2. *Minim*: a friar of the Mendicant order. The reference is to a Minim whose Lenten sermons at Aix were laughable.

hasn't the art to follow out great undertakings. I think *Mélusine* is in a trough; we hear not a single word about her. He also says that if only he were thirty years younger he would be after M. de Grignan's third rib.[3] The bit where you said he has two broken ribs tickled him to death. We always wish you will have some funny adventure to amuse you. But we are afraid that this one has been better for us than for you. After all, we pity you for only hearing about God in this way.

Ah, Bourdaloue! I have been told he preached a more perfect Passion sermon than anything you can imagine; it was last year's which he had revised to meet the advice of his friends that it might be inimitable. How can one love God when one never hears about Him? One needs more special grace than others. The other day we heard the Abbé de Montmor. I have never heard such a good sermon from a young man; I wish you could have the same instead of your Minim. He made the sign of the cross, spoke his text, didn't scold us, didn't call us names. He bade us not to fear death since it was the only route we had for rebirth with Christ, and we agreed. We were all pleased. There is nothing in him to shock. He imitates Monsieur d'Agen but without copying him. He is daring, he is modest, he is learned, he is devout. In fact I was extremely pleased with him.

Mme de Vauvineux sends you a thousand thanks; her daughter has been very ill. Mme d'Arpajon embraces you a thousand times, and above all M. Le Camus adores you. And what do you think I am doing, my poor dear? Loving you, thinking of you, giving way to emotion at every turn more than I would like, concerning myself with your affairs, worrying about what you think, feeling your sufferings and pains, wanting to suffer them for you if possible, removing anything unpleasant from your heart as I used to clear your room of any tiresome people I saw haunting it; in a word, my dear, understanding deeply what it means to love someone more than oneself – that's what I am like. It is something often thrown off as a remark, and people misuse this expression. I repeat it without ever profaning it. I feel it all within me and it is true.

I have just had your big, lovely letter of the 24th. M. de Grignan must be joking to say that they are only read with difficulty; he does

---

3. *Grignan's third rib*: joke about his third wife.

himself an injustice. Does he expect us to believe that he has not always read yours with rapture? If that was not so he was quite unworthy of them. As for me, I love them to distraction. I read and re-read them. They delight my heart and make me weep. They are written as I like them. Only one thing is not quite right; there is no reason for all these praises you lavish on me. Neither is there any for the length of this letter; I must finish it and set a limit to what would never have any if I had my way. Good-bye, my dearest. Count on my affection which will never end.

To Madame de Grignan

[Paris, Wednesday 8 April 1671]

I am beginning to get your letters on Sundays, a sign that the weather is fine. How good your letters are, my dear! There are passages fit to print; one of these days you will find that one of your friends has pirated you.

You are in a retreat. You have found our poor Sisters and have a cell there. But don't dig too deeply into your mind. Reflections are sometimes so gloomy that they lead to death; you know we have to glide a little over the surface of thoughts. You will find joy in that House of which you are mistress.[1] I am amazed at the attire of your ladies for communion; it is extraordinary and I could never get used to it. I believe that you will have to lower your own coiffes more. I can understand that you would have far less trouble not curling your hair than keeping quiet about what you see.

Your description of the ceremonies is a finished piece of art. But do you realize that it makes me so angry that I am amazed that you can put up with it. You think I should be admirable in Provence and would do wonders with my little kindnesses. Not at all, I should be downright rude; unreasonableness irritates me and bad faith offends me. I should say to them, 'Madame, let's get this clear, am I to see you out into the street? If so, don't hold me up and don't let us waste time and our breath; if not, excuse my lack of formality.' And if they did not, I should

1. Order of the Visitation at Aix. The Order founded by Mère de Chantal, great-grandmother of Mme de Grignan.

speak your private thoughts out loud. I am not surprised that this sort of play-acting puts you out of patience, I should have far less patience than you.

A word or two about your brother. He has been sent packing by Ninon. She is tired of loving and not being loved in return. She asked for her letters back and they have been returned. I was very glad about this separation. I had always breathed a word to him about God, reminded him of his former virtue and begged him not to stifle the Holy Spirit in his heart. Had it not been that he let me put in a word or two now and again I would not have agreed to receive his confidences in this way for I didn't want them. But that is not all. When one breaks off one relationship one hopes to catch up on another. The young wonder[2] has not broken off so far, but I think she will. This is why: yesterday my son came from the other end of Paris to tell me about the mishap that had befallen him. He had found a favourable opportunity, and yet, dare I say it? *His little gee-gee stopped short at Lérida.* It was an extraordinary thing; the damsel had never found herself at such an entertainment in her life. The discomfited knight beat a retreat, thinking he was bewitched. And what will strike you as comic was that he was dying to tell me about this fiasco. We laughed a lot, and I told him I was very glad he had been punished in the part where he had sinned. He then turned on me and said I had given him some of the ice in my composition, that he could well do without that resemblance, which I would have done better to pass on to my daughter. He wanted Pecquet to put him to rights again. He said the silliest things in the world, and so did I. It was a scene worthy of Molière. What is true is that his imagination has had such a setback that I don't think he'll get over it for a long time. In vain did I assure him that the empire of love is full of tragic stories, he is inconsolable. The little *Chimène* says she sees he doesn't love her and consoles herself elsewhere. Altogether it is a mix-up I find laughable, and I wish with all my heart it would lead him away from the unfortunate situation he is in with regard to God.

The other day he told me that a certain actor wanted to get married although he suffered from a somewhat dangerous malady. His friend said to him, 'Good God, wait till you're cured, or you will be the death of us all!' I thought that was very epigrammatical.

2. *The young wonder*: La Champmeslé, the actress; see List of Persons.

Ninon told my son the other day that he was an old pumpkin fricasseed in snow. You see what it means to move in high society, you pick up a thousand elegant endearments.

I haven't yet let your apartment, although people come to view it every day and I have offered to let it go at less than five hundred écus.

Now for news of your child. I thought she looked pale recently, and I found that the nurse's breast never seemed too full. I took it into my head that she hadn't enough milk, so I sent for Pecquet, who thought I was very clever and said we should have to see in a few days. He came back two or three days later and found that the child was getting worse. Off I went to Mme du Puy-du-Fou. She came here, thought the same thing, but as she never comes to a conclusion said she would have to see. 'See what, Madame?' I said. I happened to meet a woman from Sucy, who said she knew an admirable nurse there. I got her to come. That was on Saturday. On Sunday I went to see Mme de Bournonville and told her how sorry I was to be obliged to send back her pretty nurse. M. Pecquet was with me to explain the child's condition. After dinner one of Mme de Bournonville's maids came, and without saying anything about why she had come, asked the nurse to step round to Mme de Bournonville's. She did so. She was taken away in the evening and told she would not be returning, and she was heartbroken. Next day I sent her ten gold louis for four and a half months, and that was settled. I went to Mme du Puy-du-Fou, who approved of my action. And on Sunday I put the child into the hands of the new nurse. It was a joy to see her take the milk! She had never sucked like that before. Her old nurse hadn't much milk, this one has as much as a cow. She is a fine peasant woman with no nonsense about her, fine teeth, dark hair, bronzed skin, aged twenty-four. Four months' milk, her own child beautiful as an angel. Pecquet is delighted to think that the child needs nothing more. It was clear that she did lack something and was still looking for it. I have achieved a great reputation over this business; at any rate, like M. de Pourceaugnac's doctor,[3] I am expeditious. I couldn't sleep in peace for thinking that the child was sickening, and also because of the upset of sending away that nice woman who looked quite charming and only lacked milk. I am giving this one two hundred

3. In Molière's comedy *Monsieur de Pourceaugnac*.

and fifty livres per year, with clothes found, but modest ones. This is how we manage your affairs.

I am off in about a month or five weeks. My aunt stays here and will be delighted to have the child – she is not going to La Trousse this year. If the nurse were willing to go a long way from her home I think I should take her to Brittany, but she didn't even want to come to Paris. Your little girl is getting very nice, and people take to her. In a fortnight she will be a snow-white ball laughing all the time. These are a terrible lot of details, my dear, I'm a real old gossip, and you won't recognize me laying the law down throughout the neighbourhood. To tell you the truth, I'm a different person when I am responsible for something on my own from when I share it with others. Don't thank me for anything, keep your ceremonial for your ladies. I love your little family tenderly. It is a pleasure and not at all a burden, nor of course to you. I don't notice it. My aunt has done well, too, and has been with me to various places; thank her and tell little Deville all about it. I meant to write to her. Send a word to Segrais in your next letter, too.

A certain Mme de La Guette, who gave me the nurse, asks you to find out from Cardinal de Grimaldi whether he would allow the founding of an order of the Daughters of the Cross at Aix. They teach girls and have been found very useful in many towns. Don't forget to answer this.

Marans said the other day at Mme de La Fayette's, 'Oh dear, I must get my hair cut.' Mme de La Fayette boldly replied, 'Oh Lord, Madame, don't do that, it only suits young people.' If you don't like remarks like that, do better yourself. Here is a letter from Monsieur de Marseille.

M. d'Ambres is transferring his regiment to the King for 80,000 francs and 120,000 livres; that makes 200,000 francs. He is very glad to be put out of the infantry, that is to say of penury. Oh my dear child, try to avoid that. Don't live so well; people refer to it here as excess. M. de Monaco can't stop talking about it. Try above all to sell some land, there is no other way for you. I think of nothing but you and if, by a miracle I neither hope for nor want, you were out of my thoughts, I feel I should be completely empty, like one of Benoît's figures.[4]

Here is a letter I have had from Monsieur de Marseille, and here is

4. Benoît, a famous waxwork artist.

my answer. I think you will approve since you want it to be so open and sincere and in keeping with this friendship you have sworn to each other, 'the link of which is dissimulation and your interests the foundation'. This is from Tacitus, and I have never seen anything so fine. So I enter into this sentiment and approve, since I must.

[9 o'clock in the evening]

I have come back to seal up my packet after a walk in the Tuileries in stifling heat, which saddens me because I feel you must be hotter still. I have come back to M. Le Camus, who is writing to M. de Grignan, sending him M. de Vendôme's answer. The business of the secretary has not been without difficulty. M. de Grignan's civility was most necessary for this year. What is done is done. But for the other, in all good faith M. de Grignan must solicit the governor's secretary. Otherwise it will look as if what your husband has offered was just words; he must avoid not suiting actions to those words. You must also get hold of Monsieur de Marseille and persuade him that he is one of your friends, whatever he thinks, and that he will be your man of affairs of the coming year. I approve of the attitude you want to take with him. I see perfectly well that it is necessary. I see it better than I did.

I have just had yours of 31 March, which so far I have not been able to read without emotion. I see all your life, and that nobody but M. de Grignan understands you. *So you aren't beautiful, you are not very intelligent, you don't dance well?* Alas, is that my dear child? I should be hard put to it to recognize you from that portrait.

I shall tell M. de La Rochefoucauld all the funny things you say about the canons, and how you think *it is on this account that the pious sex has been called feminine.* It is a pleasure to write this nonsense to you; you answer it very well, and I am so grateful to you for thanking me for your fans while taking a share in the pleasure I have in giving them to you; that alone must make you like them. Ah, my dear, heap treasures on me and you will see whether I shall be satisfied with letting your nurse have some carpet slippers.

My dear Grignan, as you find your wife so beautiful, look after her. It is bad enough to be hot this summer in Provence, without being pregnant there. You think I should work miracles there, but I assure you that I am not up to what you think. Constraint is as much against my nature as against yours, and I think my daughter does better than I could.

Mme de Villars and all those you name in your letters send so many friendly messages that I should never end if I mentioned them all; you are not forgotten so far.

Good-bye, my dearest one. You kiss and embrace me so tenderly! Do you think I don't receive your caresses with open arms? Do you think I don't also kiss with all my heart your lovely cheeks and bosom? Do you think I can embrace you without infinite affection? Do you think that affection can ever go further than mine for you?

Let me know how you are on the 6th of this month. Your beautifully made clothes, that figure so beautifully formed in its natural state, preserve it for my journey to Provence. You know well that I shall not fail you.

I wish it even more than you, my dear Comte. Give me a kiss, be assured that I love you and that all my daughter's happiness is in you.

To Madame de Grignan

[Paris, Wednesday 22 April 1671]

Are you really afraid that I prefer Mme de Brissac to you? Do you fear that her manner pleases me more than yours? That her mind has found the way to appeal to me? Is it your opinion that her beauty eclipses your charms? In fine, do you think there is anyone in the world who can, to my taste, surpass Madame de Grignan, even without all the interest I take in her? Think about all this at your leisure and then be assured that it is just what you believe. That is my full reply which you will know from your own answer, if sincere.

Let us talk a bit about your brother, my dear. His weakness makes one sick, he is whatever other people want. Yesterday it amused three of his friends to take him out to supper at a house of ill fame, and there he went. These gentry are too clever to want to risk their own money, so they tell Sévigné to pay, and I mean beggar himself. Wretched though he still is, he pays, then he comes and tells me all, saying that he makes himself sick, and I tell him he makes me sick too. I make him ashamed of himself and tell him this is not the life of a decent gentleman, that he will find some dupe, and through exposing himself get caught. I go on to moralize a bit. He agrees with everything and does neither more nor less. He has left the actress, having loved her on and off. When he saw her or wrote to her he was in earnest; a moment later he laughed himself silly at her. Ninon has dropped him. He was miserable when she loved him, he is in despair because she loves him no more, especially as she refers to him with scant respect. 'His soul is just made of pulp,' she says, 'his body is made of wet paper and his heart is a pumpkin fricasseed in snow.' I've told you that already. The other day she wanted him to give her the actress's letters; he gave them to her. She was jealous and wanted to give them to a lover of this grand lady, so as to deal her a few little jabs. He came and told me about it. I told him it was infamous to have dealt such a blow to this poor little thing because she had loved him, that she had not sacrificed her letters, as he was given to believe, in order to pain him, but had freely given them back to him, that it was a hideous treachery, low and unworthy of a gentleman, and that even in unsavoury matters there was some decency to be observed. He agreed with my reasons and rushed off to Ninon, and in one way or another, half by skill, half by force, he got back the letters of this poor creature and I had them burned. You see from this how much the word actress means to me. It is a bit like the Visionary of the comedy;[1] she would have done the same, and I am acting like her. My son has told M. de La Rochefoucauld all about his goings-on, as he is interested in odd characters. He agreed with what I said to him the other day that my boy is not mad in the head but in the heart. His emotions are quite genuine and quite false, freezing cold and burning hot, quite villainous and quite sincere; in fact his heart is crazy. We laughed a lot about it, even with my son, for he is good company and can cap anything. We get on very well together. I am in his confidence, and I keep this questionable position which brings me such questionable confidences, so as to have the right to tell him what I think about

1. *Les Visionnaires*, by Desmarets de Saint-Sorlin; a very popular comedy to which Molière was indebted.

everything. He believes me as much as he can and asks me to put him right, which I do like a friend. He wants to come to Brittany with me for five or six weeks; if there is no camp in Lorraine I shall take him. All this is very silly, but as you take an interest in it I thought it wouldn't bore you.

You refer very tenderly and kindly to a journey to Provence. Rest assured once and for all that that is what the Abbé and I wish for, and it is one of the pleasantest hopes we have. It is a matter of fitting it in both for you and us. Our d'Hacqueville said the other day, hearing us discussing our peregrination from Brittany to Provence, that he didn't advise us to go this year, that we should go to Brittany and do all our business there and return here at All Saints and cast an eye on my son again, and also the little Adhémar girl, of whom I am getting very fond; that we should change houses, that is I should, and set myself up in a place where I can bring you back; then that towards spring I should go off to Burgundy, where I have all kinds of business, and thence to Provence. Chalon, the Saône, Lyons, the Rhône and there I am at Grignan in no time. I should be with you without fear of leaving you because apparently I should bring you back with me and it would not involve a second separation, which I find killing. He said moreover that he himself would find this arrangement far better than the other, where he saw a ridiculously long journey right in the middle of yours, pressed to return for my business and by my son, to whom I am far from useless, and with the grief of leaving you again. He saw no sense in the first plan and a great deal in the one he was suggesting to us. We listened to these arguments and approved. He said he would advise you to agree, and I think you will from your last letter, in which you point out that you would find it very unpleasant for me to leave after a short time with you. I feel sure you will enter into this arrangement. On my side I can't ever see without pain any postponement of the time and joy of seeing you, but neither will it ever be without some inner joy that I shall preserve the hope of doing so. On this hope and love I shall build all my consolation, and by means of it I will try to calm part of my impatience and natural hastiness. Let me know what you think, and rest assured that the difference between going to Provence without having a home here, and having one all fitted out with an apartment set aside for you is the strongest of our reasons.

Everything you write about the Marans woman is delightful, and the punishments she will have in hell. But do you realize you will accompany her if you continue to hate her – just think that you will be together for all eternity. Nothing more is needed to persuade you to seek your salvation. It has most fortunately occurred to me to put this thought to you; it is an inspiration from God. The other day she came to Mme de La Fayette's. M. de La Rochefoucauld was there and so was I. Behold she enters with nothing on her head. She had just had her hair cut like a chit of a girl, and was all powdered and curled. The first curlers had been taken out barely a quarter of an hour before. She was very put out, sensing that she would be disapproved of. Mme de La Fayette said, 'Really, you must be off your head. Don't you realize, Madame, that you look quite ridiculous?' M. de La Rochefoucauld: 'Oh Ma, upon my soul, Ma, we shan't let things rest at that. Come a little nearer, Ma, so that I can see whether you are like your sister, whom I have just seen.' She had had her hair cut, too. 'Yes, Ma, you look ever so nice.' You recognize that tone, and the words are straight from life. She was so out of countenance that she could not withstand this attack. She put her head-covering on again and sulked until Mme de Schomberg came to pick her up, for hers is the only carriage she has left. I think this story will amuse you.

The other day we spent a very pleasant afternoon at the Arsenal. There were men of all ranks there, and Mmes de La Fayette, de Coulanges, de Méri, La Troche and I. We took a walk, spoke about you several times and in very flattering terms. We sometimes go to the Luxembourg too. M. de Longueville was there yesterday, and he asked me to assure you of his most humble services. As for M. de La Rochefoucauld, he loves you tenderly.

I have received your gloves via the gentleman, but, my dearest, you overwhelm me with presents. These are part of my stock for Brittany, and they are excellent. I kiss you with all my heart by way of thanks, my darling.

I am delighted that you approve of my letters. Your approval and sincere praise give me a pleasure far beyond any from elsewhere, and why shouldn't daughters like you make so bold as to praise a mother like me? A strange kind of respect – you know how I value your taste.

I greatly approve of your lottery and I hope you will tell me what you have won. Your plays must give you enjoyment too. Do let yourself be entertained, dear, and go with the current of such pleasures as can be had in Provence. I approve strongly of your refusal to see visitors right out into the street; it would have been mortal. Let these ladies take their revenge and not see you off either, and then a horrible custom will be abolished.

The letter you wrote to your brother is admirable. How I love your letters! I am off now to Saint-Germain, and would have presented it to all the courtiers, the outside was addressed to them.

I have seen the Chevalier,[2] handsomer than the hero of a novel and worthy to be the frontispiece of the first volume. He had had his twinge of pain. I have noticed that he always has a fresh attack just before a journey, I wonder why? Monsieur le Duc is going to travel to Burgundy after entertaining the King at Chantilly. I think he'll make some fine conquests there. You had at any rate a victory over M. de Monaco. Where had he picked up the pronunciation *nend*? We know more about it than he does. After that I shall undertake to teach our Venetian ambassador Italian. Alas, by the way, he is leaving us and is in despair.

I have come back from Saint-Germain with d'Arpajon and d'Huxelles. The whole of France was there. I saw Gacé, drew him to one side and asked for news of you with a pleasure far greater than that of being at Court. He says that you are beautiful, gay and that it is a pleasure to see the understanding between you and M. de Grignan. He even refers to your return. I couldn't leave him, and he will come and see me. He has been in the country with his brother, who has lost his eldest son and is very upset.

There was a great hubbub at Saint-Germain. Everyone was going off, either to go home or because the King was leaving. Marans looked ridiculous to the last degree, people were laughing outright at her hair style. She didn't dare to speak to me. She was totally routed, and the final blow is the loss of your good graces. Two appalling little stories have been told me about her, but I am suppressing them for the love of God, and also it would be poaching on Adhémar's[3] preserves.

2. *the Chevalier*: Charles-Philippe de Grignan (1642–72), a younger brother of the Comte.

3. *Adhémar*: Joseph de Grignan (1641–1713), brother of the Comte, who will be called the Chevalier after the early death of Charles-Philippe.

Anyway, she seems routed. There is a portrait of you at Mme de La Fayette's; Marans dare not look up at it.

My son has leave to come to Brittany with me for five weeks; that will make me set out a little earlier than I thought.

A thousand people have asked me to kiss your hand: M. de Montausier, Maréchal de Bellefonds and many others. Monsieur le Dauphin gave me a kiss for you and I send it on.[4] Good-bye, my dearest, it is late and I am producing prose with a facility that will be the death of you. I embrace my dear Grignan, and you, my pet, more than a thousand times.

To Madame de Grignan

[Paris, Friday 24 April 1671]

We are having the loveliest weather in the world. It set in yesterday after appalling rains. It is the King's luck, as we have often observed, and this time it is also good luck for Monsieur le Prince, who has made preparations at Chantilly for the summer and the spring – the day before yesterday's rain would have made all this outlay ridiculous. His Majesty arrived yesterday evening and is there today. D'Hacqueville has gone there, and he will tell you the story when he is back. I am expecting a little tale this evening; I shall send it on with this letter, which I am writing in the morning before going to Gossip,[1] and I shall seal it up when I get there. If people say, my dear, that in our letters we chatter about the weather they will be right. I have started with quite a chapter on the subject.

You don't tell me enough about yourself. I am greedy for it, as you are for funny stories. I wish you could hear all the ones I hear. Those I tell aren't any good now that you don't help me; you inspire me, and sometimes I inspire you, too. It is one long sadness constantly renewed to be so far from somebody like you. I said my good-byes to people some days ago; I can find plenty of courage for that. What is amusing is that I feel I shall not find courage to say good-bye to you from here as I leave for Brittany. You will be my real pain at leaving, and if I were

4. The Dauphin was then aged nine!
1. *to Gossip*: pun on *bavarder*, to gossip, and Mme de *Lavardin*.

deceitful I could turn that into a great honour for my friends. But people can see through my words, and I don't want to disguise in any way my feelings for you. So I shall be saddened to see that it is not enough to be two hundred leagues from you; I have got to be three hundred, and every step I take will go towards the third hundred. It is too much, it makes my heart bleed.

Yesterday, while I was at Mme de Richelieu's the Abbé Têtu came in. His gaiety put his absent friends to shame. I mentioned my journey to him, my dear, and he didn't change his tone, but with a smiling face: 'Well, Madame,' says he, 'we shall see each other again.' That is not very funny to write, but it was to hear, and we all laughed heartily. Anyhow, that was all he thought about, and he passed lightly over all my absence and only found one word to say. We use it now in our farewells and I use it to myself when I think of you. But not so gaily, and the length of the separation is not a circumstance I forget.

I have bought for a day-dress a material like your latest skirt. It is lovely. There is some green, but purple predominates – in a word, I succumbed. They wanted me to have it lined with a flame colour, but I thought that looked like the last judgement. The top is fragility pure and simple, but the lining would have displayed a determined will-power which appeared unseemly to me, so I have gone in for white taffeta. Very little expense. I have no respect for Brittany, but only want to lay out money for Provence, so as to uphold the dignity of a middle-aged wonder, to which you have raised me.

Mme de Ludres was wonderful to me at Saint-Germain the other day – no absent-mindedness. She is fond of you, too: '*Ah! pour matame te Grignan, elle est atorable.*' Mme de Beringhen happened to be next to Ludres, who cut her out somewhat; her looks seem weird to me. Brancas told me about some dealings[2] M. de Grignan had last winter with Monsieur le Premier: 'I am for Grignan, I have seen their letters.' This Brancas has written you the deuce of a long letter, pleasant but illegible. He told me bits of it, we shall need a whole day to read it all.

Your child is a dear. She has a perfect nurse who is becoming a very fine fountain – fountain of milk this time, not of crystal.

M. de Salins has sacked a doorkeeper. People are saying all sorts of things. There is talk of grey cloaks, four o'clock in the morning, blows

2. All imaginary. Brancas, a notoriously absent-minded and unreliable chatterer.

with the flat of the sword, *et l'on se tait du reste.** There is mention of a certain apostle who plays similar tricks. Anyway, I am saying nothing, so I shan't be accused of chattering. I know how to hold my tongue, thank God! If this end seems a bit of a muddle to you, you will like it all the better for that. Good-bye, my dearest one, I love you more than can be imagined. I will let you have some news soon when I seal up my packet.

[Paris, Friday evening 24 April 1671 at M. de La Rochefoucauld's]

So I am finishing my letter here. I had intended to tell you that the King arrived at Chantilly yesterday evening. He hunted a stag by moonlight; the lanterns were wonderful. The fireworks were a little dimmed by the light of our friend the moon, but the evening, the supper, the gaming all went off perfectly. The weather we have had today gave grounds for hoping for a continuation worthy of such a pleasant beginning. But now I learn, on coming here, something I can't get over and which drives out of my head what I am writing. It is that Vatel, the great Vatel, maître d'hôtel to M. Foucquet and now to Monsieur le Prince, this man whose ability surpassed all others, whose mental capacity was capable of carrying all the cares of a state – this man, then, whom I knew, seeing at eight o'clock this morning that the fish had not come, was unable to face the humiliation he saw about to overwhelm him and, in a word, stabbed himself. You can imagine the horrible disorganization such a terrible occurrence brought about in this festivity. Reflect that the fish probably arrived later, as he was dying. I know no more yet, but I think you will find this enough. I don't doubt that the confusion has been enormous; it is an annoying thing to happen to a fête costing fifty thousand écus.

M. de Ménars is marrying Mlle de La Grange Neuville. I don't know how I have the courage to mention anything else except Vatel.

*'But of the rest not a word.'

97

To Madame de Grignan

[Paris, Sunday 26 April 1671]

It is Sunday 26th of April and this letter will not go until Wednesday, but this is not a letter, it is a story Moreuil has just told me for your benefit about what has happened at Chantilly concerning Vatel. I wrote to you last Wednesday that he had stabbed himself; here is the affair in detail.

The King arrived on Thursday evening. Hunting, lanterns, moonlight, a gentle walk, supper served in a spot carpeted with daffodils – everything was perfect. They had supper. There was no roast at one or two tables because of several unexpected guests. That upset Vatel, and he said more than once, 'I am dishonoured; this is a humiliation I will not bear.' He said to Gourville, 'I don't know where I am, I haven't slept for twelve nights. Help me give orders.' Gourville comforted him as far as he could, but this roast missing, not from the King's table but from the twenty-fifth down, constantly came back to his mind. Gourville told all this to Monsieur le Prince. Monsieur le Prince went to Vatel's room and said to him, 'Vatel, everything is all right, nothing was so perfect as the King's supper.' But he answered, 'Monseigneur, your kindness is overwhelming, but I know that there was no roast at two tables.' 'Not at all,' said Monsieur le Prince, 'don't upset yourself, everything is going splendidly.' Night falls. The fireworks are a failure owing to fog, and they cost 16,000 francs. By four in the morning Vatel was rushing round everywhere and finding everything wrapped in slumber. He found a small supplier who only had two loads of fish. 'Is that all?' he asked. 'Yes, Sir.' He did not know that Vatel had sent round to all the seaports. Vatel waited a short time, the other suppliers did not turn up, he lost his head and thought there would be no more fish. He went and found Gourville and said, 'Sir, I shall never survive this disgrace, my honour and my reputation are at stake.' Gourville laughed at him. Vatel went to his room, put his sword up against the door and ran it through his heart. But that was only at the third attempt, for the first two were not mortal. Then he fell dead. Meanwhile the fish was coming in from all quarters. They looked for Vatel to allocate it, went to his room, broke in the door and found him lying in his own blood. They rushed to Monsieur le Prince, who was terribly upset. Monsieur le Duc wept, for the whole of his trip to Burgundy depended on Vatel. Monsieur le Prince told the King very sadly, explaining that it was a matter of honour as he saw it; he was greatly praised. His courage was both praised and blamed. The King said that he had been putting off his visit to Chantilly for five years because he realized what an extreme embarrassment it would be. He told Monsieur le Prince that he ought only to have two tables and not undertake all the rest. He swore that he would not allow Monsieur le Prince to take all this trouble, but it was too late for poor Vatel. However, Gourville tried to make up for the loss of Vatel. He did so, and there was a very good dinner, light refreshments later, and then supper, a walk, cards, hunting, everything scented with daffodils, everything magical. Yesterday, Saturday, the same thing and in the evening the King went on to Liancourt, where he had commanded a *medianoche*; he is to stay there today.

That is what Moreuil told me, to be passed on to you. I don't know how to end this, not that I know anything about it. M. d'Hacqueville, who was present at everything, will no doubt tell you the tale, but as his writing is not as legible as mine I am writing all the same. I have gone in for a lot of details but I am sending them because on a similar occasion I should like them myself.

[Begun in Paris, Monday 27 April 1671]

I have a very bad opinion of your listlessness. I am one of the spiteful gossips and I think the worst; it is what I feared. But, my dear child, if this misfortune is confirmed do look after yourself. Don't shake yourself up in these early days by your journey to Marseilles; let things settle a bit. Think of your delicate state and that it is only by dint of being careful that you have managed to go full term. I am already very worried about the upset the journey to Brittany will cause to our relationship. If you are pregnant you know that my only object will be to do what you want. I shall make your desires my rule and shall leave any other arrangement or consideration a thousand leagues away.

I think that the tale about your brother has entertained you. He is at present more or less in a state of equilibrium. However, he sees Ninon every day, but just as a friend. The other day he went with her into a place where there were five or six men. Their expressions convinced her that they thought he was in possession. She saw what they were thinking and said, 'Gentlemen, you are making a mistake if you think there is anything going on between us. I assure you we are like brother and sister.' It is true that he is quite 'fricasseed'. I am taking him to Brittany, where I hope I shall help him to recover a healthy body and soul. La Mousse and I are contriving to get him to make a good confession.

M. and Mme de Villars and little Saint-Géran are just leaving and send you their kindest regards. They want a copy of the portrait of you on my mantelpiece to take to Spain with them. My little girl has been in my room all day, dolled up in her fine lace and doing the honours of the establishment, this establishment that reminds me so much of you, where you were virtually a prisoner a year ago, this place that everybody wants to view, that everybody admires but nobody wants to rent.[1]

I had supper the other day with the Marquise d'Huxelles, and the Maréchale d'Humières, Mmes d'Arpajon, de Beringhen, de Frontenac, d'Outrelaise, Raymond and Martin were there. You were not forgotten.

I do beg of you, my child, to let me know the truth about your health, your plans and what you would like me to do. I am sorry about your condition and I am afraid you will be too. I can see many troubles ahead and have a whole lot of thoughts in my mind that are no good either for night or for day.

[Livry, Wednesday 29 April 1671]

Since I wrote the beginning of this letter I have made a very pretty journey. I left Paris early yesterday morning and had dinner at Pomponne. There I found our old friend[2] waiting for me; I would not have wanted to miss saying good-bye to him. I found him even more saintly, which surprised me; and the nearer he draws to death the holier he becomes. He scolded me very seriously and in an access of zeal and affection for me said I was mad not to think of coming back to a

1. *everybody admires, but nobody wants to rent*: pun on *louer*, to admire or praise, and *louer*, to rent or hire.
2. *our old friend*: Arnauld d'Andilly, then aged eighty-two.

Christian way of life, that I was a fine old pagan, that I set you up as an idol in my heart, that this kind of idolatry was as dangerous as any other, although it might appear less criminal to me, in fact that I should think about myself. He said all this so vehemently that I was quite silenced. At length, after six hours of very pleasant though very serious conversation I left him and came here, where I found all the triumph of the month of May.

> Le rossignol, le coucou, la fauvette,
> Ont ouvert le printemps dans nos forêts.*

I walked about all the evening quite alone, and relapsed into all my gloomy thoughts, but I don't want to talk about them any more. This morning I was brought your letters of the 22nd of this month. What a long way they have to come when they reach Paris! I set aside part of this after-dinner period to write to you in the garden, where I am being deafened by three or four nightingales over my head. This evening I go back to Paris and make up my packet to send to you.

It is true, my dear, that my friendliness was a bit lacking when I met the chain of convicts. I should have gone with them to meet you instead of writing, and I reproach myself. What a pleasant surprise it would have been for you at Marseilles to find me in such good company! But are you going there in a chair? What an odd notion! I knew a time when you only liked them when they were at a standstill; you have changed a lot. I am entirely in agreement with the gossips, and the only honourable conclusion I can draw is to believe that you never would have used this conveyance if you hadn't left me and if M. de Grignan had stayed in his Provence. How sorry I am about this misfortune, but how clearly I foresaw it. Do take care of yourself, my dearest. Remember that the *Guisarde beauty*, wanting to show off with a happy delivery, had a bad accident and was at death's door for three days; that's a fine example for you. Mme de La Fayette is always fearful for your life because of your perfections. She willingly yields you first place in my heart. When she is in a good mood she says it is not without difficulty, but anyway that is all settled and agreed, and this justice makes her worthy of second place. She has it. La Troche is dying of jealousy.

*'The nightingale, the cuckoo, the warbler
Have declared spring open in our forests.'

I still go on my way, and my way takes me to Brittany. We certainly shall be leading very different lives. Mine will be very bothered by the States, which will come and torment me at Vitré at the end of July, and this annoys me very much. Your brother will no longer be there then. My dear, you wish Time would fly. You don't know what you are doing, and you'll get overtaken. He will obey you too literally, and when you want to hold him back you will no longer have the power. Long ago I made the same mistakes as you; I have regretted it, and although Time has not done me all the ill he has done to others, a thousand little enjoyments he has taken away show that he leaves all too many marks of his passage.

So you think that your actors are clever enough to speak lines of Corneille? There certainly are some thrilling ones. I have brought a volume of him here that I enjoyed very much yesterday evening. But didn't you think that the five or six fables of La Fontaine in one of the books I sent you were good? The other day at M. de La Roche-foucauld's we were thrilled with them. We learned 'Le Singe et le Chat' by heart:

> D'animaux malfaisants c'était un très bon plat;
> Ils n'y craignaient tous deux aucun, quel qu'il pût être.
> Trouvait-on quelque chose au logis de gâté,
> On ne s'en prenait point aux gens du voisinage:
> Bertrand dérobait tout; Raton, de son côté,
> Était moins attentif aux souris qu'au fromage,*

and so on. That is true to life. And 'La Citrouille' and 'Le Rossignol'. They are as good as the first volume. But I am silly to write such nonsense; it is having nothing to do at Livry that bores one to death.

You wrote an excellent letter to Brancas. The other day he wrote you a whole quire of paper, quite a good outpouring. He read it to Mme de Coulanges and me. I said to him, 'Send it to me in a finished state

---

*"They were a fine pair of wicked animals:
Neither feared anyone, whoever he might be.
Was there something broken in the house?
Nobody blamed the folk round about.
Jacko pinches everything; Puss, on his part,
Was less interested in the mice than in the cheese.'
La Fontaine, *Fables*, IX, 17 ('The Monkey and the Cat').

for Wednesday.' He said he would do nothing of the kind, didn't want you to see it, it was too silly and feeble. 'Who do you take us for? You've read it to us!' 'The fact remains that I don't want her to read it.' That's all the sense I could get out of him. He never was so absurd. He asked for a case to be brought up the other day at the second session; his case was judged at the first. This idiocy tickled the senators very much, and I think it won his suit for him.

My dear child, what do you think of the endless wanderings of this letter? I could go on writing until tomorrow if I wanted. Look after yourself, my dear, that is my continual chorus. Mind you don't fall; stay in bed sometimes. Since I gave my little girl a nurse like those of the time of François I, I think you should honour all my advice. Do you think I shan't come and see you this year? I had settled all that another way, and even for love of you, but your chair throws me all into a muddle again – how can I not rush to see you this year if you would like me to? Alas, I am the one who must say that I have no fixed country left except where you are. Your portrait reigns over my mantelpiece; you are an object to worship now in Provence and in Paris, and at Court and at Livry. So anyway, my dear, you have to be ungrateful, for how could you return all that? I kiss you and love you and will keep on saying so because it is always the same. I would kiss that rascally Grignan if I weren't angry with him.

Old Paul died a week ago; our garden is all forlorn.

To Madame de Grignan

[Les Rochers, Sunday 31 May 1671]

At last, my love, here we are in our dear old Rochers. How can I see these paths again, these carved mottoes, this little study, these books, this room, without dying of sadness? There are happy memories, but there are also some so vivid and emotional that they are hardly bearable, and those I have of you are of this kind. Do you not realize the effect that can have on a heart like mine?

If you go on keeping well, my dear child, I shan't come and see you until next year. Brittany and Provence are not compatible. Long journeys are strange things. If we were always feeling as we do at the end of them we should never leave the spot where we are. But Providence bestows forgetfulness, the same that helps women over childbirth. God bestows this forgetfulness so that the world should not come to an end and one should undertake journeys to Provence. The one I shall make will give me the greatest joy I can have in my life, but how sad a thought to see no end to your stay there! I admire your good sense and applaud it more and more. Although, to tell you the truth, I am deeply touched by this impossibility, yet I hope that by then we shall see things in another light. We must hope so, for without that consolation there would be nothing to live for. Sometimes in these woods I go off into reveries of such gloom that I come back more shaken than if I had had the fever.

It seems to me that you had a good time in Marseilles. Don't forget to let me know what sort of welcome you get at Grignan. Here they had arranged a sort of triumphal entry for my son. Vaillant had put more than fifteen hundred men under arms, all well turned out and with new ribbons at their necks. They marched in good order to wait for us about a league from Les Rochers. Now for a nice story: M. l'Abbé had written that we should arrive on Tuesday and then at once forgot all about it. These poor folk waited on Tuesday until ten o'clock at night, and after they had all gone home very dashed and very perplexed, we quietly arrived on Wednesday without any idea that they had put an army in the field to welcome us. This contretemps annoyed us, but what could be done? That is how we started.

Mlle du Plessis is exactly as when you left her. She has a new woman acquaintance at Vitré whom she is very proud of because she is a bluestocking who has read all the novels and has received two letters from the Princesse de Tarante. I was naughty enough to get Vaillant to say that I was jealous of this new friend, that I wouldn't let anything show but that my heart was wounded. All she said about it was worthy of Molière. It is funny to see how carefully she handles me and how skilfully she guides the conversation so as not to mention my rival in front of me. On my side I play up for all I'm worth.

My little trees are astonishingly beautiful. Pilois is raising them to the skies with admirable rectitude. But seriously, nothing is so beautiful as these avenues you saw being planted. You know I gave you a sort of motto to suit you. Here is something I wrote on a tree for my son when he came back from Candia: *vago di fama*;* isn't that nice for such a short word or two? Only yesterday I had inscribed in honour of lazy people: *bella cosa far niente*.†

Alas, my dear, how dreary my letters are! Where is the time when I talked about Paris like everybody else? You will have nothing but news of me, and such is my conceit that I am persuaded you prefer that to any other.

The company here appeals to me very much. Our Abbé is ever more admirable; my son and La Mousse get on very well with me and I with them. We are always looking for each other, and when business cuts me off from them they are in despair and think I am absurd to prefer a farmer's accounts to the *Contes* of La Fontaine. They are all passionately devoted to you, and I think they will be writing to you. So I am making the first move, as I don't like talking to you in a crowd. My dear girl, don't stop loving me, for love is my life and soul; as I said to you the other day, it makes all my joy and all my grief. I declare that the rest of my life is overshadowed by gloom and sadness when I think that so often I shall spend it far away from you.

To Madame de Grignan

[Les Rochers, Wednesday 15 July 1671]

If I were to write down all my reveries for you I should always write you the longest letters in the world. But that is not very easy. So I content myself with what can be written and I dream whatever should be dreamed; I have the time and place for it. La Mousse has a little swelling on the teeth and the Abbé a little swelling on the knee, which leave me free in my avenue of trees to do what I please. And what I please means to walk up and down there in the evening until eight o'clock. My son has gone now and that leaves a silence, tranquillity and solitude that I don't think it is easy to find anywhere else.

> Oh! que j'aime la solitude!
> Que ces lieux sacrés à la nuit,

---

*'In love with glory.'
†'It is a lovely thing to have nothing to do.'

Éloignés du monde et du bruit,
Plaisent à mon inquiétude!*

I won't tell you, my dear, whom I am thinking of and with what affection; to those who guess there's no need to speak. If you were not pregnant and the hippogriff still existed in the world it would be a kind of never-to-be-forgotten act to be brave enough to climb on him and come and see me sometimes. Alas, dear, it wouldn't be much trouble: he can circle the earth in two days. You could even come sometimes and have dinner here and get back to supper with M. de Grignan; or have supper here for the sake of the walk, for which I should love to have you, and the next day you would be back in time to be in your gallery for Mass.

My son is in Paris, but he won't be there long. The Court is back and he must show himself. The loss of the Duc d'Anjou seems very serious to me. I am told that my granddaughter is very pretty, that her nurse takes good care of her and the little household is running perfectly. I hope I shall find it all settled in at my house in Paris. It is absurd how I already feel that this small person is the fruit of my body once removed. Mme de Villars writes quite often and always mentions you. She is affectionate and understands love, so understands my feelings for you, which makes me fond of her. She asks me to send you a thousand nice things on her behalf; her letter is full of admiration and kindness. Answer her with a little half-page that I can send on. This is a fine detour to get to her, but the urgency of the things you have between you doesn't call for any more haste. Little Saint-Géran has written me some scrawl I can't read. I reply with rudeness and insults which tickle them and me too. This feeble joke is not yet quite stale. When it is I shall say no more, for I should get very tired of any other style with her.

We still read Tasso with pleasure. I am sure you would not mind if you made a third with us. There is a great difference between reading a book on one's own or with people who appreciate and pick out the

*'Oh, how I love solitude.
How these places, dedicated to night,
Far from the world and its noise
Soothe my restlessness.'
Saint-Amant, 'Ode à la solitude'.

fine passages and so keep one's attention from flagging. This *Morale* of Nicole is admirable, and *Cléopâtre* is going along nicely, but in no hurry; it is for odd moments. Usually it is reading this that lulls me to sleep – the large print pleases me much more than the style. As for the sentiments, I admit that they please me too, and their perfection fulfils my conception of noble souls. You know too that I am not averse to great deeds of the sword so that all is well, provided you don't give away my secret.

Mlle du Plessis often honours us with her presence. She was saying yesterday that in Lower Brittany the food is admirable, and that at the wedding of her sister-in-law they ate twelve hundred chickens in one day. At this exaggeration we were all turned to stone. I plucked up my courage and said, 'Mademoiselle, think a moment, don't you mean twelve? Everyone makes mistakes sometimes.' 'No, Madame, it was twelve hundred, or eleven hundred. I won't swear to you whether it was eleven or twelve, for fear of telling a lie, but I am sure it was one or the other.' And she repeated that a score of times, and wouldn't knock off a single chicken. We felt that there must have been at least three hundred dressers to prepare the birds with larding fat, and that the scene must have been a big field in which marquees had been set up, and that if they had numbered only fifty they would have had to start a month in advance. This table-talk was good and you would have enjoyed it. Have you got some exaggerating female like that?

And now, my dear, that watch you gave me, which was always an hour or two fast or slow, has become so exactly right that it doesn't differ a second from the clock. I am delighted with it and thank you all over again. In a word, my dear, I am all yours. The Abbé tells me he adores you and wants to do something for you but doesn't quite see when; but anyway he loves you as much as he does me.

To Madame de Grignan

[Les Rochers, Wednesday 5 August 1671]

Well, I am very glad that M. de Coulanges has sent you some news. You will also learn about M. de Guise, which overwhelms me when I think of Mlle de Guise's grief. You can well see, my dear, that this death can only upset me through my imagination, for otherwise nothing can less affect the peace of my life. You know how afraid I am of self-reproach; Mlle de Guise has nothing to reproach herself for except the death of her nephew. She never agreed to his being bled. Excess of blood caused his stroke, and that's a pleasant little circumstance for you. It seems to me that as soon as you fall ill in Paris you fall down dead – I've never seen such mortality. I do urge you, my dearest, to look after yourself. If any child at Grignan is stricken with smallpox, send it to Montélimar. Your health is the object of all my wishes.

I must tell you a bit of news about our States as your penalty for being Breton. M. de Chaulnes arrived on Sunday evening to the sound of all the din that Vitré can muster. On Monday morning he wrote me a letter and sent it by one of his gentlemen. I answered by going to dine with him. Food was served at two tables in the same room, which made a pretty good feed with fourteen covers at each table. Monsieur presided at one, Madame at the other. There was far too much to eat, roasts were taken back again as though untouched. For the pyramids of fruit the doorways had to be raised. Our forefathers never foresaw mechanics like these, since they didn't imagine a door had to be higher than themselves. A pyramid wants to come in (one of those pyramids that mean you are obliged to write notes from one side of the table to the other, not that there is anything upsetting about that, on the contrary it is very pleasant not to see what they conceal). This pyramid, with twenty dishes, was so satisfactorily knocked down at the door that the din drowned the violins, oboes and trumpets.

After dinner Messieurs de Locmaria and de Coëtlogon, with two Breton ladies, danced wonderful passepieds and minuets with an air that our good dancers do not have by a long way; they do gypsy and Low Breton steps with a delicacy and precision that are delightful. I am always thinking of you and I recalled your dancing and the things I had seen you dance with such tenderness that this pleasure became quite painful to me. They talked a lot about you. I am sure that you would have been delighted to see Locmaria dance. The violins and passepieds at Court make you sick in comparison. It is quite extraordinary; they do a hundred different steps, but always with this quick, exact rhythm. I have never seen a man dance this kind of dance as he does.

After this little ball there entered all those coming in crowds to open the States on the morrow: the First President, the Prosecutor and Advocates of the Parlement, eight bishops, MM. de Molac, La Coste and Coëtlogon senior, M. Boucherat from Paris and fifty Lower Bretons gilded up to the eyes, a hundred communities. In the evening Mme de Rohan was to arrive from one direction and her son from another, and M. de Lavardin, which surprises me. I did not see these last because I wanted to come here to sleep, after going to La Tour de Sévigné to see M. d'Harouys and MM. Fourché and Chésières, who had just come. M. d'Harouys will write to you. He is overwhelmed by your kindnesses, having had two of your letters at Nantes, for which I am even more obliged than he is. His house will be the Louvre of the States: there is gaming, good food and freedom day and night, which attracts everybody. I had never seen the States; it is quite a fine affair. I don't believe there are any more impressive than these. This province is full of nobility. Not one of them is away at the war or at Court except your brother, who may come back here one day like the rest. I shall go and see Mme de Rohan some time. Lots of people would come here if I didn't go to Vitré. It was a great joy to be at the States. I didn't want to see the official opening, it was too early in the morning. The States should not go on long. It is only a matter of asking what the King's will is. Not a word is said and the thing is done. As for the Governor, he picks up more than 40,000 écus due to him, I don't know how. All kinds of other presents, road repairs and town restorations, fifteen or twenty huge tables, continual gaming, eternal balls, plays three times a week, lots of showing off, and there you have the States. Oh, and I am forgetting four hundred pipes of wine drunk there, but if I forgot that little item others wouldn't, and it is the main one. Well, my dear, all this is too boring for words. But it trips off the pen when you are in Brittany and have nothing else to say. A thousand greetings to you from M. and Mme de Chaulnes. I am always wholly yours, and await Fridays, when I get your letters, with an impatience equal to the extreme affection I have for you. Our Abbé embraces you, as I do my dear Grignan and whatever else you like.

To Madame de Grignan

[Les Rochers, Sunday 9 August 1671]

You aren't sincere when you praise me so highly at the expense of your own worth. It would ill become me to write your panegyric back to you, and you don't want me to speak ill of myself, so I won't do the one or the other. But all the same, my dear, if you have grounds for complaint against me it is not for failing to see good qualities and the sum of all the virtues in you. You can thank God for all He has given you, for as to me I haven't enough merit to give any of it away.

However that may be, you are putting your reflections into practice at a very suitable time. What you say about the anxieties we suffer so often and so naturally about the future, and how imperceptibly our inclinations change and modify themselves through necessity is most suitable matter for a book like Pascal's. Nothing is so solid and useful as these kinds of meditations. Well, who are the people of your age who can make them? I don't know of any. You have a fund of reason and courage that I honour. I haven't so much, especially when my heart takes a part and upsets me. My words are quite good (I class them with those of people who speak well), but the tenderness of emotions kills me. For example, I was not deceived about the pains of separation from you. I imagined them as I now feel them. I have realized that nothing would fill your place for me, that the memory of you would always make my heart ache, that I should be bored in your absence, that I should worry about your health and fret about you day and night. I feel all that as I had foreseen. There are some subjects on which I haven't the strength to insist. All my thoughts slip in that direction, as you say so well, and I haven't found that the proverb, *choose a garment suitable for the cold*, applies to me; I haven't any garment for that kind of cold. However, I find amusement and the time passes, and this particular fact doesn't upset the general rule, which is always true and always will be: *We almost always fear evils which lose that name with changes of our thoughts and inclinations*. God preserve your health of mind.

You want to love me both on your own behalf and on your child's, but, my dear, don't take on so many things. Even if you could succeed in loving me as much as I love you, which is not possible or even in

God's order of things, my little girl would have to have the advantage; it is the overspill of the love I feel for you. My aunt has been to see her, she will have a new dress this summer. She is pretty and well favoured, and her nurse has too much milk.

But here is one thing that has surprised me very much, it is that Mme de Lavardin is not budging. She is staying in her Paris house. She has been seen, she is very brave. Her son is at Vitré, entertains lavishly, and to please people laughs and sings as though nothing had happened. I went to see him recently. I thought he would throw himself weeping on my neck, but nothing of the kind, I was more upset than he was. He chatted quite normally and I left the Abbé and La Mousse with him to have dinner, and they came back full of wise remarks.[1]

I dined on Monday with M. de Chaulnes, who has had the States sitting twice a day for fear of their coming to see me. I daren't tell you the honour they are paying me at these States; it is absurd. Yet I haven't slept there yet, and I can't leave my woods and walks, however much they implore me. Chésières has double tertian fever. All fever frightens me, but I shall go to see him tomorrow. I have been here four days. The weather is so lovely that I can't shut myself up in a little town.

But, my dear, who is to deliver the baby if you have it at Grignan? Will you get help from a distance? Don't forget last time and don't forget what happened the first time, and how you needed a skilled and quick-acting man. Sometimes you are worried about how you can prove your affection; here is just the occasion when I am asking you for a proof. Moreover I shall be so grateful if for love of me you will take a great deal of care of yourself. Ah, my dear, how easy it will always be to pay your debt to me! Could treasures and all the wealth in the world give me as much joy as your affection? But also, if you reverse the medal, hell is no worse than the opposite.

Your letter to Mme de Villars is excellent. One would have to be deaf to fail to recognize you, but all the same it doesn't seem quite as pointed in style as others I have read of yours. But she will be very pleased with it, and nobody writes better than you. When the Coadjutor's foot is better I beg him to be so good as to make some answer

---

1. Mme de Lavardin had just lost her brother-in-law, the Bishop of Le Mans, uncle of her son mentioned here.

to Monsieur d'Agen about this nun who is turning all his diocese topsy-turvy. I will count that letter as addressed to me and will give him three months' grace. I find his turns of expression baffling, like those of M. de La Rochefoucauld. They are very different from those one achieves by working to deserve them. Isn't all this a bit labyrinthine? Do you understand it? This is what is called subtlety.

But what is this you are saying about a pain in the hip? Might your little boy have turned into a girl? Never mind, I'll help you to expose her on the Rhône in a little basket of rushes, and she will come ashore in some realm where her beauty will be the subject of a romance. Look at me, just like Don Quixote! There are some horrible places in *Cléopâtre*, but fine ones as well, and strict virtue is certainly on her throne. We have finished Tasso with pleasure and regret; and we are left anchorless. I must wait until the States are over before taking on anything else.

Was it to you that I wrote the other day that it seemed as if all the paving-stones had turned into gentlemen? I have never seen so many people. I can't imagine that the States of Languedoc can be finer. But give me news of what is going on round you. Aren't you feeling the burden of your position? It overwhelms me and I think the earlier one was better.[2] Aren't you hoping for the same grace in your Assembly? How do you stand with Marseille? Oh dear, how very Provençal I am getting, and how that country has become my own! Oh, my darling, did my life have to be planned and marked out so far from yours?

[To Monsieur de Grignan]

There was nobody but you, my dear Comte, who could persuade me to give her to a Provençal, but in truth that is how it is. I call Caderousse and Mérinville to witness, for if I had found as much eagerness and readiness in my daughter's heart for the latter as I found for you and had I not been the queen of chicanery through my fear of settling things, all would have been done.[3] So never doubt my true affection

2. *the earlier one was better*: at the time of his marriage Grignan's position was Lieutenant-General of Languedoc, which was not so exacting, not having a residence stipulation.

3. Françoise-Marguerite de Sévigné had nearly married Mérinville in 1666.

and very special esteem; a moment's reflection will show you I am speaking the truth. I am not surprised that my daughter tells you nothing about me, for she was the same with me about you last year. So do believe, without her telling you, that I never forget you. Now she is scolding you and saying that you use this pretext as an excuse for your laziness. I leave that debate to the two of you, and assure you that although you are of all men the most fortunate in being loved, you have never been loved, nor can be, by anybody more sincerely than by me. I wish you were here in my mall every day, but you are proud, and I see quite well that you want me to come and see you first. You are very fortunate that I am not an old granny. I assure you that I shall devote the rest of my health to undertaking this journey. Our Abbé wants it even more than I do, and that is something. He kisses your hands and our dear La Mousse. Good-bye, my dear Grignan, love me, let me catch a glimpse of you and I will let you have some of my woods.

My poor dear, I return to you. So you didn't have all that mob you were expecting? But you want war. I guess why this confusion might be good for you. Have you given up thinking of selling that piece of land? Ah well, why haven't you all I wish for you, or why myself haven't I everything I haven't got?

M. d'Andilly has sent me the collection he has made of the letters of M. de Saint-Cyran; it is one of the finest things in the world. They are really Christian maxims or aphorisms, and so well turned that you know them by heart, like those of M. de La Rochefoucauld. When it is issued get Mme de La Fayette or M. d'Hacqueville to ask M. d'Andilly for one for you; he will be most obliged for this mark of confidence. When you think that he has never had a penny for any of his books and that he gives them all away, you will see that it really is obliging him to want one from his hands. I challenge M. Nicole to express better what you have written on the changing of our passions; there is not a word more or less than is necessary.

To Madame de Grignan

[Vitré, Wednesday 12 August 1671]

Well, my dear, here I am in the middle of the States, otherwise the States would be in the midst of Les Rochers. Last Sunday, as soon as I had sealed my letters, I beheld four coaches and six in my courtyard, with fifty horse-guards, several led horses and several mounted pages. It was M. de Chaulnes, M. de Rohan, M. de Lavardin, MM. de Cöetlogon, de Locmaria, the Barons de Guais, the Bishops of Rennes and Saint-Malo, MM. d'Argouges and eight or ten I don't know; I am forgetting M. d'Harouys, *who need not be mentioned*. I received all these. Lots of things were said and replied to. Then, after a little tour they enjoyed very much, there appeared from one end of the mall an excellent and genteel collation, especially some Burgundy, which went down like Forges water. They were persuaded that all that happened at a wave of the wand. M. de Chaulnes begged me to go to Vitré. So I came here on Monday evening. Mme de Chaulnes entertained me to supper, with the play *Tartuffe* not at all badly done, and a ball where the passepied and minuet almost made me cry. It makes me think so much of you that I can hardly stop myself, and have to find something quickly to take my mind off it. People talk about you very often, and I don't have to cast about for my answers, for I'm thinking of you at the very same moment, and I always think people can read my thoughts through my bodice.

Yesterday I received the whole of Brittany at my Tour de Sévigné. I went to the play again. It was *Andromaque*, and that made me shed more than half a dozen tears, which is quite enough for a rustic company. Supper in the evening and a dance. I wish you had seen the way M. de Locmaria carried himself, and the way he doffs his hat and puts it on again. What grace, what perfect timing! He can challenge all the courtiers and confound them, upon my word. He has sixty thousand livres a year and has just left riding-school. He is a model of good looks and would like to marry you. For the rest, don't suppose that your health is not drunk here. This is no great obligation, but such as it is you owe it every day to the whole of Brittany. They begin with me and then Mme de Grignan comes quite naturally. M. de Chaulnes pays you a thousand compliments. The civilities paid to me are so ridiculous, and the women of these parts so silly that it leads one to suppose that I am the only one in the town, although it is crammed. Among people you know here are Tonquedec, Comte des Chapelles, Pomenars, the Abbé de Montigny, who is Bishop of Saint-Pol-de-Léon, and countless others. But these talk to me about you, and we laugh a bit at our neighbours. The neighbours are amusing here, particularly after dinner; I've never seen so much good food. Mme de Coëtquen is ill here with a fever. Chésières is better, and a deputation from the States came to compliment him. We are at least as polite here as the polite Lavardin. He is much loved here, he has a solid merit like Graves wine. My Abbé is busy building and doesn't want to come and stay in Vitré, but comes over to dine. I shall still be here until Monday and then go and spend a week in my humble solitude, then back here to say good-bye, for all will be over by the end of the month.

Our contribution has been made already, over a week ago. We were asked for three million, we offered two million five hundred thousand livres without haggling, and it was settled. And the Governor will have fifty thousand écus, M. de Lavardin eighty thousand francs and the rest of the officers in proportion, all for two years. One must suppose that as much wine flows into the bodies of our Bretons as water under the bridges, since it is on this that they get the vast amount of money that is given away at each States. Now you are fully informed, thank God, about your homeland, but I have none of your letters and consequently no answers to give you. I am quite naturally telling you about what I see and hear.

Pomenars is wonderful. There is no other man I would more willingly wish to have two heads, for his own will never last the end of the journey. For myself, my dear, I wish I were at the end of the week already, so as to retire gracefully from all the honours of this world and enjoy my own company at Les Rochers. Good-bye, my dearest. I always wait impatiently for your letters. Your health is a matter that touches me very intimately. I believe you know that, and so without falling back on 'it is right and proper to believe', I can finish my letter and sleep in peace on what you think of my affection for you. Will you tell M. de Grignan that I embrace him with all my heart?

To Madame de Grignan

[Paris, Wednesday 13 January 1672]

Good gracious, my dear, what are you talking about? What pleasure can you get from speaking ill of yourself and your intelligence, from running down your own good actions, from thinking anyone must be very kind to remember you at all? Although you certainly don't believe all that, yet I am hurt and annoyed, and although perhaps I should not rise to things you only say as a joke, yet I can't help scolding you rather than getting on with the things I have to tell you. You're a nice one, too, when you say you are frightened of great minds. Alas, my dear, if you realized how small they are when seen close to, and how awkward they sometimes are, you would soon cut them down to a reasonable size. Do you remember how weary you sometimes were of them? Take care that distance doesn't magnify things; that is a fairly usual effect.

I have supper every evening with Mme Scarron. She has an agreeable and marvellously sensible mind. It is a pleasure to hear her discussing the horrible disturbances of a region she knows well, the desperation of that d'Heudicourt just when her position seemed so miraculous, the continual ravings of Lauzun, the black despondency or miserable troubles of the ladies of Saint-Germain. And perhaps the most envied of them all is not always free from them.[1] It is a most interesting thing to hear her talk about all this. This discussion sometimes takes us far and wide, from one moral to another, sometimes Christian, sometimes political. We often talk about you. She loves your wit and manners, and when you are back here you need have no fear of being a back number.

I feel you are a bit tired of your Provençal people. Shall we compose a ditty against them? Anyway, they have proved obedient, though with a bad grace. If they had believed M. de Grignan at the outset it would not have cost them any more and they would have satisfied the courts. Charming manners! You are right to say it is not your fault and you don't know what to do; this remark is very amusing.

But listen to this example of the King's goodness and the pleasure

1. Mme de Montespan.

of serving such a good master. He summoned the Maréchal de Belle-fonds to his private apartment and said, 'Monsieur le Maréchal, I want to know why you wish to quit my service. Is it religion? Is it a desire to retire? Or is it the burden of your debts? If it is this last I want to straighten it out and go into the details of your affairs.' The Marshal was very touched by this kindness. 'Sire,' he said, 'it is my debts. I am ruined. I cannot watch the troubles of some of my friends who have helped me and whom I cannot satisfy.' 'Very well,' said the King, 'we must clear what is owing to them. I will give you 100,000 francs on your house at Versailles and a guarantee of 400,000 which will act as insurance in the event of your death. You will pay what is outstanding out of the 100,000, and that being so you will remain in my service.' One would indeed have to be very hard-hearted not to obey a master who entered into his servants' interests with so much consideration. And the Marshal did not resist, so he is back in his place and has been showered with favours. All these details are true.

Every evening at Saint-Germain there are balls, plays and mas-querades. The King shows an assiduity for entertaining Madame which he never showed for her predecessor. Racine has written a tragedy called *Bajazet* which raises the roof; indeed it doesn't go from bad to worse like the others. M. de Tallard[2] says it is as far above the plays of Corneille as those of Corneille are above those of Boyer. That is what you might call praise; it doesn't do to keep truths hidden. We shall decide later with our own eyes and ears.

I have been to Livry. Alas, my dear, how I have kept my word to you and thought of you with love! It was very warm there for the cold season. But the sun shone; all the trees were decked with pearls and crystals; this diversity is not unpleasing. I walked a great deal. The next day I went to Pomponne to dinner – how can I ever repeat what took five hours to say? I enjoyed myself there very much. M. de Pomponne will be here in four days' time. It would be very distressing for me if I had to go and talk to him about your affairs in Provence. Really he wouldn't listen to me – you see I'm setting myself up as an expert. But honestly, my dear, nothing comes up to Monsieur d'Uzès, he is what you call the big noise. I've never seen a cleverer man nor a wiser

2. *M. de Tallard*: Camille d'Hostun de La Baume, Comte de (1652–1728). Later became distinguished French soldier, defeated and taken prisoner by Marlborough at Blenheim.

counsellor. I'm waiting for him so as to tell you what he has done at Saint-Germain.

You ask me to write you long letters. I think you should be satisfied, my dear, for sometimes I am appalled by their immensity. It is all your flattery that gives me such confidence.

I do urge you, dear, to keep yourself in this happy state and not go from one extreme to the other. Do take time to get right again and don't tempt God with your dialogues and your continual visiting.

Mme de Brissac has made very good provision for her winter, namely M. de Longueville and the Comte de Guiche, but it is all above board, only for the pleasure of being adored. The Marans is no longer to be seen at Mme de La Fayette's, nor at M. de La Rochefoucauld's. We don't know what she is up to, and sometimes make up rather wild theories. Last summer she had this idea of being raped; she was determined to be raped. You know this kind of obsession. My idea is that she never will be. Lord, what madness! And how long have I been seeing her as you do now!

It is not my fault that I don't see Mme de Valavoire. And there is no need to say, 'go and see her'. It suffices for her to have seen you to make me go running after her. But she is running after someone else, for however much I beg her to wait for me I can't attain this good fortune. You should give your pun to Monsieur le Grand; it is a good one. Here Châtillon gives us some of the most awful ones every day.

To Madame de Grignan

[Paris, Friday evening, 15 January 1672]

I wrote to you this morning, my dearest, by the post which is bringing you all joys and happiness for your affairs in Provence, but I mean to write again this evening lest it should be said that a post comes without bringing you a word from me. I really think, my dear, that you like my letters. You say you do – why would you want to deceive me as well as yourself? For if by chance it were not so, one would have to pity you for being overwhelmed by the abundance of mine. Yours are a joy to me. I haven't answered about your great soul (it is Langlade who says *great soul* by way of teasing), but honestly you have a very great one. Perhaps it is not one of those souls in the very first class, like that Roman who went back to the Carthaginians to keep his word and was martyred, but below that you can pride yourself on being in the top rank. I find you so perfect and so well thought of that I don't know what to say except admiration, and advice to back up your reason with your courage and your courage with your reason, and to take chocolate, so that the most unpleasant company seems good to you.

Racine's play seemed beautiful to me, we went to see it. My daughter-in-law[1] struck me as the most wonderful actress I have ever seen; she is a hundred leagues ahead of the Desoeillets, and as for me, who am considered pretty good on the stage, I am not worthy to light the candles when she appears. She is plain close to, and I am not surprised that my son was overcome by her presence, but when she recites verse she is adorable. *Bajazet* is very fine, but I do think it is a bit muddled at the end. There is plenty of passion, and not such unreasonable passion as in *Bérénice*. But to my taste I don't think it comes up to *Andromaque*, and as for the finest plays of Corneille, they are as much above those of Racine as Racine's are above all the others. Think that over and remember that silly remark, and believe me, nothing will approach (I don't say surpass) the divine moments of Corneille. The other day he read us a play[2] at M. de La Roche-foucauld's which recalls the Queen Mother. I wish, my dear, that you had come with me after dinner; you would not have been disappointed. You might even have shed a little tear, as I shed more than a score. You would have admired your sister-in-law. You would have seen the *Angels* in front of you, and the Bourdeaux, who was got up like a little girl. Monsieur le Duc was behind, Pomenars up above with the footmen, his coat turned up to his nose because the Comte de Créance wants to hang him, whatever resistance he puts up; all the young fashionables were on the stage.[3] The Marquis de Villeroy was in full evening dress, the Comte de Guiche with a belt as twisted as his wit. All the others looked like highwaymen. I have seen the count twice at M. de La Rochefoucauld's; I thought he was very entertaining and less other-worldly than usual.

1. *My daughter-in-law*: La Champmeslé, who for a time was Charles's mistress.
2. *Pulchérie*. The opening of the play might recall the Queen Mother and Mazarin.
3. *young fashionables were on the stage*: this practice, which annoyed Molière so much, persisted well into the eighteenth century. Voltaire finally put a stop to it.

Our Abbé, with whom I am staying, says he has received the plan of Grignan and is very pleased with it, and he is already walking about there in advance. He would like to see the elevation. As for me, I shall wait until I am there. I have a thousand compliments for you from all who have heard the kind words of the King for M. de Grignan. Mme de Verneuil is the first who comes to mind. She has been very ill.

Good-bye, my darling. What can I say about my love and all the interest I take in you for twenty leagues round, from the biggest to the smallest things? M. de Harouys has arrived. I have delivered all your answers. A kiss to the admirable Grignan, the prudent Coadjutor and the presumptuous Adhémar – isn't that what I called them the other day?

To Madame de Grignan

[Paris, Wednesday 20 January 1672]

The *Maximes* of M. de La Rochefoucauld have now been revised, corrected and augmented, and I am sending them to you on his behalf. There are some wonderful ones and, to my shame, some I don't understand. God knows how you will.

There is a fuss going on between the Archbishop of Paris and the Archbishop of Reims over a ceremony. Paris wants Reims to ask permission to officiate, Reims swears he will do nothing of the kind. It is said that these two men will never agree unless they are thirty leagues apart, so they will always be at loggerheads. This ceremony is the canonization of a Borgia Jesuit. All the music of the opera was raging, and there were lights as far as the rue Saint-Antoine – it was packed to suffocation. Old Mérinville died before he could get there.

Are you not mistaken, child, in the opinion you have of my letters? The other day some horrible man, seeing my immense letter, asked me whether I thought anyone could read it. I trembled, but with no intention of mending my ways, so abiding by what you say about them I shan't spare you a single trifling incident, small or large, that might amuse you. My life and sole pleasure is the correspondence I keep up with you; all other things are far behind.

I am worried about your young brother. He is very cold in camp and has been advancing towards Cologne for an infinite time. I was hoping to see him this winter, and there he is. So it turns out that Mlle d'Adhémar[1] is the consolation of my old age. I wish you could see her affection for me and how she addresses me and embraces me. She is no beauty but she is very nice. She has a lovely voice, her complexion is white and clear. In fact I love her. You sound mad on your baby son, and I am very glad. You can't have too many hobbies, smelly or not, no matter.

There is a ball tomorrow at Madame's. I have seen a lot of jewels about at Mademoiselle's. It reminded me of our past tribulations, and would that we still suffered them. Could I be unhappy with you? My whole life is full of regrets. Monsieur Nicole, have pity on me and make me see clearly the dictates of Providence. Good-bye, my dear girl, I daren't say I worship you, but I can't imagine a degree of affection beyond mine. By your kind and sweet assurances of love you mitigate but also add to my sorrows.

To Madame de Grignan

[Paris, Friday 12 February 1672]

I cannot but be most grieved for you, my dear, when I think of the sorrow you will be feeling over the death of the poor Chevalier. You saw him recently, and that is enough to be very fond of him and get to know still better all the fine qualities God had given him. Certainly no man was better born or had more upright and enviable qualities, with a handsome face and a great affection for you. All this made him attractive to you and everybody else, and I do understand your grief very readily because I feel it too. Nevertheless, my dearest, I am going to try to interest you for a quarter of an hour, both in things that do interest you and in the tale of what is going on in society.

Monsieur d'Uzès has written an admirable memorandum about everything he thinks it proper to inform M. Colbert about, as he dare not speak to him because of the idea that his name carries smallpox. One can only admire everything Monsieur d'Uzès does, and you cannot put your interests into better hands. He adds to, takes away

1. *Mlle d'Adhémar*: used in fun for Marie-Blanche, then aged two.

from, rectifies all your thoughts, and altogether one cannot wish for anything beyond what he does. I spoke to him the other day about the little difficulty you are placed in by the affair of the secretaries. He thinks with me that it is quite ridiculous that you should give a hundred écus to satisfy the whim of M. Davonneau, not because of the money itself but because it is wrong and might have repercussions. M. Davonneau has forgotten that he had all last year's money, and it is forcing M. de Grignan's hand to say that he can't make a civil gesture to M. de Vendôme the next year, and that M. Davonneau, with various perquisites moreover, and showing some attachment to his master, wants to influence the mood of the Assembly against M. de Grignan and leaves him to use his own money to satisfy him. Frankly this seems to me neither fair nor honest as a way of going on. You are obliged to pay out so much money that I find it very hard to want you to do what you are not obliged to, and I am amazed at your docile, sheeplike consent. If you take the line of saying, 'What are a hundred écus more or less?' that kind of talk exposes you to all kinds of knavery. I am not paying court to M. Davonneau, but your interests do concern me and I think I am right. At any rate Monsieur d'Uzès is no less severe than I am in this matter. Well that is that and I shall say no more, but I thought I could tell you what I think.

I have had a long conversation with M. Le Camus; he has a great respect and affection for you. He is extremely learned, and the Bishop might well cross swords with him. He enters so perfectly into our interests that he gives me advice and I shall learn his ways of thinking. He is disgusted with crooked practices, and as his own are quite the opposite he has no difficulty in sharing our interests, in which straightforwardness and sincerity are the thing. This must never be forgotten whatever happens; it is a way of life that is always fitting. You can't deceive people for very long, and rogues are found out in the end, I am persuaded of that. M. de Pomponne is no less opposed to what is so unlike him, and I can assure you that if I were as clever about everything else as I am about holding forth about this my skill would be perfect. Send me some kind word sometime for M. Le Camus; it would be precious to him, especially as he is not bound to answer in any way.

Here is a letter for MM. de Maillane and de Vence, which makes up pretty well, I feel, for the Abbé de Grignan's former negligence.

Let me know if it goes down well. Rippert has his marching orders. Monsieur d'Uzès will tell you the rest – he thinks only of you, and would to God that I could with my love be as useful as he is!

Here is some news. The Marquis de Villeroy has left for Lyons, as I told you. The King let him know through Maréchal de Créquy that he was to go away, it is thought because of remarks made at Madame la Comtesse's. Anyway, *On parle d'eaux, de Tibre, et l'on se tait du reste.**

The King asked Monsieur, just back from Paris, 'Well, brother, what are they saying in Paris?' Monsieur said, 'Sir, they are talking a lot about that poor Marquis.' 'And what are they saying about him?' 'They are saying, Sir, that it is because he wanted to speak for another poor wretch.' 'What poor wretch?' asked the King. 'The Chevalier de Lorraine,' said Monsieur. 'But,' said the King, 'are you still thinking about the Chevalier de Lorraine? Do you care for him, would you like somebody to restore him to you?' 'Indeed, Sir,' he answered, 'it would be the greatest pleasure I could have in my life.' 'Very well,' said the King, 'I mean to make you this present; the letter went off two days ago. He will return, I give him back to you again, and want you to feel under this obligation to me for the rest of your life and love him for love of me. I will go further, and appoint him Field-Marshal in my army.' Thereupon Monsieur threw himself at the King's feet and embraced his knees for a long time, and kissed his hand with unspeakable joy. The King raised him up, saying, 'Brother, that is not the way brothers should embrace,' and embraced him fraternally. All these details come from a very reliable source, and nothing could be truer. From all this you can make your own observations, draw your own conclusions and redouble your fine passions for the service of the King your master. It is said that Madame is making the journey and several ladies with her. Feelings vary in Monsieur's circle. Some have faces half a foot long, others equally shortened. It is said that the Chevalier de Beuvron's is very long indeed.

M. de Navailles comes back too and will act as Lieutenant-General in Monsieur's army with M. de Schomberg.

The King said to Maréchal de Villeroy, 'Your son had to pay this little penalty, but the trials of this world are not endless.' You can be

*'There is talk of water, of Tiber, but of the rest not a word.' Corneille, *Cinna*, IV, 4 (on the discovery of a conspiracy).

sure that all this is true. I hate false details but I love true ones, and if you don't share my taste, my dear, you are lost, for here they go on for ever.

Marans was alone the other day, wearing her cloak, at Mme de Longueville's; she was not approved of. Langlade informs you that another time, in order to please you, he reproved her about silly things she had told him, and that he wished you had been behind the door; I wish you had been! Mme de Brissac was inconsolable at Mme de Longueville's, but unfortunately the Comte de Guiche began talking to her. She forgot her part – that of desolation on the day of the death – for at a certain moment she was supposed to faint away, but she forgot to, and recognized perfectly the people coming in.

Good-bye, my dearest. Don't you feel we have been separated for a very long time? This grief nags at me so incessantly that it would be unbearable if I didn't love you as much as I do, whatever the sorrows.

La Troche came yesterday; she adores you. Our Abbé is entirely yours and so is La Mousse. My aunt is consoled by memories of you. She is always in great pain and my cousin's fear and despair are pitiful.

Good-bye, dear, I am all yours, and nothing must be subtracted from that. Barillon[2] is here and sends much love. Mme de La Fayette has written to you. She meant to give me her letter, but it was inadvertently posted. There is only *Madame de Grignan* on it, and she is afraid it may be lost. Much love to my dear Grignan.

To Madame de Grignan

[Paris, Wednesday 16 March 1672]

You refer to my departure. Ah, my dear daughter, I am clinging to that delightful hope. Nothing keeps me here except my aunt, who is dying of grief and dropsy. She is breaking my heart with the state she is in and by all the affectionate and sensible things she says. Her courage, patience, resignation are all admirable. M. d'Hacqueville and I watch her illness day by day. He reads my heart and the pain I feel at not being free at present. I follow his advice and between now and Easter

2. Paul de Barillon, Ambassador to England from 1677; he was active in negotiations between Charles II and Louis XIV.

we shall see. If her illness gets worse, as it has done ever since I have been here, she will die in our arms; if she makes any improvement and gets into a lingering condition I shall set off as soon as M. de Coulanges gets back. Our poor Abbé is in despair as I am. We shall see how this grievous trouble turns out in April. This is all I can think of. You can't be as anxious to see me as I am to embrace you; curb your ambition and don't think you will ever be able to equal me in this.

My son tells me that they are miserable in Germany and don't know what they are doing. He was very upset by the death of the Chevalier de Grignan.

You ask me, my dear child, whether I am still fond of life. I admit that I think it has some acute sorrows. But I am even more repelled by death and I feel that I am so unfortunate to have to finish all this by death, and that if I could go backwards I would ask for nothing better. I find I am in the midst of an undertaking that embarrasses me; I was launched upon life without my consent. I have got to leave it and that overwhelms me. And how shall I leave it? Which way? Through which door? When will it be? In what frame of mind? Shall I suffer thousands and thousands of pains and die in desperation? Shall I have a stroke? Shall I die in an accident? How shall I stand with God? What shall I have to present to Him? Will fear or necessity bring me back to Him? Shall I have no other emotion than that of fear? What can I hope for? Am I worthy of paradise? Am I only fit for hell? What an alternative! What a puzzle! Nothing is so silly as to pin one's salvation to uncertainty, but nothing is more natural, and the stupid life I lead is the easiest thing in the world to understand. I am lost in these thoughts, and I find death so terrible that I hate life more because it leads me there than because of the thorns to be met with on the way. You will say I want to live for ever. Not at all, but if my opinion had been consulted I would have liked to die in my nurse's arms; it would have spared me many troubles and brought me to heaven quite safely and easily. But let us change the subject.

I am extremely sorry you have had *Bajazet* from others rather than me. It's that wretch Barbin,[1] who hates me because I don't write *Princesses de Clèves* and *de Montpensier*. You have judged it rightly and very well, and you will have seen that I share your opinion. I wanted

1. *Barbin*: Paris publisher of many writers, including Mme de La Fayette.

to send you the Champmeslé to warm it up for you. The character of Bajazet is stone cold. The Turkish manners and customs are badly observed – they don't make that much fuss there about marrying. The dénouement is not at all well prepared and no reasons are given for this mass slaughter. Of course there are some good things in it, but nothing perfectly beautiful, nothing that carries you away, none of those speeches of Corneille that thrill you. My dear, let us be careful not to compare Racine to him, let us appreciate the difference. There are cold and weak parts, and he will never go further than *Alexandre* and *Andromaque*. *Bajazet* is less good in the opinion of many people and in mine, if I may make so bold as to quote myself. Racine is writing plays for the Champmeslé and not for future ages. If ever he is no longer young or in love, it will not be the same thing. Long live our old friend Corneille! Let us overlook some bad lines in favour of the divine and sublime beauties that transport us; these are the touches of the master that are inimitable. Despréaux has more to say about this than me, and in a word this is what good taste means. Stick to that.

Here is a witticism of Mme Cornuel which tickled the pit very much. M. Tambonneau junior has abandoned the legal robe and put a strap under his belly and hindquarters. With this dashing look he wants to go to sea; I don't know what the land has done to him. So somebody said to Mme Cornuel that he was going off to sea. 'Alas,' she said, 'has he been bitten by a mad dog?' It was said without malice, which is what made everybody laugh uproariously.

Mme de Courcelles is in a great state, all her requests are being refused. But she says she hopes somebody will take pity on her, as her judges are men. Our Coadjutor would not have mercy on her at present; you say he is just now involved in the occupations of Saint Ambrose.[2]

It seems to me that you should be happy that your daughter is made in his image and likeness. Your son also wants to be like him but, with no offence to the beauty of the Coadjutor, where is the fine mouth of this little boy? Where are his charms? So he resembles his sister; you embarrass me by this resemblance. I love you dearly for not being pregnant. Console yourself for being beautiful *uselessly* with the pleasure of not being ill all the time.

2. *occupations of Saint Ambrose*: i.e. it is in Lent.

I can't pity you for having no butter in Provence because you have admirable oil and excellent fish. Oh my dear, how well I understand what people like you find to do and think in the middle of your Provence. I shall think of it as you do, and pity you all my life for spending some of your finest years there. I am so little anxious to shine in your Provençal court, and I can form so just an opinion of it from that of Brittany, that for the same reason as after three days of Vitré I longed for nothing but Les Rochers, I swear to God that the object of my desires is to spend the summer with you at Grignan. That is my aim, and nothing beyond that. My Saint-Laurent wine is at Adhémar's, and I shall have it tomorrow morning. For a long time I have been thanking you for it *in petto*; it is most kind.

Monsieur de Laon is very fond of this way of being a Cardinal. It is alleged that the other day M. de Montausier, speaking to the Dauphin about the dignity of the Cardinals, told him that it depended upon the Pope, and that if he wished to turn a stable-boy into a Cardinal he could. Thereupon enter Cardinal de Bonzi. The Dauphin said to him, 'Sir, is it true that the Pope would make a stable-boy a Cardinal if he wanted to?' M. de Bonzi was surprised, but guessing what was up he answered, 'It is true, Sir, that the Pope chooses whom he pleases, but so far we have not noticed that he has taken Cardinals out of his stable.' Cardinal de Bouillon told me this story.

I have had a lot of discussion with Monsieur d'Uzès. He will let you know about the conference he has addressed; it is admirable. He has a balanced mind and he measures his words, which have great weight on these occasions. His actions and words are excellent in every case.

What you have been told about Jarzé was being said, but it is unconfirmed. It is said that the lady's joy at the return of the Chevalier de Lorraine is unbounded. It is said, too, that the Comte de Guiche and Mme de Brissac are so over-subtle that they would need an interpreter to understand each other. Write something to our Cardinal; he loves you. The town loves you, Mme Scarron loves you. She is spending Lent here and is in this house almost every evening. Barillon is still here, and would that you were too! Good-bye, my child, I am rambling on and on. I defy you to comprehend how much I love you.

To Madame de Grignan

[Paris, Wednesday 30 March 1672]

Aren't you being too kind? At any rate, my dear, you like my letters, you want them to be long and you flatter me with the thought that you don't like them as much when they are short. But poor Grignan has a job to be accommodating enough for you to read such volumes. I still remember seeing him wonder how one could read long letters; he really has changed. Anyhow, I trust you not to show him anything that might bore him.

I must make you an apology. I thought you hadn't answered the Cardinal; you have done so very well. I must also confess that I very wickedly said nothing about compliments from Mme de Villars. I have told you about her in my letters, and I took care to tell you everything she said to me. Don't be angry with her; she is fond of you and admires you. I see her quite often. She likes talking about you and reading extracts from your letters, which gives me a very natural liking for her. She will set off at Easter in spite of the war, and will just have to come back again if the Spaniards misbehave. As these Villars have lots of money, comings and goings with crowds of retainers are not worth bothering about.

It is said that the English have routed five Dutch vessels, and that the Ambassador has told the King that the king his master had begun the war on the sea and now begged him to keep his word and begin it on land.

You know, my dear, what the name of Roquesante means for me and what veneration I have for his virtue. You can take it that his re-commendation and yours count considerably with me, but my credit is not up to my good intentions. You have said so many good things about the President in question that one would deem it an honour to serve him if he had any voice in the chapter. I will mention him in passing, but, truth to tell, everything is so secret at Versailles that one can but wait in peace for the oracles that issue therefrom. As for M. de Roquesante, if you don't remember me particularly to him, you and I are mortal enemies.

You shudder at our Abbé's fever; thank you very much. But as you were the only one to shudder and the Abbé didn't shudder at all, you will realize that I didn't shudder either. His illness was a continual anxiety, but there were no untoward accidents. He looked after himself wisely, and I am sure he will now be well for twenty years. God grant it! I have given him your love, and he is very touched.

My aunt talks of nothing but thanking you. Her condition is heart-breaking even to the most indifferent. Her swelling gets bigger day by day and remedies have no effect. She recently said to me, 'Well, my dear, you see what is called a lost woman.' She is preparing to die and speaks of it without fear; she is only astonished that so much pain is required to kill such a feeble person. There are some very harsh and cruel ways of dying, and hers is one of the most pitiful you could see. She accepts my nursing with great affection, which I return similarly, and I am so extremely touched by her sufferings and the horrible desolation of my cousin that I cannot refrain from weeping.

Here is a thought that occurs to me about the losses you are incurring at gambling and those of M. de Grignan. Do be careful, my dear, it is not pleasant to be taken in, for you can rest assured that continual ill-luck or continual good luck are not in the natural order of things. Not long ago I was told about the three-card trick at the Hôtel de Vieuville; do you remember that swindle? You must not suppose that everyone plays like you. It is my concern about you that makes me say this. As it comes from a heart that belongs to you I am sure that you will find it good advice.

Don't you also think it good to know that Kéroualle,[1] whose fortune had been read before she set off, has followed it out very precisely. The King of England has slept with her. She happened to be disposed not to hate him. Anyway, she is now eight months gone, which is strange! The Castlemaine is in disgrace. That is how things are done in that kingdom.

While we are on that theme I will tell you, with all due respect to M. de Grignan's virtue, that the young son of F— and the Chevalier de Lorraine (I hope I make myself clear) is being brought up higgledy-piggledy with the children of Mme d'Armagnac, quite openly. And great play was made of family likenesses when the Chevalier returned.

1. Louise de Kéroualle. Mistress of Charles II, created Duchess of Portsmouth.

He confirmed all that was said on that score, and found the boy so pretty and took such a liking to him that at last they told him the truth. He was delighted, and Mme d'Armagnac is continuing her kindness and bringing him up in the name of Chevalier de Lorraine. If you already know all this you will be very bored. Adhémar is in a position to tell you these trivialities. Incidentally I feel I have been rather slack about news, knowing he is much better placed for recounting it to you.

I have just had your letter of 23rd, written simply for the sake of it like mine of Friday. Ah, my girl, how lovely it is although it's not an answer, but a thousand times better, for it is what you write when you have nothing to tell me. That is what I find enchanting; you say lots of loving things and I confess I just let myself be gently flattered by this lovely truth. Who is this Breton you are helping for love of me? It is true that all Provençaux now mean something to me.

Today is the poor Abbé's examination.[2] What nonsense it is! They are all going to argue against him, torment him, haggle over details, and he has to answer everything. I am persuaded that nothing is more unfair than things of this kind, and that they make the mind insufferably boorish and argumentative.

You talk about the weather. We have had a lovely winter: three months of beautiful frost. Now it is over and spring is beginning. Nothing is so well-behaved as we are; why are you so extravagant?

I am horrified by the infidelity of M. de Vardes. It developed as his passion waned, with no reason except that his love had gone. That is upsetting, but I would prefer that sorrow to being left for another woman – that is our old bone of contention. There are many other reasons for my not approving of M. de Vardes. If Corbinelli wishes I were in Provence he is doing what I do every day of my life.

M. and Mme de Coulanges are too honoured by all the kind things you write, and they will be writing to you. I see them go with great sorrow. M. de Coulanges means to see *Jacquemart et Marguerite* once again before he dies. As for Mme de Coulanges, she will go to Grignan. We shall see her there when she has done us the honours of Lyons.

I have not seen d'Hacqueville for a week. I forgive him and am no

2. Public oral examination on the Abbé de Grignan's thesis. He would not be a Doctor of Theology until 1680.

less fond of him. As for you, my dear child, you know that I am yours and that your affection is the real joy of my life and your absence the real grief.

My dear Grignan, alas, must we spend our lives without seeing the people we love most in the world? I was told this evening that the Abbé de Grignan had done wonders in the Sorbonne. Our Cardinal is delighted.

To Madame de Grignan

[Paris, Friday 1 April 1672]

My dear, I am full of tenderness for you because you have written things to Guitaut about the joy you are hoping for when you see me in Provence, things that transport me with joy. You can imagine what pleasure it is to learn things like this indirectly, even though one knows them already. Alas, it can only add to the extreme desire I have to be off, which is now unparalleled. Only my aunt is delaying me, she is so ill that I don't understand how she can last long in this state. I will give you news of her, as it is the only big preoccupation I have at present.

Your prelate doesn't call on me much just now, although he has been so pleased with me. It seems to me that he didn't want so much to see me as to have seen me – it gave him something to write and talk about, for he had not the satisfaction of convincing me that you were wrong in the slightest degree. In fact in the matter of the baptism I even embarrassed him with his own arguments. He said that the Coadjutor had got a man to ask him to dress suitably, but that the man said nothing to him about it. Which was why the Coadjutor was right to be vexed when he saw him wearing a cassock, having asked him to do the opposite; he had not thought of these little matters. I also maintained that a governor should not divulge orders he asked for in court, and which he thought necessary for obtaining obedience on certain occasions, and that this confidence was a betrayal of the service of the King. Anyhow, my dear, one cannot describe everything said in one hour, but I think that this prodigy you wanted to send me would have been pleased. I assure you that many people here know this prelate, and that he has been described to the life in very high places.

Yesterday I saw Mme de Verneuil, safe back from Verneuil and death; the milk diet has restored her. She is good-looking, with a fine figure, there is no longer any difference between her waist-line and mine and she is neither red nor bloated as she was. This state makes her attractive. She is affectionate, obliging and speaks well of people. She asked me to send a thousand good wishes to you.

Yesterday morning there was a service for the Chancellor[1] at Sainte-Elisabeth. I wasn't there because they forgot to bring me my ticket, but all the rest of the habitable world was there. Mme Fieubet overheard this: The Choiseul stepped in front of the Bonnelle. 'Ah,' said the Bonnelle, 'here is a jumped-up female who has had over a hundred thousand écus of our clothes.' The Choiseul turns round and, like Harlequin, 'Hee, hee, hee,' she says, laughing in her face, 'that's how you answer crackpots,' and passes on. When that is as true as it is in this case it is extremely funny.

Mme de Coulanges and M. de Barillon acted yesterday the scene of Vardes and Mlle de Toiras. We all felt like weeping; they surpassed themselves. But the Champmeslé is so amazing that you never saw anything like her in your life. People go to see the actress and not the play; I saw *Ariane*[2] for her sake alone. The play is feeble, the actors are awful, but when Champmeslé comes on you hear a murmur, everyone is transported and sheds tears at her despair.

The other day the Chevalier de Lorraine went to see Fiennes. She was by way of acting the forsaken maiden. The Chevalier, with that fine open face I like and you don't, wanted to save her from any kind of embarrassment and said, 'Mademoiselle, what is upsetting you, why are you so sad? What is so extraordinary about all that has happened to us? We have loved each other and now we don't, fidelity is not a virtue in people of our age. It is much better for us to forget the past and resume ordinary tones and manners. That's a nice little dog, who gave it to you?' And that was the dénouement of this grand passion.

What are you reading, my dear? I am reading the discovery of the Indies by Christopher Columbus, which I am finding extremely entertaining. But your daughter appeals to me still more. I love her and I don't really see how I can help it. She makes a fuss of your portrait

1. *the Chancellor*: Séguier.
2. *Ariane*: a play by Thomas Corneille.

and pats it in such a funny way that you have to rush and kiss her. I am surprised that even then you did your hair in that way. Your fingers wanted to turn it all up and curl it; in fact it was a prophecy. Good-bye, dearest and best. I shall never believe anyone can love more passionately than I love you.

To Madame de Grignan

[Paris, Wednesday 6 April 1672]

Here is the prettiest of the fans that Bagnols intended for his *Chimène*; I was glad to win it and loved Fortune for this little favour she granted me just when I needed it. Amuse yourself by looking at it carefully. Enjoy a visit from the Pont-Neuf, your old friend, for as you won't come and see it, it goes to you to pay its respects. I have never seen anything so pretty. But if I am happy to have this little favour from Fortune I hate her on the other hand for muddling me up and upsetting all my plans. My aunt's illness means that I simply don't know where I am. The Abbé and I are fuming, and have made up our minds, if her illness just goes on and on, to set off for Provence, for how long can natural goodness last? For my part I know nothing but you, and I am so impatient to set off to see you that my feelings towards others are distinctly curtailed thereby. You can always rest assured that I am more anxious to set off than you are for me to do so. You think that that is saying a lot, and so do I, but I can't exaggerate my feelings about you. I don't fail to give my aunt all your kind regards. She believes her end is near, but thanks to her kind nature she is controlling herself even unto death and pretending to hope for something from remedies that no longer do any good, so as to save my cousin from despair. But when she can say a word without being overheard, one can see what she really thinks, and it is death that she is contemplating calmly, with the greatest virtue and courage.

In the face she is like a retarded child, and in the belly like a woman nine months pregnant; she still gets up because she feels suffocated in bed. We cannot see what future my cousin has, and think we have ideas which we don't really believe in at present. We can envisage a convent with very reasonable charges, and an increase in the allowance her brother might consent to give her. But we are all very embarrassed about it.

As for M. de La Mousse, I have impressed upon him how much you want to see him. He is only afraid of the bothers of the journey. Write to him as you intend to, and for our part we shall be very happy to add his company to our own and encourage him with the joy he will be giving you. I assure you, my dear, that I wish to be in that little cool room you are having built for me more than anywhere else in the world, but after that I would very much like to see you in an apartment I am going to have fitted up for you.

I am expecting the tuberoses; a delightful present. Our Sévigné uncle is giving us some.

M. de Grignan is asking for a very good jerkin. This is a matter of seven or eight hundred francs. What has become of a very fine one he had? Do let me remind you, my love, that one doesn't exactly give away rags of this kind and that even the pieces are good. For God's sake do save at least some of the excessive expense. Without knowing exactly what effect it will have, do keep a general eye open so as not to let anything be lost and not to relax your efforts about anything. Don't, as they say, throw away the handle after the axe. Look at Canada as a good thing no longer available. M. de Frontenac possesses it, and others don't always have the same resources. But whatever your philosophy leads you to suppose, it's a dreary business to live in another climate with people you would hate to know in this one. 'We belong to all countries ' – that is from Montaigne, but while saying that he was very glad to be in his own home. And do, please, my dear, forgive these tirades of reflections of mine and put them down to my excessive love for you. You must either tear out this heart that loves you or let me take a great and urgent interest in you; the two things can't be separated.

The troubles in Provence terrify me. Your child is saved from smallpox by the death of the other, but what about the plague? I am very frightened. It is quite unlike any other disease, and your sunshine won't be much help against it. I trust that the Governor will give the best orders he can about it.

I am astonished at this affliction of one of M. de Grignan's gentlemen. What! Delirium with no temperature? It's frightening. But I was also rather astonished to hear reference to *one of M. de Grignan's gentlemen* who is no La Porte. Well really, what next? Have people only got to throw themselves into a household? Must we be so weak as to welcome what is determined to belong to us by force? I am addressing myself to M. de Grignan. As for you, my dear, take a hand in this, and don't dismiss these increases as of no account. And you, Monsieur le Comte, employ your mind and even your honour in saving your household, your wife and your children and paying off your debts (these are the sentiments you should be feeling) and not letting yourself be sucked dry by people who will drop you when you are no further use to them. I am prepared for M. de Grignan to be annoyed with me provided he agrees in the end with my sentiments and accepts that loving you both as I do I am giving you the advice of a true friend; and those who speak differently are no friends of yours. But tell me if this upsets either of you, for in that case, since it would be useless, I should not be in a hurry to tell you anything unpleasant. Answer me sincerely.

I am so glad you are not pregnant. Alas, dear, do at least have the pleasure of being in good health and enjoying a restful life. Don't add this worry to so many others you find on your way.

Old Madame has died of an apoplexy which she had been suffering from for a year. So the Luxembourg is Mademoiselle's and we shall be able to go there. She had all the trees cut down in the garden on her side, simply out of contrariness. That beautiful garden had become ridiculous, but Providence has stepped in. Both sides will have to be cleared and Le Nôtre set to work to make it like the Tuileries. Mademoiselle would not go and see her dying stepmother, which is neither Christian nor noble.

M. de Lorraine's settlement has been broken after being well advanced, so your poor friend has had a setback. M. de Bâville is marrying a Mlle de Chalucet from Nantes, and getting 400,000 francs. M. d'Harouys is playing the principal part in it. I have given your compliments to the Duras and Charosts. The Marquis de Villeroy will not leave Lyons this campaign; the Marshal has had this assurance by asking leave to rejoin the army. We don't understand the cause of this misfortune.

On Saturday Monsieur le Duc gave a hunting party to the *Angels* and a supper at Saint-Maur of the finest fish. They returned to a little house near the Hôtel de Condé where, as soon as midnight had struck, and so more scrupulously than we do in Brittany, they served the most wonderful *medianoche* in the world, with exquisite food. This little extravagance was not well received, and Mme de Grancey's gracious tolerance about it has been much admired. There were present the Comtesse de Soissons, the Coëtquen, the Bourdeaux, several men as well as the Chevalier de Lorraine, oboes, musettes and violins. Of Madame la Duchesse or Lent, never a word. One was in her apartment and the other in the cloisters. All these ladies are dark, but we think it needed some yellow to set them off well.

M. de Coulanges is desolate at the death of the painter. Didn't I say he would die? It is all beautiful at the beginning of the story, but this dénouement is sad and upsetting for me, as I was hoping to have this beautiful *Madeleine with naturally wavy hair*.

M. de Morangis is dead, and the Barillons are very afflicted and very rich. That silences the natural feelings. The elder nephew has asked for the post of *Conseiller* for himself and his own post for his brother. Send me your compliments for them.

I shall say no more about Monsieur de Marseille. I call Monsieur d'Uzès as witness to all my reactions: whether I lost sight of your interests for a single moment, or whether he took me in over the slightest thing, or whether his manners and duplicity were not always clear to me throughout what he said, or whether I was ever at a loss for an answer on the main points, or whether all my friends haven't done their duty, or whether I doubt the sincerity of your behaviour and the *galonetonnerie*[1] of his. Anyway, I have opened my heart to Monsieur d'Uzès and have not been proved wrong over anything. I have good witnesses and a certain minister has failed to find me suborned against your interests. The Bishop himself is somewhat embarrassed about me, for you know he likes putting the goats among the cabbages. He has mismanaged the goat and won't even eat the cabbages. That is all I shall say about it, and you can believe whatever you like. Monsieur d'Uzès will tell you the remainder and I shall be at rest with a clear conscience and a heart which can never let me be found wanting in anything to do with you. All the same, we see a fellow who has gone visiting before anybody in Paris is awake, we see an Archbishop of Aix, we see a man we need for the Abbé de Grignan and we conclude that

1. *galonetonnerie*, word made up from the name Ganelon, the traitor in the *Chanson de Roland*.

if Monsieur d'Uzès can make a good and lasting peace in the place it will be to the advantage of both parties. There is no question about it here. Would that you were here to see things as we do!

You describe that affected wit perfectly. I wouldn't like him any more than you, but I wouldn't be surprised if the Comte de Guiche got on well with him. You are both right.

While we are on the subject of disagreeable wit, M. de La Rochefoucauld has relapsed into such a terrible attack of gout and such a terrible fever that you never saw him so ill. He asks you to have pity on him. I would defy you to see him without wanting to cry.

My very dear child, I must leave you. After wishing you an *adamantino* heart I regret it; I should be very sorry if you didn't love me as much as I love you. Don't wish for such a thing either, my dear, let us keep our hearts as they are. You know the only thing that can touch mine.

I embrace M. de Grignan and thank him for his nice thank-yous and exclamations. He can rest assured that I shall never quit the service of his kingdom of Micomicona. Please, dear, don't thank me any more for the little things I give you; pity me for not giving you more, and come and let me kiss you. What joy when it really happens! I shan't send you the Pont-Neuf any more; it's up to you to come and see it. I send you a hundred thousand little Cupids, which are a hundred times nicer. You will find your little children here, and I believe you will think they are pretty.

For my Beauty.

To Madame de Grignan

[Paris, Friday 6 May 1672]

My dear, I must tell you all about it. It is a sign of dotage I can't avoid.

I went yesterday to a memorial service for the Chancellor at the Oratory. It was painters, sculptors, musicians and orators who contributed, in a word the four liberal arts. There was the finest decoration imaginable; Le Brun had designed it. The Mausoleum reached to the vault, adorned with a thousand lights and several figures appropriate to the man to be honoured. At the base four skeletons bore the marks of his dignities, as though they had borne away his honours with his life. One carried his mortar, another his ducal coronet, another his order, another his Chancellor's maces. The four Arts, Painting, Music, Eloquence and Sculpture, were bathed in tears, overcome at losing their patron. Four Virtues supported the base of the representation: Strength, Justice, Temperance and Religion. Above, four Angels or genies received this noble soul. The Mausoleum was further adorned with several angels supporting a chapel of rest fixed to the vault. Never was seen anything so magnificent or so well conceived; it is Le Brun's masterpiece. The whole church was adorned with pictures, devices and emblems bearing upon the arms or the life of the Chancellor. Some of his principal acts were depicted. Mme de Verneuil wanted to purchase all this decoration at an exorbitant price. The whole family resolved to adorn a gallery with it and bequeath this token of their gratitude and magnificence to eternity.

The congregation was numerous and impressive, but perfectly orderly. I was near to Monsieur de Tulle, M. Colbert, M. de Monmouth,[1] as handsome as in his days at the Palais-Royal, who incidentally is off to the army to join the King. A young Oratorian father came to deliver the funeral oration. I told Monsieur de Tulle that he should make him come down from the pulpit and go up in his place, because nothing but the power of his eloquence could sustain the beauty of the spectacle and perfection of the music. Well, my dear, the young man began nervously and everyone else was nervous too. To begin with he had a Provençal accent (he comes from Marseilles and his name is Laisné). But once over his nerves he followed a road of such shining truth, set out his discourse so well, gave such well-measured praise to the dead man, passed over all the delicate places with such tact and threw light so well on everything that could be admired, displayed eloquence and masterly touches with such aptness and such good grace that everybody, and I mean everybody without exception, broke into applause, and each one of us was charmed by so perfect and finished a performance. He is a man of twenty-eight, an intimate friend of Monsieur de Tulle, with whom he went off afterwards. We wanted to call him the Chevalier Mascaron, but I think he will surpass his senior.

1. The Duke of Monmouth had reputedly been in love with his aunt, Henriette, first wife of Monsieur.

The music was indescribable. Baptiste[2] had done the utmost with all the King's musicians. His *Miserere* was extended, and there was a *Libera* which brought tears to all eyes. I don't believe there can be any other music in heaven.

Many prelates were present. I said to Guitaut, 'Let's look out for our friend the Bishop of Marseilles.' We did not see him, and I whispered to Guitaut, 'If this were the funeral oration of somebody living he wouldn't miss it.' This little joke made Guitaut laugh, without any regard for the funeral solemnities.

My dear, what sort of a letter is this? I think I must be a bit out of my mind. What's the point of such a long tale? Really I have been satisfying the desire I had to tell a tale.

The King is at Charleroi and will stay there quite a long time. There is still a shortage of forage and all the horses take famine with them. At the very outset of the campaign they are in trouble.

Guitaut has shown your letter to me and the Abbé: *Send Mother to me*. My darling, how sweet of you and how beautifully you justify the extreme love other people see I have for you. Alas, I think of nothing but setting off; leave it to me. I have my eye on everything, and if my aunt decided to linger on I really should go. You alone in the world can make me decide to leave her in such a pitiful state; we shall have to see. I live from day to day and haven't the courage to come to a decision. One day I'm off, the next day I daren't. In fact, my dear, what you say is true: there are some very unkind things in life.

You ask me not to consider you when I move house, but I ask you to believe that I never think of anything else but you and that you are so extremely dear to me that you are the sole preoccupation of my heart. Tomorrow I shall sleep in that pretty apartment where you will be put without upsetting me. Ask the Marquis d'Oppède, who has seen it; he says he is off to see you. Lucky man, alas! I am expecting letters from Pomponne. We have no First President.

Good-bye, my sweet little one. You are at the far end of the earth and you are travelling. I fear your taste for adventure, and don't trust either you or M. de Grignan. As you say, it is a strange thing after travelling two hundred leagues to be at Aix, and at Saint-Pilon after

2. *Baptiste*: Lully, the composer. This beautiful *Miserere* exists on a gramophone record.

climbing so high. Sometimes there are some very funny bits in your letters, but sometimes you write sentences like Tacitus. I have discovered this comparison, and nothing is truer.

I embrace Grignan and kiss him on his right cheek just below his hairy mole.

To Madame de Grignan

[Paris, Monday 30 May 1672]

I had no news from you yesterday, poor child. Your journey to Monaco made you incapable of anything, and I suspected that this little misfortune would befall me. I send you news of M. de Pomponne; already the vogue for being wounded is setting in. My heart is very heavy with fear of this campaign. My son writes quite often; he is quite well so far. My aunt is still in a deplorable state, and yet we have the courage to envisage a date for our departure, putting on a hope that we don't really feel. I am still in the state of finding some things very badly arranged; there are big boulders in the way, too heavy to be shifted. I think we shall get over them, but not without trouble. The comparison is a just one.

I shall not take my granddaughter. She is doing very well at Livry, where she will stay all the summer. The beauty of Livry is beyond everything you have seen; the trees are wonderfully green and there is honeysuckle everywhere. I am not yet tired of this scent. But you look down on our humble shrubs compared with your forests of orange trees.

Here is a tragic story from Livry. You will remember that self-styled very religious man who never dared turn his eyes or his head – I said he seemed to be carrying a glass of water on it. Well, his piety has turned his brain. One fine night he stabbed himself five or six times and knelt down naked and covered in blood in the middle of his bedroom. They go in and find him in this state: 'Oh God, brother, what are you doing? And who has done this to you?' 'Father,' he says coldly, 'I am doing penance.' Then he falls in a dead faint. They put him to bed, dress his wounds and find his condition very grave. He is restored to health after three months of care, then sent back to his family at Lyons.

If that head doesn't seem sufficiently crazy for you, you only have to say so and I will give you Mme. Paul, who has gone quite off her head and has fallen in love with a great oaf of twenty-five or twenty-six whom she had taken on to do the garden. He really has made a fine match; the woman is marrying him. This fellow is a mad brute, and will soon beat her, in fact he has already threatened to. No matter, she wants it that way. I've never seen so much passion. All the most violent sentiments you could imagine. But they are only sketched out like a rough picture. All the colours are there, they only need arranging properly. I have been very interested meditating on these vagaries of love, but I have quite frightened myself looking at such attacks. What insolence to attack Mme Paul, that is to say austere, fierce, ancient and elemental virtue. Where is safety to be found? Here are some fine stories for you, my dear, instead of your genteel narratives.

Mme de La Fayette is still in a poor state of health. M. de La Rochefoucauld is still limping about. Sometimes our conversations are so gloomy that it seems as if the only thing left is to bury ourselves. Mme de La Fayette's garden is the prettiest thing in the world. Everything in flower, everything scented. We spend many evenings there because the poor soul doesn't dare go in a carriage. Sometimes we wish you were behind a screen to overhear certain tales of certain unknown lands we think we have discovered. Anyhow, dear girl, pending the happy day of my departure, I go from town to my aunt's fireside and from my aunt's fireside to this miserable town.

Please, my dear, don't forget M. d'Harouys altogether, his heart is a masterpiece of perfection and he adores you.

Good-bye, dearest and nicest. I am extremely anxious to hear your news and about your son. It is very hot where you are, and this season frightens me for him and for you much more, for it hasn't yet crossed my mind that one could love anything more than you.

Love to my dear Grignan. Does he still love you a lot? I beg him to love me too.

To Madame de Grignan

[Paris, Monday 13 June 1672]

My poor little one, alas, you have been very ill. I understand this illness and it alarms me as one of the most terrifying. Were it not for M. de Grignan's kindness in writing to me I confess I would have been in a mortal panic, but he loves you so passionately that I would think he'd be little inclined to think of allaying my fears had you been in danger for a single moment. I wait impatiently for tomorrow's news. I hope you will tell me yourself how you are and why you have been so angry. I feel so too against those who have given you cause.

Here is a letter from my son which will amuse you; it is the details that are interesting. You will see that the King is so perfectly fortunate that henceforth he will only have to say what he wants in Europe, without bothering to go himself at the head of his army; everybody will be glad to give it to him. I am told that he will cross the Ijssel as if it were the Seine. Terror prepares an easy victory everywhere; the joy of all the courtiers is a good augury. Brancas writes that they laugh from morn till eve. Here is a little story that I must tell you. As soon as old Bourdeille was dead M. de Montausier asked the King for the office of Seneschal of Poitou on behalf of his brother-in-law M. de Laurière. The King granted this. Shortly afterwards young Matha asked for it and told the King that this office had been in his family for a long time. The King asked M. de Montausier to return it to him, assuring him that he would give something else to M. de Laurière. M. de Montausier answered that for himself he would be delighted to be able to do so but that, his brother-in-law having now received the official compliments due to him, it was impossible, and that His Majesty could bestow other benefits upon young Matha. The King seemed annoyed and said, 'Very well, I will leave him the office for three years, but after that I give it to young Matha for good.' This setback has been irritating for M. de Montausier. I should have addressed this to M. de Grignan. Never mind, these two letters belong to both of you, and are not the equivalent of a good one.

You will not have a Provençal for First President, I am told. Monsieur de Marseille came to see me yesterday with the Marquis de

Vence and two deputies; it seemed to me like an official deputation. I also saw M. de Tourette and said good-bye to M. de Laurens, who is going to like you very much, by what he says.

Good-bye, dearest one. Do be glad to see me, whenever that will be. Do try to banish those beastly bed-bugs from my room; the very thought of them frightens me to death. I am plagued with them here and don't know what to do. It must be far worse in Provence. My dear, this is a silly little letter. I had better go to bed.

To Madame de Grignan

[Paris, Friday 17 June 1672, 11 o'clock at night]

My dear, I have just heard some sad news, the details of which I shall not go into because I don't know them. But I do know that during the crossing of the Ijssel under Monsieur le Prince, M. de Longueville was killed, and this news is shattering. I was at Mme de La Fayette's when the news was brought to M. de La Rochefoucauld, and of the wounding of M. de Marsillac and the death of the Chevalier de Marsillac. This storm broke upon him in my presence. He was grievously afflicted and wept in his heart, and only his strength of character prevented his bursting into tears.

After this news I couldn't waste time to ask anything else. I rushed to see Mme de Pomponne, who reminded me that my son is in the King's army, which played no part in this expedition; that was reserved for Monsieur le Prince. It is said that he is wounded, it is said that he crossed the river in a small boat, it is said that Nogent is drowned, it is said that Guitry is killed, it is said that M. de La Feuillade and M. de Roquelaure are wounded and that a vast number have perished in this grim affair. When I know the details I will write to you.

Now Guitaut has sent me a gentleman from the Hôtel de Condé. He tells me that Monsieur le Prince is injured in the hand. M. de Longueville had forced the barricade, where he was the first to attack and so the first to be killed on the spot. All the rest is very similar. MM. de Guitry and de Nogent drowned, M. de Marsillac wounded as I told you, and a large number of others not yet known. But at last the Ijssel has been crossed. Monsieur le Prince has now crossed it three or four times by boat quite peacefully, giving orders everywhere with that godlike valour for which he is renowned. We were assured that after this initial difficulty no more enemy were to be found; they had retired to their positions. M. de Marsillac's wound is a musket ball in the shoulder and another in the jaw, but the bone is not broken. Good-bye, my dearest child, my mind is a bit unhinged although my son is in the King's army, but there are so many possibilities that it makes one tremble and die of fear.

To Bussy-Rabutin

[Paris, Sunday 19 June 1672]

I have at this moment in my room that big boy of yours. I sent my carriage to bring him to dinner with me. My uncle the Abbé, who was here too, first presented my nephew with a large folded document, and on opening it he found it was a genealogy of the Rabutin family. He was quite delighted, and at the moment he is having a good time finding where he comes from. If he goes on to amuse himself by meditating on where he is going, we shall not dine very early. But I shall save him the trouble of this meditation by assuring him that he is going straight to death, and a pretty early death if he takes up your profession (as appears very likely). I am certain that this thought will not put him off his dinner; he comes from too good a stock to be upset by such sad news. But still I don't understand how one can expose oneself a thousand times (as you have done) and not be killed a thousand times as well.

Today I am very full of this reflection. The death of M. de Longueville, that of Guitry, Nogent and many others, the wounds of Monsieur le Prince, Marsillac, Vivonne, Montrevel, Revel, of the Comte de Sault, Termes and countless unknown people, give me a very gloomy idea of war. I don't understand at all how one can swim across the Rhine. To plunge in on horseback like hounds after a stag, and be neither drowned nor knocked out on landing, so passes my imagination that it makes my head spin. God has preserved my son so far. But can one count on those who are at war?

Good-bye, dear cousin, I am going to dinner. I think your boy is very good-looking and pleasant. I am so glad you like my letters. To be to your taste makes one very conceited.

To Madame de Grignan

[Paris, Sunday 3 July 1672]

I am off to take my little girl to Livry. Don't worry about her at all, I look after her extremely well and I'm sure I love her much more than you do. I shall go tomorrow and say good-bye to M. d'Andilly, and shall be back on Tuesday to finish a few odds and ends and set off what you might call at once. I am leaving this letter to dear Troche, who undertakes to send you all the news, which she will do better than me. The interest she has in the army makes her better informed than anyone else, and particularly than someone who for four days has seen nothing but tears, mourning, services, burials, in fact death.

I confess I was quite overcome with sorrow when my manservant came and told me there were no letters for me in the post. This is the second time that I have had no word from you. I think it might be the fault of the post or of your travelling, but it still is very unpleasant. As I am not used to the pain I suffer on these occasions I am bearing it with rather a bad grace. You have been so ill that I keep feeling some disaster will befall you, and you have been so surrounded with disasters since you have no longer been with me that I have reason to fear them all, just because you don't fear any. Good-bye, my dearest, I would say more had I had news from you.

[Livry, Sunday evening, 3 July 1672]

Ah well, my dear, I have lots of apologies to make for the letter I wrote you just before leaving for here. I hadn't had your letter; my friend in the post had told me there were none for me. I was in despair. I left it to Mme de La Troche to write you all the news, and then set off.

It is ten at night. And M. de Coulanges, whom I love like my own life, and who is the nicest-looking man in the world, has sent on your letter, which he had in his packet. And to give me this joy he doesn't hesitate to send his manservant by moonlight. He has certainly not made a mistake in thinking he has given me great pleasure. He is very delicate-minded, I must say, and I think you are in no doubt about that.

I am vexed that you have lost one of my packets; as they are full of news it throws things out and breaks the thread of what is happening.

You must have had some very correct accounts that have shown you that the Ijssel was badly defended; the great miracle was to swim across it. Monsieur le Prince and his Argonauts were in a boat and the squadron they attacked was asking for quarter when ill-fortune willed that M. de Longueville, who probably couldn't hear and was spurred on by furious ardour, leaped on to his horse that he had dragged after him and, wanting to be first, breached the barricade behind which they were entrenched and killed the first man who came to hand; but at the same moment he was run through five or six times. Monsieur le Duc followed him, Monsieur le Prince followed his son and all the others followed him. That is how the killing happened, which as you can see could have been avoided had they known these men's willingness to surrender. But everything is ordained by Providence.

M. le Comte de Guiche brought off a successful feat which covers him with glory, for if it had turned out otherwise it would have been criminal. He was sent to reconnoitre whether the river was fordable. He said it was, but it wasn't. Whole squadrons swam across without breaking ranks and he was at their head, it is true. It had never been risked before, and it succeeded. He surrounded some squadrons and forced them to surrender. You see his luck and his courage did not part company. But you must have some good accounts of all that.

A certain Chevalier de Nantouillet had fallen off his horse. He went to the bottom, came up again, sank back and came up yet again. At last he found a horse's tail and clung to it. This horse took him to the bank, he leaped on to it, was in the scrimmage, received two blows on his helmet and came up quite perky. That is coolness for you, and it reminds me of Orontes, Prince of the Massagetes.

It is absolutely true that M. de Longueville had been to confession before setting off. As he never boasted about such things he had not even tried to gain his mother's favour by telling her. But it was a confession conducted by our friends,[1] with absolution deferred for

---

1. *confession conducted by our friends*: our friends were the Jansenists.

146

more than two months. It has proved to be so true that Mme de Longueville cannot doubt it, and you can imagine what a consolation it is. He did all sorts of kindnesses and charities that nobody knew about and that he did only on condition that they were never mentioned. Never did a man have such solid virtues. He only wanted a few worldly failings, such as a little pride, vanity and haughtiness. But never did anyone come so near to perfection: *Pago lui, pago il mondo.** He was beyond praise; so long as he satisfied himself, that sufficed. I often see people who are still very far from getting over this loss. But for the ordinary run of people it is all past. This sad news stunned people for only three or four days; the death of Madame lasted much longer. The personal interests of each one in what goes on in the army prevent much attention to the misfortunes of others. Since this first battle it has constantly been a matter of cities surrendering and deputations coming to appeal for permission to be counted among those newly conquered by His Majesty.

Don't forget to drop a little line to La Troche about her son's having distinguished himself and swum across the river – he was commended in the presence of the King as one of the bravest. It doesn't look as if any will defend themselves against such a victorious army. The French really are splendid. Nobody comes near them for acts of glory and courage, and there is no other river now that will act as a defence against their magnificent valour.

If my letters are lost at this moment you will miss more than at any other time.

Why do you believe, my dear, that I am not setting off until next winter? I mean to return about then with you and M. de Grignan. Our Abbé is brave enough to face the hot weather, and I am only concerned for him. Don't prevent our setting off by saying you don't expect us. Alas, it no longer depends on my poor aunt. We have done our last duties by her with many tears, so you can excuse me from paying her all your compliments.

I think we shall put poor Mlle de La Trousse at the Daughters of the Cross in the Faubourg Saint-Antoine, as they are not so meticulous as our Sisters. The poor thing only hopes for death and paradise. She is right.

* Roughly 'If he was satisfied, the world would be satisfied.'

There's a lot of news for you. I had brought my little pussy here for the summer, but I have found that it is all dried up here, there's no water. The nurse is afraid of having nothing to do. What do I do, in your opinion? I shall quietly take her back home the day after tomorrow. She will be with old Jeanne who will look after the little household. Mme de Sanzei will be in Paris and she will go and walk in her garden. She will have lots of visitors, and I shall often get news of her. So that's settled; I've changed my mind. My house is pleasant, and she will not lack anything. One must not suppose that Livry is as charming for a nurse as for me. Good-bye, my lovely child. Overlook my sadness at having missed your letters twice. I have only had one, but it's enough for me. My love, I embrace you most affectionately. Your letters are so pleasant to me that only you can console me for not having more of them.

To Madame de Grignan

[Auxerre, Saturday 16 July 1672]

Well, my girl, here we are. I am still a very long way from you, yet I am already feeling the pleasure of being nearer. I left Paris on Wednesday disappointed at not having heard from you on Tuesday. I am consoled by the hope of seeing you at the end of such a long course. Everyone relished assuring us that I was bent on causing our dear Abbé's death by exposing him to a journey to Provence in the middle of the summer. He was brave enough to laugh at all this talk, and God has rewarded him with the loveliest weather you could wish for. There is no dust, it is cool and the days last for ever. And that is all you could wish for. Our Mousse is taking heart. We travel rather solemnly; M. de Coulanges would have come in handy to amuse us. The only reading matter worth our while that we have found has been Virgil, not *burlesqued*,[1] but in all the majesty of the Latin and Italian. To be really joyous we must be with joyous people; you know I am all sorts of things but cannot invent anything.

I am sad at having lost touch with what is going on in Holland. When

---

1. *Virgil, not burlesqued*: refers to a parody of Virgil by Scarron, *Virgile travesti*. Mme de Sévigné had read Virgil in Latin with the help of an Italian translation.

I left they were between peace and war. It was the most serious pass France has been in for a long time. Both private and state interests are involved.

So good-bye, my dear child. I hope I shall find news from you at Lyons. You owe a great deal to our dear Abbé and La Mousse, but to me none at all.

To Madame de Grignan

[Paris, Friday 8 December 1673]

I must begin, my dearest, with the death of the Comte de Guiche; that is what is in everybody's mind at the moment. The poor fellow died of sickness and general decline in the army of M. de Turenne. The news came on Tuesday morning. Père Bourdaloue announced it to Maréchal de Gramont, who had guessed it already, knowing his son's parlous condition. He sent everybody away from his room. He was in his little apartment just outside the Capucines. When he was alone with the priest he fell on his neck saying that he guessed what he had to tell him, that it was a mortal blow which he accepted from the hand of God, that he had lost the only true object of his love and natural affection, that he had never had any real joy or violent pain except through his son, who had admirable qualities. He threw himself on to a bed in utter despair, but not weeping, for one doesn't weep in that state. The priest himself was weeping, though so far he had said nothing, then he spoke to him of God, as you know he can speak. They were together for six hours and then the priest, to crown his sacrifice, took him into the church of the good Capuchin nuns, where the office for the dead was being said for his beloved son. The Marshal staggered in, shaking and more dragged and pushed than on his own feet, and his face was unrecognizable. Monsieur le Duc saw him in this state, and he was weeping as he told us at Mme de La Fayette's. The poor Marshal came back eventually to his little room. He is like a condemned man. The King has written to him. Nobody sees him.

Mme de Monaco is quite inconsolable and refuses to see anybody. The Louvigny is inconsolable too, but that is because she is not afflicted. Don't you admire the good fortune of this woman? Behold her shortly to be the Duchesse de Gramont. The Chancellor's wife is transported with joy. The Comtesse de Guiche is behaving very well. She weeps when told about the kind things her husband said when he was dying, and the apologies he made for his conduct, and says, 'He was a very lovable man, and I should have loved him passionately had he loved me just a little. His contempt caused me great pain. His death touches me and moves me to pity. I always hoped his feelings for me would change.' That is the truth, there is no play-acting there. Mme de Verneuil is genuinely touched. I think that by asking me to give her your compliments you will have done enough. So you need only write to the Comtesse de Guiche, Mme de Monaco and Mme de Louvigny.

D'Hacqueville has had the job of going to Frazé, thirty leagues from here, to break this news to the Maréchale de Gramont and give her a letter from the poor fellow, who has made an entire confession of his past life. He has asked publicly for forgiveness and written to Vardes many things that will perhaps be of advantage to him. In fact he has made a very good end to the comedy and left a rich and happy widow. The Chancellor's wife is so deeply conscious of the little or no satisfaction her granddaughter has had during her marriage that she will henceforth think of nothing else but atoning for this misfortune, and if a king of Ethiopia presented himself she would even sacrifice her shoe to give him her granddaughter. We cannot envisage a husband for her. You will name M. de Marsillac as we do, but neither he nor she wants the other. The other dukes are too young. M. de Foix is destined for Mlle de Roquelaure. Look round in your part of the world, for the matter is urgent. Here is a lot of detail, my dear, but you have told me sometimes that that is what you like.

The Orange affair prompts a very agreeable stir here for M. de Grignan. This great quantity of nobles who have followed him simply out of their attachment to him, this great expense and successful outcome does him great honour and gives joy to his friends here, who are by no means few. This general talk is very gratifying. The King said at supper, 'Orange is taken, Grignan had seven hundred gentlemen with him. They fired from inside the walls and surrendered on the third day. I am very pleased with Grignan.' This little speech, which La Garde knows even better than I do, was reported to me. As for that Archbishop of Reims of yours, I don't know who he was up against. La Garde thought of mentioning the expense to him. 'Ah yes,' he said, 'the expense, that is what they always say. People love complaining.' 'But, Sir,' he said, 'M. de Grignan couldn't do without it, with so many noblemen who had come for love of him.' 'Say rather for the service of the King.' 'Sir,' he said, 'that is true, but there was no order to that effect, and it was to follow M. de Grignan on the occasion of the King's service that all that assembly gathered.' Anyway, my dear, it doesn't matter, you know he is a very good friend. But there are days of bad temper, and those days are miserable.

I have had news about the States in Brittany. M. le Marquis de Coëtquen the younger thought fit to attack M. d'Harouys, saying that he was the only rich man while the whole of Brittany groaned in poverty, and that he knew of people who would do the job better. M. Boucherat, M. de Lavardin and everybody in Brittany were for stoning him and were horrified at his ingratitude, for he is deeply indebted to M. d'Harouys. Thereupon he received a letter from Mme de Rohan requesting him to come to Paris because M. de Chaulnes has an order to forbid his attending the States; so he disappeared the day before the Governor's arrival. He is held in abomination for the horrible accusation he tried to level against M. d'Harouys. All this, my dear, is what you are obliged to listen to because of your name.

Don't run down your own letters. Sometimes we think our own letters are no good because we are in a muddle of conflicting ideas, but the confusion is in the head, while the letter is clear and natural. And that is what yours are. Some parts of them are so good that those who are honoured by my letting them see them are delighted.

I have just seen M. de Pomponne. He was alone, and I spent a good two hours with him and Mlle Ladvocat, who is very pretty. We read with pleasure a good part of your letters, and you were admired both for your style and the interest you take in certain affairs. M. de Pomponne understood perfectly what we would like him to do if a letter comes, and he will do it no doubt. But he says one thing that is true, namely that your syndic will be appointed before the break-up of your council is known here; he thinks that it is all over already. All the paper in my portfolio would not suffice for telling you all the pleasant and kind things said about you and what delightful conversations I have had with the minister. In a word, I am extremely pleased with him, and you must be so too on my recommendation. He will be very glad to see you and is counting on your return.

Good-bye, my very dear child. I am expecting your brother any day, and as for your letters, I should like some every hour.

To Madame de Grignan

[Paris, 15 December 1673]

When I told you that you would not be thought any the worse of here for not having carried off the syndic affair and that I was belittling this small victory as much as I could, be assured, my dear, that I was doing so out of pure calculation and following out a plan premeditated between ourselves, so that if you lost your little battle you would not resolve to hang yourself. But now that from your life-restoring letter we see your triumph virtually certain, I can freely confess that taken all round it is the pleasantest thing in the world to have carried this affair off in the face of all the precautions, prophecies, prayers, threats, entreaties, corruptions and boasts of your enemies. It really is delightful, and shows just as much as the siege of Orange how well thought of M. de Grignan is in the province. M. de Pomponne, d'Hacqueville, Brancas, the Grignans and many of your friends were particularly interested in the outcome of this affair and did not think it as unimportant as I wrote in my letter, but we were all agreed about this way of treating it so as to keep up your spirits in case of a defeat. Mlle Ladvocat is in this business up to the eyes and, truth to tell, I sent the first two pages of your letter to M. de Pomponne and to d'Hacqueville who was with him, so as to cheer them up. So don't think we saw things so very differently from you – anything touching one's honour looks much the same anywhere. Don't be annoyed with us but rather praise our good intentions and do believe that we are completely in agreement with all your sentiments, and particularly I, who have no others.

You explain sufficiently what prevents your undertaking the journey to Paris, but when I reflect that the Coadjutor is ready to leave, having handed over his abbey for two years, wanting to live on air, get rid of his servants and horses, and that sometimes one can do things by black magic, it makes me believe that you must do as others do this year or never. This is how I reason: you will appear victorious on all kinds of scores, and moreover you will have effaced the exclusion of your friend.

I am expecting my son at any moment. Yesterday I dined at Gourville's with Monsieur le Duc, M. de La Rochefoucauld, Mme de Thianges, Mme de La Fayette, Mme de Coulanges, the Abbé Têtu, M. de Marsillac and Guilleragues. You were toasted and missed, and then we listened to the *Art Poétique*[1] of Despréaux, which is a masterpiece.

M. de La Rochefoucauld has no mark of favour except that conferred on his son, who is very well placed. The other day, as I have told you already, he went to a concert at Mme de Montespan's. They made him take a seat – the least they could do. It doesn't mean anything at all. Mme de La Fayette sees Mme de Montespan when she goes once a month to Saint-Germain, and I don't think that is much of a favour. The Queen's young ladies are going off each to her own place, as I have also told you. The Chevalier de Vendôme has asked in fun for quarter from M. de Vivonne, who went on and on about the horror he felt about fighting, so peace is patched up and no more is being said about it. Soyecourt asked Vivonne yesterday, 'When is the King going hunting?' Vivonne answered sharply, 'When are the galleys setting off?' I am on very good terms with this general. He doesn't think he has the Swiss; he had said on his side as I on mine that they were pictorial coats of arms. Mme de La Vallière no longer talks of retirement, suffice it that it has been mentioned. Her maid threw herself at her feet to stop her doing so – who could resist that?

D'Hacqueville has got over sticking a knife into the Maréchale de Gramont.[2] He is so upset about the death of the Comte de Guiche that he can't be sociable any more. I doubt whether he will write to you today.

La Garde still wants you to come instead of M. de Grignan, if he cannot come himself, and for that I refer you to that black magic of the Coadjutor's I have spoken about. You are clever, and you would now play quite a different part from that of a young lady of eighteen.

I have Corbinelli here; he is as excited about your affairs as if he were at Grignan. We shall be overjoyed about the syndic, and when we have won publicly people can talk about conciliation as much as they like; we must be lenient after victory.

1. *Art Poétique*: not published until July 1674. It was a common practice for authors to give readings in advance to selected audiences.
2. By telling her of the death of her son.

Despréaux will enchant you with his verses. He is most kind to poor M. Chapelain; I tell him he is tender in prose and cruel in verse.

Good-bye, dearest child; how grateful I shall be if you come here and embrace me! There is a lot of fuss at our States in Brittany; you are much better behaved than we are.

Bussy is under orders to go back to Burgundy. He has not made his peace with his principal enemies. He still wants to marry his daughter to the Comte de Limoges; it is hunger and thirst together, but he is fascinated by the beauty of the name. I expect my son at any moment.

To Madame de Grignan

[Paris, Monday 8 January 1674]

I have never seen nicer letters than yours, dearest Comtesse; I have just read one that enchants me. I have heard you say that I have a way of turning the most trivial things. Really, my dear, it is you who have it. There are five or six places in your last letter the brilliance and charm of which touch the heart. I don't know where to begin to answer you.

Chauvigny comes to mind first; I am no less annoyed than you by the silly things he has said. I shall see him, perhaps, at M. de Pomponne's, and I shall have a word with him about it and get one out of him. It is true, my dear, that it is irritating to do as well as you do and then meet fools on the way who can't distinguish you from evil-doers; it puts you off doing your duty. But what I notice in you is that this injustice upsets you too much and that you at once fly to extremes. If you ever bring that kind of mood here it will be amusing to make you lose your temper. I very much like your Intendant and his reply to that muddler; it is characteristic of a straightforward, honest man, an enemy of all dissimulation, *Qui nomme un chat un chat et la Grêle un fripon.** That suffices, provided he sees and retains what he sees. It is true that there was consummate iniquity in the opposition of the guards, and you will see from my letters that it is even greater than you think. *Rain* is ashamed for his friend, and talks pretty frankly about it to his lady, but all that between ourselves. The other day I saw

* 'Who calls a cat a cat and Hail a rogue.' (Parody of '*J'appelle un chat un chat et Rollet un fripon.*' Boileau, *Satire*, I.)

Monsieur de Meaux, who never tires of deploring this contemptible and even clumsy act. You wouldn't believe the injustice it does him. You are fortunate that the Intendant sees everything. He must console you for the one-sidedness of his wife; I wouldn't ever have believed she would have had the courage to oppose you. Your First President told me the other day that the King had encouraged him to hope for the position of Intendant this spring, on M. Rouillé's return. I will speak to M. de Pomponne about it. I am off tomorrow to Saint-Germain with Mme de Chaulnes, simply to see him. I am fond of him naturally, as you know, and I don't think he has any aversion from me.

Yesterday I saw the *Torrent* and the *Dew* at Mme de La Fayette's. There was much talk about you of a kind not likely to make you angry, for they did you justice over everything. They both wore very becoming mourning: *Le deuil enfin sert de parure*.* Two plain bonnets, two plain cornets, high and billowing to the floor; knots of crêpe everywhere, ermine everywhere, *Dew* more than *Torrent*. Both quite consoled and looking well turned out. It has been suggested that the *Torrent* mixed with the *Snow* and that the *Fire* inflamed the *Dew*. This vision has done them both a great deal of harm. It was thought that it was enough for the *Torrent* to be here, having forgotten the one who was so lovable; this last choice has done no credit to her taste.

I want to talk to you about your fine earthworks and pretty walks. You are right to say that I am married a second time in Provence. I shall make it one of my countries, so long as you don't cut this one out of the list of yours. You say all sorts of nice things about the new year; my dear, nothing can be more pleasant for me. You are everything to me, and my one study has been to behave so that everybody doesn't see how true that is. I spent the beginning of this year pretty brutally, without saying one tiny word to you. But you can take it that this year and all those of my life are yours – the whole fabric of a life is devoted to you to the last breath.

Your moral reflections are admirable. It is true that time flies everywhere and flies fast. You are crying after it because it is always bearing away something of your lovely youth. But you still have plenty left, whereas I see it fly by with horror, bringing me on its flight hideous old age, inconveniences and death at the end. Those are the

* 'Finally mourning itself is used for adornment.' La Fontaine, 'La Jeune Veuve'.

colours of the reflections of a person of my age. Pray to God, my dear, that He make me find the benefits Christianity teaches us.

This great journey of Monsieur le Prince and M. de Turenne to relieve M. de Luxembourg has come to nought. They now say the departure has been abandoned and that M. de Monterey's army has made its *retirote* – the very word that His Majesty used two days ago, meaning that, that army being put out of action, M. de Luxembourg found himself freed. Only my son has left. I have never seen such prudence, foresight and impatience as his. He will take the trouble to come back; it is not important. All the other warriors are here. M. de Turenne brought many of them back and M. de Luxembourg will bring the rest.

The ladies of the palace are required to serve for a week. This obligation to be four for dinner and supper is wonderful for pregnant women: there will always be midwives behind them and on all journeys. The Maréchale d'Humières will be very vexed at always having to stand beside those who are seated; if she sulks she will be out of favour, for the King requires submission. I don't think they take it very seriously in Mme de Montespan's circle, but it is true that at least they pay great attention to not separating any woman from her husband or her duties; they don't like scandal unless they cause it themselves.

The new princes have not yet been seen, so nobody knows what they are like. Some have been at Saint-Germain, but they did not appear. There will be plays at Court and a ball every week. There is a dearth of female dancing partners. The King will dance, and Monsieur will lead out Mlle de Blois,[1] so as not to take Mademoiselle his own daughter, whom he leaves to Monsieur le Dauphin. On Thursday there is to be the opera, which is a prodigy of beauty; already parts of the music have melted me to tears.[2] I am not the only one to find them harrowing; Mme de La Fayette's soul is also disturbed.

I think that the former lover of *Whirlwind* is no longer in love at all. The patience with which he puts up with the *Fog* looks to me like an infallible sign. One must be very indifferent and concerned only with one's own career to put up with such liaisons.

1. *Mlle de Blois*: daughter of the King and La Vallière; then aged eight.
2. Lully, *Alceste*.

I think it is admirable that our worthy Archbishop is acting on the strength of a rumour of a reconciliation. Yet he seems very pleased with all your successes and loudly praises the courage and tenacity all three of you have shown; he keeps on talking about it. He is right, you have wrought miracles. It was correct for you to take a vigorous and hazardous line as it is correct that he should always show prudence, foresight and wisdom. Stay as you are, all of you, you couldn't be better. You couldn't know what to do at the wedding of the *Hail*'s cousin; you haven't forgotten anything. Perhaps it is an arrangement of Providence useful to us.

I often see Corbinelli; he is one of your adorers, and holds forth magnificently about your qualities. He is the one who really understands my feelings about you, and I love him even more for that. I very much respect Barbantane; he is one of the best men in the world, romantically valorous, and I have heard Bussy mention him many times. He was his friend, they have had many a laugh together and are brothers in arms. Mme de Sanzei still has measles, but it is nearly over. M. de Coulanges has not left home. Mme de Coulanges is with Mme de Bagnols, who is in our old house. My heart aches unbearably when I am in that big room where I have seen so much of my beloved child. I hardly need touch on that subject without being touched myself to the quick.

I am expecting news of your peace. *Justitia et pax osculatae sunt:** *do you know Latin*? You are most amusing. Good-bye, my child, good-bye, my heart's love. You are not forgotten anywhere. Your brother is very sure of your affection, he loves you passionately, he says, and I believe him.

From Coulanges

Aren't you afraid of the measles? For that, in a word, is what has prevented my writing to you all these days, and your mother's writing is in such good odour that I hope it will disinfect mine. Yet I was bursting to wish you a thousand prosperities at the beginning of this year. So herewith, Madame, all my wishes and offerings, and please do believe that I am yours more than anyone in the world. Good day,

* 'Justice and peace have embraced.' Psalm 84.

good year; find me some little portraits in copper about the size of an écu. It is my craze at the moment and I'm doing wonders at it. Those you sent me are well set out. Come and see them soon. My compliments to the Comte your husband. Your oil is lovely, one could put it on one's handkerchief. It would not be the first time I had paid that honour to Provence.

[Monday, after sending my packet to the post]

M. d'Hacqueville has just come in and told me some news we want you to know by this post. It is that Monsieur the Keeper of the Seals is Chancellor. Nobody doubts that it is in order to give the Seals to someone else. We shall know this news officially in four days' time. It is very important and will lend great weight to the party concerned.

Monsieur le Prince leaves in two days, also M. de Turenne, even with gout, to advance to their rendezvous at Charleroi. It is not true that M. de Monterey has drawn back, nor that M. de Luxembourg has disengaged. So we take away the false news so as to put you back into the true.

To Madame de Grignan

[Paris, Wednesday 19 June 1675]

I assure you, my dearest, that after the farewell I bade you at Fontainebleau, which cannot be compared with any other, there was no more painful one I could make than the one to Cardinal de Retz at M. de Caumartin's, four leagues from here. I went there to dinner on Monday and found him surrounded by his three faithful friends. Their gloomy faces brought tears to my eyes, and when I saw him so steadfast, yet with all his kindness and affection for me, I could not bear it. After dinner we went and talked in the loveliest woods in the world, and were there until six with all kinds of talk, so kind, tender, affectionate and obliging both to you and to me that I am deeply moved. And I repeat yet again, my child, that you could not love him and honour him too much.

Mme de Caumartin arrived from Paris and, together with all the men who had stayed in the house, came and joined us in the woods. I wanted to return to Paris, but they persuaded me to stay without much trouble. I slept badly. In the morning I embraced our dear Cardinal with many tears and without being able to say a word to the others. So I have come sadly home, and can't yet get used to this separation. It found the fountain of tears well in play, but would certainly have turned it on even had it been turned off. Madame de Savoie's must have opened all its taps. Aren't you quite amazed at the death of the Duc de Savoie, so sudden and unexpected at forty?

I am sorry that what you have written about the clerical assembly has not been read at all – the promptness of the post is sometimes a nuisance. The prelates are giving 4,500,000 livres, as much again as the other assembly. The way affairs are conducted is admirable; the Coadjutor will tell you all about it. I thought what you say about Lannoi very amusing, also what is being asked for under the guise of establishment. I will remember you to Mmes de Villars and de Vins; it is all a matter of who is mentioned in my letters.

There are plenty of little gripings in Brittany, and at Rennes there has even been a violent colic. M. de Chaulnes tried to disperse the crowd by his presence, but was chased home with a hail of stones, which is very insolent, I must say. The *young person* writes to her sister that she wishes she were at Sully and is frightened to death every day. You know quite well what she is after in Brittany.

Monsieur le Duc is besieging Limburg. Monsieur le Prince has stayed with the King; you can imagine the horrible state of worry he is in. I don't think my son is at that siege or at that of Huy; he sends you his love. I am still waiting for letters from him, but for yours, my child, with the greatest impatience. I find like you, my dear, and perhaps more than you, that it is a long time from one post to the next. Time, which sometimes annoys me by flying so fast, stops quite still, just as you say. In fact we are never satisfied. I still can't get used to not seeing, finding, running into or hoping for you. I am obsessed by your absence and can't get it out of my mind. Our Cardinal might have blurred the memory of you a little but you are so involved in our relationship that after looking closely into it I find that it is you who make him seem so much to me, so I am not benefiting by your philosophy. I am very glad that you also feel you have a little human weakness.

Here is a portrait of the Cardinal that has been dashed off hurriedly. The person who has written it is no close friend of his. He does not want him to see it, nor that it be shown to all and sundry; he has not made a point of praising him. For all these reasons it has seemed good to me. I send it to you and beg you not to give away copies of it. One is so tired of praises sung to one's face that it is stimulating to be able to know that there has been no intention of pleasing and that this is what comes when one speaks the simple truth, naked and unadorned.

News is expected from Limburg and Germany; everyone is on tenterhooks.

Good-bye, dear girl. Your portrait is lovely, and one wants to kiss it, so well does it stand out from the canvas. I am amazed where I find my pleasure nowadays.

I embrace M. de Grignan and am yours, my dear, with an affection you can scarcely believe.

Portrait of M. le Cardinal de Retz by M. le Duc de La Rochefoucauld

Paul de Gondi, Cardinal de Retz, is a man of great sublimity and breadth of mind, with more ostentation than true greatness of soul. He has an extraordinary memory, more forcefulness than elegance in his words, an easygoing temperament very open to influence and weak enough to bow to his friends' complaints and criticisms, little piety but some externals of religion. He looks ambitious, but is not, for vanity and the influence of others have made him undertake great things, almost always in opposition to his declared profession, and thereby he has stirred up the greatest mischief for the state without having any fixed aim to profit from it himself; and far from declaring himself the enemy of Cardinal Mazarin in order to step into his shoes, his only object was to seem to be feared by him and preen himself on the false glory of being his opponent. Nevertheless he cleverly contrived to take advantage of public troubles and become a cardinal. He suffered imprisonment courageously, and only regained his freedom through his own daring. Through sheer indolence he remained for several years in an ostentatious position of nomadic retirement. He held on to the archbishopric of Paris in defiance of Cardinal Mazarin's power, and yet after that minister's death he gave it up without realizing what he was doing and without utilizing the event in his friends' or his own interests. He has been a member of various conclaves, and has always behaved in such a way as to add to his own reputation. His natural tendency is to be idle, yet he will toil energetically when matters are pressing, only to sit back nonchalantly as soon as they are settled. He has great presence of mind, and he is so adroit at turning to his own advantage whatever opportunities fortune offers that it looks as though he had foreseen and wished for them. He loves telling tales and is so anxious to dazzle all and sundry with amazing adventures that often his imagination supplies more than his memory. Most of his qualities are bogus, and what has contributed to his renown more than anything else is his art of displaying his own defects in a flattering light. Hatred and friendship find him equally indifferent, however hard he may have tried to appear interested in one or the other. He is incapable of envy or avarice, possibly through virtue, possibly through lack of interest. He has borrowed more from his friends than any private person could hope to repay, and has made rather a point of honour of finding so much credit and undertaking to clear off the debt. He is devoid of taste and delicacy, finds everything amusing but enjoys nothing, and skilfully avoids revealing that his knowledge of everything is of the most superficial kind. The retirement he has just gone into is the most ostentatious and least genuine action in his life, a sop to his own pride disguised as piety, for he is leaving a court in which he cannot find a position, and turning his back on a world that is turning its back on him.

To Madame de Grignan

[Paris, Friday 19 July 1675]

Guess where I'm writing from, my dear. From M. de Pomponne's house. You will see I am there from the little note Mme de Vins will enclose.

I have been with her, the Abbé Arnauld and M. d'Hacqueville to see the Sainte-Geneviève procession go by.[1] We got back quite early,

1. The procession was intended to stop a month of rain. (It worked, she says.)

it was only two o'clock, but many of them won't come back until this evening. Do you know that this procession is a remarkable affair? All the religious orders, every parish, every shrine, all the parish priests, all the Canons of Notre-Dame, and the Archbishop pontifically, on foot and blessing all to right and left, proceeding to the Cathedral. Yet he only has the left-hand place, for on the right is the Abbot of Sainte-Geneviève, barefoot, preceded by a hundred and fifty monks, with his crook and mitre like the Archbishop, also giving blessings, also barefoot, but modestly and piously and fasting, with an air showing that he is the one who is going to say Mass in Notre-Dame. Parlement, red-robed, and all the independent companies follow this shrine, which is gorgeous with precious stones and borne by twenty men in white, barefoot. There were left at Sainte-Geneviève the Prévôt des Marchands and four councillors by way of hostages until the precious treasure was returned. You will ask me why it was brought down; it was to make the rain stop and the warm weather come. Both things happened as required, so that, as it is generally to bring us all sorts of good things, I think it is to her we owe the return of the King. He will be here by Sunday. I will let you know on Wednesday everything there is to be told.

M. de La Trousse is taking a detachment of six thousand men to M. de Créquy to join M. de Turenne. La Fare and the others are staying with the Dauphin's men-at-arms in the army of Monsieur le Prince. I shall be very glad to have La Garde. Ladies here await their husbands more or less *pro rata* to their impatience.

The other day Madame and Mme de Monaco picked up d'Hacqueville at the Hôtel de Gramont and went off *incognito* round the streets and into the Tuileries. As Madame is not given to gallantry she is not worried about her dignity.

Mme de Toscane is expected at any time – yet another of the benefits bestowed by the shrine of Sainte-Geneviève. I saw yesterday one of your letters to the Abbé de Pontcarré, which is one of the loveliest letters in the world, everything in it is to the point and witty. He has sent a copy to His Eminence, for the original is kept like the shrine. You write quite perfectly, I assure you.

I think we shall sell our bureau. If so leave it to me; our bed will begin. I wish you had a good coachman, it seems important to me. You were well recommended to the moustache of the Cardinal's coachman;

you wouldn't have found him an impressive seigneur. I don't understand with what equipage you went to Pierrelatte.*

I expect letters from you tomorrow, my dearest; they are my one joy
and consolation for your absence. It is a strange thing, this absence.
You have said what can be said about it, but since it is true that time
bears us away and brings death, I think we are right to weep instead
of laughing as we would if our poor life did not pass away; I often
meditate on this. But we must pass over that as lightly as we can and
call Mme de Vins to say something to you.

From Madame de Vins

Don't think it is Mme de Sévigné who is the reason for my writing.
If I followed my own heart, I assure you, Madame, that you would often
hear about me. Don't think you will get away with this little word, you
will get more as soon as possible. And although it is said that there is
nothing like hating each other to make you write, I think that friendship
can produce that effect unaided.

From Ambassador Courtin[2]

Madame your mother is doing herself the utmost violence by yielding
the pen to me. I am snatching it from her hands to tell you, Madame,
that what little good sense remains to you in a land where the brain
easily dries up, you had better use to come back to Paris at the end of
October. The whole Court, which only survived last winter thanks to
Madame de Sévigné, entreats you to come, and I more than anyone,
although I haven't made so bold as to approach you. You will still find
more than one Eminence there. There will be two in this city who will
gladly wait upon you. And since the Pope favours us by keeping the
third for us, I don't despair of seeing him again where I was so glad
to meet him before. But already I am being reproached for holding on
to the pen too long; I am not being given any more time except to assure

* This obscure and semi-facetious passage refers back to more serious discussions
about helping the Grignans with their perennial debts.

2. Honoré Courtin (1628–1705), Ambassador to London, 1665 and 1676–7.

you that there is nobody in the world who honours you more than I do, nor who is more respectfully and genuinely entirely yours than I am.

Courtin

Good-bye, my dearest and perfectly loved. You are so truthful that I don't discount a word of all you say about your love, and you can deduce whether I am touched by it.

To Madame de Grignan

[Paris, Wednesday 31 July 1675]

What you say about the weather is marvellous, my dear daughter. It is true that *nobody is ever seen stopping in the middle of a month because he can't manage to cross it; these are quagmires you get out of*. But the quagmire holds us up and time goes on. I am very glad that you are peacefully at Grignan until October; Aix would have seemed strange to you after living here. The solitude and peace of Grignan attenuate our ideas a little; you were quite right. M. de Grignan is company for you now, your castle will be full of people and your music brought to perfection. One could die of laughter at what you say about the Italian aria; the massacre your singers made of it, corrected by you, is a martyrdom for poor *Vorrei*[1] which shows the punishment he deserves. Do you remember where you heard it and the pretty boy who sang it and so quickly caught your eye? I beg M. de Grignan to learn this aria all through. Do urge him to make this effort for my sake, and we will sing it together.

I did tell you, my dearest, how our upsets in Brittany held me up for some days. M. de Forbin is to set off with six thousand men to punish this province, that is to say, ruin it. They are going via Nantes, which is why I shall take the Le Mans road with Mme de Lavardin. We are considering together the time we must take. M. de Pomponne has told M. de Forbin that he has property in Brittany and has given him the name of my son's.

The shrine of Sainte Geneviève is giving us wonderful weather here. Saint-Géran is on the road to heaven. The worthy Mme de Villars has not had your letter, which is a pity.

1. Vorrei scoprirti, aria by Luigi Rossi.

Here is a little story that happened three days ago. A poor haber-dasher in the Saint-Marceau district was taxed at ten écus for duty on his mastership. He hadn't the money. They press him and press him again. He asks for time, time is refused. They take away his poor bed and his poor bowl. When he saw himself in this state madness seized his heart; he cut the throats of three children who were in his room. His wife saved the fourth and fled. The poor fellow is in the Châtelet; he will be hanged in a day or two. He says that his only regret is not to have killed his wife and the child she saved. Just think, this is as true as if you had seen it yourself, and since the siege of Jerusalem such a frenzy has never been seen.

They were to set off today for Fontainebleau, where the entertain-ments were to become boring by their very multiplicity. Everything was ready when a bolt fell from the blue that shattered the joy. The populace says it is on account of *Quantova*, the attachment is still intense. Enough fuss is being made to upset the curé and everybody else, but perhaps not enough for her, for in her visible triumph there is an underlying sadness. You talk of the pleasures of Versailles, and at the time when they were off to Fontainebleau to plunge into joys, lo and behold M. de Turenne killed, general consternation, Monsieur le Prince rushing off to Germany, France in desolation. Instead of seeing the end of the campaigns and having your brother back, we don't know where we are. There you have the world in its triumph and, since you like them, surprising events. I am sure you will be very touched by this. I am appalled by the predestination of this M. Desbrosses. Can one doubt the existence of Providence and that the cannon which picked out M. de Turenne from afar out of ten men round him had been loaded through all eternity? I am going to give this tragic story to M. de Grignan in exchange for that of Toulon. Would to God they were equal!

You should write to Cardinal de Retz; we all write to him. He is well and leading a very devout life. He attends all the offices and eats in the Refectory on fast days. We advise him to go to Commercy. He will be very upset by the death of M. de Turenne. Write to Cardinal de Bouillon. He is inconsolable.

Good-bye, my dear child, you are all too grateful. You speak ill of your own soul, but I think you do realize that a nobler and better does not exist. You are afraid I might die of affection; I should be ashamed of wronging the other love in this way, but let me love you in my own way. You have written an admirable letter to Coulanges; when I am fortunate enough to see one I am delighted. Everyone is hunting out everybody else to talk about M. de Turenne. People gather together. Yesterday everyone was in tears in the streets; all other business was suspended.

To Monsieur de Grignan

[Paris, Wednesday 31 July 1675]

I am writing to you, dear Comte, to tell you one of the most grievous losses that could befall France; it is the death of M. de Turenne. If I am the first one to tell you this I am sure you will be as deeply moved and desolate as we are here. This news reached Versailles on Monday. The King was grief-stricken, as one must be at the loss of the greatest captain and finest gentleman in the world. The whole Court was in tears, and Monsieur de Condom almost fainted. They were all ready to go on a pleasure jaunt to Fontainebleau, and everything was cancelled. Never has a man been mourned more sincerely. All the neighbourhood where he lived and all Paris and all the people were afflicted and full of woe; everyone was talking to everybody else in groups and lamenting this hero. I now send you a true account of what he did in the last days of his life. The last day of his glory and his life came after three months of miraculous conduct which professionals never weary of admiring. He had the joy of seeing the enemy routed in front of him. On the 27th, Saturday, he went up on to a little eminence to observe their movements. He planned to fall upon their rearguard, and wrote to the King at noon that with that in mind he had sent word to Brisach that forty hours of prayers should be said. He mentioned the death of young d'Hocquincourt and that he would send a messenger to tell the King the outcome of this undertaking. He sealed up his letter and dispatched it at two. He went up on this little hill with eight or ten others. The enemy fired, from a distance and at random, just one wretched cannon-ball which struck him in the middle of the body, and you can imagine the cries and lamentations of this army. The messenger set off at once. He arrived on Monday as I told you, so that within an hour the King had a letter from M. de Turenne and the news of his death.

166

One of M. de Turenne's gentlemen has come since and says that the two armies are quite close to each other, that M. de Lorges is in command in his uncle's place and that nothing can compare with the violent affliction of the whole of this army. At the same time the King has ordered Monsieur le Duc to post there pending the arrival of Monsieur le Prince who is to go there. But, as his health is none too good and the road is long, there is everything to be feared in the interval. It is a cruel thing to imagine all this fatigue for Monsieur le Prince. God grant that he return! M. de Luxembourg is staying in Flanders as commander-in-chief. The lieutenants-general of Monsieur le Prince are MM. de Duras and de La Feuillade. M. le Maréchal de Créquy stays where he is. On the very day after this news M. de Louvois proposed to the King that this gap should be filled and that, instead of appointing one general, eight should be appointed (which is a gain). At the same time eight Marshals of France were created, namely: M. de Rochefort, to whom the others owe thanks, MM. de Luxembourg, Duras, La Feuillade, d'Estrées, Navailles, Schomberg and Vivonne; that makes a good eight. I leave you to meditate on this.

The Grand Master was in despair; he has been made a duke. But what is the good of this dignity to him? He already has the freedom of the Louvre through his office; it won't get through Parlement because of the consequences, and his wife only wants her official seat at Bouillé. However, it is a favour, and if he were widowed he could marry some young widow.

You know the hatred of the Comte de Gramont for Rochefort. I saw him yesterday; he is furious. He wrote to him and told the King he had done so. Here is the letter:

Monseigneur,
La faveur l'a pu faire autant que le mérite.[*][2] That is why I shall say no more.

       Comte de Gramont.
Good-bye, Rochefort.

---

[*]'Favour may have managed to do as much as merit?' Corneille, *Le Cid*.

2. The insolence of this to a creature of Louvois was only possible for a favourite of the King.

I believe you will think of this compliment as we have thought of it here.

I have seen an almanac; it comes from Milan. For the month of July there is: *Sudden death of a great man*. And for August: *Ah, what do I see?* We are in a continual state of fear.

Meanwhile our six thousand men have gone off to despoil our Brittany. Two Provençaux in command, Forbin and Vins, M. de Pomponne has put in a word for our poor estates. M. de Chaulnes and M. de Lavardin are in despair and sick at heart. If ever you act the fool I hope they won't send you Bretons to correct you. Note how far my heart is removed from all thoughts of revenge.

That, M. le Comte, is all we know so far. As a reward for a very nice letter I am sending you one you will not like, but really I am as upset about it as you are. All through the winter we have heard about the sublime qualities of this hero. Never has a man been so nearly perfect, and the more one knew him the more one loved him and the more one misses him.

Good-bye, Monsieur and Madame. I embrace you both a thousand times. I am sorry you have nobody to talk to about this important news; it is natural to pass on to others everything you think about it. If you are upset you are like us here.

To Madame de Grignan

[Paris, Friday 9 August 1675]

As I only wrote a little note on Wednesday, I forgot several things that should have been said. M. Boucherat wrote on Monday evening that the Coadjutor had done wonders at a conference at Saint-Germain for clerical affairs. Monsieur de Condom and Monsieur d'Agen said the same thing to me at Versailles. I am sure he will do equally well in his speech to the King. So we still have to praise him.

So our poor friends have re-crossed the Rhine quite happily and easily and after beating the enemy; it is complete glory for M. de Lorges. We were all very anxious that the King should send him the baton after such a fine and useful action for which he alone has all the honour. His horse received a cannon-shot in the belly which went between his legs, so he was astride a cannon-ball. Providence had certainly earmarked that man and many others too. We only lost Vaubrun and perhaps Montlaur, brother of the Prince d'Harcourt, your first cousin: people now hardly mention him any more than a dog. The enemy's losses were heavy. On their own admission they have four thousand killed; we only lost seven or eight hundred. The Duc de Sault, and the Chevalier de Grignan and their cavalry distinguished themselves, and the English above all did fabulous things. So it is a great piece of good fortune.

It is reported that Montecuculi, having sent to express to M. de Lorges his grief at the loss of such a great captain, wrote that he would let him re-cross the Rhine and that he was unwilling to expose his reputation to the rage of a furious army and the valour of young Frenchmen whose first impetuous attack is irresistible. In fact the combat was not general and the troops who attacked us were defeated. Several courtiers, whom I daren't name out of prudence, offered to speak to the King about M. de Lorges, with frivolous reasons why he should be created Marshal of France at once, but their arguments were unavailing. He only has the command of Alsace and the twenty-five-thousand-franc pension that Vaubrun had. Ah, that was not what he wanted! M. le Comte d'Auvergne has the post of colonel-general of cavalry and governorship of Limousin. M. de Bouillon struts about in the Tuileries, delighted to be able to be what he likes, with nobody to say him nay. You may be sure that Mme de Bouillon shares his opinion. Cardinal de Bouillon is very upset.

Our good Cardinal[1] has written again to the Pope saying that he can't help hoping that when His Holiness has grasped the reasons in his letter he will listen to his humble prayers, but we think that the Pope, who is infallible and does nothing pointless, will not even read his letters, having answered in advance like our little friend you-know-who. Monsieur le Cardinal rises at six, says his breviary in Hebrew. You know why he goes to High Mass. He dines frugally. He reads the New Testament or writes until Vespers. He takes a walk. He eats at seven, retires at ten. His talk is edifying, and in a word he seems happy.

Let us talk a while about M. de Turenne; it is a long time since we have done so. Isn't it astonishing that we felt ourselves fortunate to

1. Retz.

have re-crossed the Rhine and that what might have been distasteful were he still here seems a stroke of fortune because we have him no longer with us? See what the loss of one man can do. Listen to something that seems grand to me; it seems as though I am reading the history of Rome. Saint-Hilaire, Lieutenant-General of the artillery, made M. de Turenne stop in his gallop to point out a battery to him; it was just as if he had said, 'Sir, stop a moment, for this is where you are to be killed.' The cannon-shot comes and takes off Saint-Hilaire's arm even as he is pointing out this battery and kills M. de Turenne. Saint-Hilaire's son threw himself upon his father and began to shout and cry. 'Stop, my son,' said his father. 'Look (showing M. de Turenne dead), that is what you must weep for eternally, that is irreparable.' And paying no attention to himself he began to weep and bewail this great loss. M. de La Rochefoucauld himself weeps out of admiration for the nobility of this sentiment.

M. de Turenne's gentleman, who had returned, was now back from Versailles and has said he saw the Chevalier de Grignan perform heroic deeds. He charged five times and his cavalry repulsed the enemy so effectively that it was this extraordinary energy that decided the combat. Boufflers did very well, too, and the Duc de Sault, and above all M. de Lorges, who really looked like a nephew of the hero on this occasion. But the gentleman's head was so full of the Chevalier de Grignan that he couldn't stop talking about him. Aren't you surprised he hasn't been wounded, being so involved and exposed so often to the enemy's fire? The Duc de Villeroy is inconsolable about M. de Turenne; he feels that fate can do no further harm after taking away the joy of being loved and respected by such a man. He had refitted a whole English regiment at his own expense,[2] and only nine hundred francs were found in his coffer. His body has been taken to Turenne, many of his servants and even his friends followed it.[3] The Duc de Bouillon has returned; the Chevalier de Coislin because he is ill, but the Chevalier de Vendôme on the eve of the battle. People are in an outcry about this, and all the beauty of Mme de Ludres is no excuse.

Here is one quite new piece of news. You know that there is no love

---

2. *at his own expense*: for the Duke of Monmouth.
3. But the King ordered it to be taken to Saint-Denis.

lost between the Chevalier de Lorraine and the Chevalier de Châtillon. *Enfin, pour éviter les discours superflus,** you know the rest of the lines. Varengeville carries out Monsieur's commands and is very attached to the Chevalier de Châtillon. The Chevalier de Lorraine claims he has grounds for complaining about Varengeville; two days ago he found him in a street and, being followed by a score of his men, said to him, 'If you go on annoying me I will have you given twenty strokes. And if you say a word to me, now, here are some gentlemen (indicating his own men) who will deal with you as you deserve.' Varengeville said nothing except: 'I have nothing to say to you, Monsieur, with such a numerous company,' and went off and complained to Monsieur, who listened to him and blamed the other one. Lorraine had boasted that once he spoke he would get Varengeville dismissed, and perhaps the Chevalier de Châtillon as well, who is the head of the cabal. Seeing that this was not turning out as he had imagined, he followed Monsieur to Versailles and in the King's presence demanded permission to quit his service, but went through all the obligations he had to Monsieur and declared that he would never serve anyone else. And called on the King to bear witness to his fidelity to Monsieur but that, seeing he preferred a petty secretary to himself, he could not bear his disgrace and would go away wherever his destiny might take him. The King, laughing to himself at the storms of this little court, did not use his authority, and after a few words to the effect that he would not speak as a master he left the prince and the favourite together. The latter went back to Paris, where he received through Mme de Monaco a most affectionate letter from Monsieur, but instead of not pursuing his anger any further and seizing his pretext for going back, he went off to Chilly, where he says he will wait some days to see what Monsieur will do to satisfy him, and later, if he is not satisfied, he will go on to Vichy to take the waters, and thence wherever it may please his unhappy fortune. That is where things are at the moment. People don't doubt that those present will create the impression, as usually happens, that those absent are in the wrong. Meanwhile Mme de Monaco is most intrigued, and the Marquis d'Effiat and Volonne have been so clever that they have handed their resignations to Monsieur, showing with great skill that they were the creatures of the Chevalier de Lorraine and

*'So, to spare you unnecessary talk.' Corneille, *Le Cid*, I, 3.

that, with him no longer there, they have lost their master. I will let you know the sequel to this fine tale. Good-bye, dearest love.

We are waiting very impatiently for this ratification. We dare not leave Paris for a single moment because we know that M. de Mirepoix and his good lady are very tempted to commit an infamy; we are very anxious about the arrival of this communication. I am so completely and devotedly yours that I find my steps usefully employed only when they have something to do with you.

I embrace M. de Grignan and you, my dear. *Montélimar*, my love.[5]

From Coulanges

When I put on your packets *Montélimar* it means 'I adore you.' In this way I say quite correctly twice a week, 'I adore you, Madame; Madame la Comtesse de Grignan, in your château of Grignan, I adore you.' It is a sort of refrain. So kindly accept this code that I have hidden from you thus far so as to keep it more secret from M. de Grignan, from whom I think it wise to hide it eternally. I have had your good and nice letter, which I am preserving like the apple of my eye.

So you have seen your husband's pictures. What do you think of them, and particularly the little sheep kicking up the dust from under their feet? Do you know what those little sheep mean? For you should profit from everything. They teach you that you've got to be a sheep like them; so be my little lamb always, and also his who bought the little sheep who adorn your room. There never was such an acquisition. Pictures are gold ingots, you can always sell them when you want. So don't be upset when you see new ones arriving at Grignan, and when you've got enough for your main rooms and all the little ones, well, adorn your courtyards and forecourts with them.

It will not be my fault if I don't go and see all these wonders in September, but Mme du Gué's illness will never let me. I shall certainly leave for Lyons at the end of this month. I am doing all I can to persuade Madame your mother to go with me. Will you allow her

5. Mme de S.'s letters were addressed to Montélimar, and went from there by messenger on foot.

to go to Brittany when the whole of Brittany is in revolt, when they pillage and burn all the châteaux and violate all the women? Good-bye, my lovely Comtesse. *Montélimar*, my lovely Comtesse, I am all yours. So now you really understand what *Montélimar* means.

To Madame de Grignan

[Orléans, Wednesday 11 September 1675]

Well, my dear, I am on the point of embarking on our Loire. Do you remember the nice voyage we had on it? I shall often think of it. Although your Rhône is *terribilis* and strikes fear into me, I wish I were also on the point of entrusting myself to its integrity. I can't hope to live happily without you. I will write to you from all the places I can. I expect a letter from you tomorrow morning early, and I have ordered it to be forwarded here to M. Riaux, head clerk in the main post office, rue des Bourdonnais, and that keeps me going. You say hope is so nice; alas, she must be much more than you say to sustain half the world as she does. I am one of the most assiduous of her courtiers.

I am taking with me some worries about my son; one cannot cut oneself off from news of the army without anxiety. I wrote to him the other day that it felt as if I were going to put my head into a bag and neither see nor hear anything going on in the world. He thinks there will be no detachment until mid October. If he assures you that there will be a detachment we know him well enough to be assured of his attachment, so you have nothing to wish for him. M. de La Trousse will be back soon, he thinks he will not get the governorship of Philippeville. We can't yet guess what fortune has in store for him – often it is a musket-shot. God save him from one of those! On the morning I left I saw the Grand Master and worthy Troche, who escorted me to Mass and to wait for my carriage at Mme de La Fayette's, where I found the Marquis de Saint-Maurice, back from England to report the death of his duke; this is the ceremony.

I am leaving Orléans to enjoy what is left and concern myself with telling you more news; you will guess the authors. It is certain that Mme de Montespan and the King have really separated, but the lady's grief is frequent and even tearful when she sees how well the King is doing without her. The only thing he bewailed was his freedom and this place of refuge from the *lady of the palace*;[1] the rest, for some reason or other, no longer interested him. He has rediscovered the company he likes; he is gay and glad to be free of upsets, while she trembles lest that means a change, and weeps. And if the contrary were the case she would weep and tremble still. So peace is banished from this place. You can make your own reflections on this as on a truth; I think you understand what I mean.

As for England, Kéroualle has missed none of her goals. She wanted to become the King's mistress; she is. He sleeps with her almost every night with the knowledge of the whole court; she has a son who has just been recognized and on whom two duchies[2] have been bestowed. She is amassing treasure, she makes everyone she can fear and respect her, but she had not foreseen finding in her path a young actress who has bewitched the King.[3] She cannot detach him from her for a moment. He shares his attentions, time and health between the two. The actress is as proud as the Duchess of Portsmouth. She defies her, makes faces at her, attacks her and often gets the King away from her and boasts of his favours. She is young, wild, brazen, shameless and amusing, she sings, dances and plies her trade openly. She has a son by the King and wants him to be recognized. This is how she reasons: 'This Duchess,' she says, 'claims to be high-class. She claims to be related to everyone in France: as soon as some grandee dies she goes into mourning. All right, then, as she is so well connected why has she become a whore? She ought to die of shame. As for me, it's my trade, it's the only thing I'm any good at. The King is keeping me, so for the time being I am his. As he has given me a son, I want him to be recognized, and I am assured he will be, for the King loves me as much as the Portsmouth woman.' This creature takes pride of place, and disconcerts and embarrasses the Duchess very much. It is odd characters like this who amuse me. I decided that from Orléans I couldn't send you anything better. At least it's all true.

I am very well, my dear. I am quite satisfied to be a substance that thinks and reads. Were it not so, our worthy Abbé would not be very amusing; you know he is very preoccupied with *les beaux yeux de sa*

1. *the lady of the palace*: the Queen.
2. *two duchies*: Richmond and Gordon.
3. Nell Gwyn.

cassette.* But while he is looking at that and examining it from all angles, Cardinal Commendon is very good company for me. Weather and roads are lovely. We are having crystal clear days when you feel neither cold nor heat. Our coach would be quite all right overland, but we go by water for the pleasure of it. Don't be worried about Marie, she is just as good as Hélène. I can forestall your anxiety: my health is perfect. I am watching it so as to satisfy you. I love you, dearest, and this love is my most delightful and charming occupation. A thousand kisses and love to M. de Grignan. *Le Bien Bon* sends greetings.

The perfume burner has been dispatched and should arrive soon. I beg M. de Grignan to put it above or beneath his study table; it is a real show-piece. Good-bye, dearest. Send your respectful thanks for it to our dear Eminence.

I don't claim to be among the friends of Monsieur le Premier, but I have seen him quite often at M. de La Rochefoucauld's, Mme de Lavardin's, in his own home and twice in mine. He finds me with his friends, and you know what sort of reverberation that makes.

To Madame de Grignan

[Les Rochers, Sunday 12 January 1676]

You can fill your letters, my dear, with whatever you like; I always read them with great pleasure and full approval. They couldn't be better written; will you believe me on that score? For my affection has no influence upon this opinion.

You say I mustn't go walking in the evening, you think I am disobedient and you scold me. You work that up into an admirable piece, but as my son is at present with me you needn't worry any more about the evening damp; I think it only comes down when I am quite alone.

I have given up telling my beads; as I become more desirous of leading a religious life so I have dropped this devotion, or rather distraction.

It delights me that you like the *Essais de Morale*. Hadn't I told you

*'The lovely eyes of his money-box.' Molière, *L'Avare* (reference to Harpagon's '*chère cassette*').

they were just what you like? As soon as I began reading them I thought all the time that I must send them to you, for you know I am eager to share and don't like enjoying a pleasure all alone. This would be a good rule to introduce to lovers, namely that instead of being jealous as they sometimes are (at least so it was said in my time), they should take it into their head not to enjoy converse with their lady-love alone but want above all to share it with their best friend. This fashion has not yet been introduced; sometimes ladies are not far away from this good nature. But look where I am wandering; let's come back to the *Essais*. You didn't possess them and you are very glad to have this book. It wouldn't be more worthy of pleasing you if it had been written specially for you. What language! What power in the arrangement of words! You feel you have never read French except in this book. And this parallel between charity and self-esteem and between the heroic modesty of Monsieur le Prince and M. de Turenne compared with the humility of Christianity! But I stop short about this book, for I should praise it from end to end and this would no longer be a letter but a dissertation. In a word, I am very glad it pleases you, for it makes me think well of my own taste. As for Josephus, you don't like his life, but it suffices that you should have approved of his actions and his history. Didn't you think that he enjoyed great good fortune in that dungeon, where they drew lots as to who should stab himself last? You are far from being as fortunate at gambling; for both husband and wife to lose always and every day, and lose all that can be lost is a whim of fortune that offends me and outrages my patience. Fickle jade! Fancy hating you as she does! Yet eight or ten pistoles when often repeated make a large sum in the end.

You don't say anything about my little girl. Why had you sent them on ahead to Aix? Did you put my dear little girl into Sainte-Marie on the very next day? You will have done well. You ask me for news of M. de Grignan. I think one shouldn't worry about a Grignan who doesn't write.

You justify yourself well about your Saint-Andiol. Why didn't you write to d'Hacqueville what you wrote to me? Yet it seems to me that they are quite pleased with you, since they have served you well in everything, both in the matter of the town house and the assembly of nobility; you could not wish for anything more than they have done. I enjoy these successes earlier than you because d'Hacqueville tells me everything. You must always believe that he is the cause, or at least he has a hand in every good thing that happens to you, for apart from being genuine he enjoys being at the centre of everything. It is certain that he has helped you very much, and I envy his good fortune. Yet you must realize that I would only have contributed by taking the same steps with him as he has done alone. You have seen the precautions he is taking to prevent your thanking M. de Pomponne, preferring to leave you in ignorance of the services he has rendered you rather than to bring out your gratitude to him too clearly. I can understand that our friend is afraid of the Forbins. Mme de Vins wrote to me that it was a pity all these unpleasantnesses fell on her connections. I took up that word *connections* and used it in more ways than one, telling her that I had seen the time when they were Monsieur d'Arles and the Grignans, that I called on M. de Vins to witness, if he cared to reflect a moment on the past, that I understood perfectly her gratitude to the opposite party, but that she, so just and reasonable, should hold the balance and restore things to the state they ought to be in.[1] This letter was much better turned than I am putting it now, and I think you would have approved of it. D'Hacqueville tells me it had a very good effect. But anyhow you are out of it all and have had satisfaction on and about everything, and I am at least as pleased as you.

We laughed till we cried about that girl who sang at the top of her voice in church that bawdy song she was confessing to having sung elsewhere; there is nothing so novel and amusing. I don't see how she could have done otherwise; the confessor wanted to hear it since he was not satisfied with the admission she had made. I can imagine the old boy being the first to roll about with laughter at the adventure. We often write nonsense to you, but we can't compare with that one. I am always talking to you about Brittany and have sent you some fine songs, and this is to give you confidence to talk to me about Provence, in which I really am more interested than in any other region. The journey I have made there prevents my being bored with anything you say about it; I know it all and understand it all perfectly.

I don't recognize you at all well beneath this dress with silver flowers; the one I know and value, and which suits you perfectly,

1. Family complication: Melchior de Vins, father of the man mentioned here, son of François, Marquis de Vins and Madeleine de Forbin, sister to Gaspard, father of the Bishop of Marseilles by his wife, an Adhémar de Grignan.

seems averse to being repeated this winter and would have been very suitable for your fine room; won't you put it there? I know the beauty of your winters; ours is a lovely one at the moment. I go out walking every day and am making a sort of new park round those wide open spaces at the end of the mall, and am planting avenues with four rows of trees all round. It will look very fine. All this part is smooth and cleared.

I shall leave in February in spite of all these charms; our Abbé's affairs are even more pressing than yours. That is what has prevented my offering our house to Mlle de Méri. She complains about it to many people, I don't understand on what grounds. The *Bien Bon* approves of everything you have decided upon to appease that devil Jabach. What can one do on these ridiculous occasions? We admire you for paying your interest so promptly and living as you do. He is transported by your letters; I often show him things that concern him. He thanks you for everything you say about the *Essais de Morale*. He was delighted and tells me so many things to tell you that he makes me quite tired. Oh, *Bien Bon*, write to her yourself, I'm not your secretary!

We still have the young person, who is still making a good impression here. She has a keen little brain, quite receptive, that we enjoy enlightening. She is absolutely ignorant, and we are making a pastime of informing her about everything: a few words about this great universe, empires, countries, kings, religions, wars, the heavenly bodies, the map. This chaos is pleasant to sort out roughly in a young mind which has never seen a town or a river and didn't believe that the world extended beyond this park. She gives us great joy. Today I told her about the capture of Wismar, and she realizes that we are sorry about it because the King of Sweden is our ally. So you see how extravagant are our amusements. But I seem to remember that twenty or twenty-five years ago you were not so innocent as not to know what day the day after the eve of Whitsun was; it is true that I may not be very clear about it myself, as you and your brother have some ancient recollections in your heads which thank God I know nothing of. The princess is overjoyed that her daughter has taken Wismar; she is a real Dane. She also writes that Monsieur and Madame send their complete exemption for warriors, so we are all saved! Oh, what a good princess!

Mme de La Fayette is very grateful for your letter; she thinks you are very kind and considerate. But don't you think it's funny that her brother-in-law is not dead after all, as you thought, and that the truth at Toulon is not known at Aix?

On the questions you ask your brother, I boldly decide that I prefer the man who is angry and says so to the *traditor* who hides his venom beneath fine, gentle appearances. There is a stanza in Ariosto depicting deceit that would fill my bill, but I haven't time to look it up.

The worthy d'Hacqueville tells me some more about Saint-Géran's journey, and to show me how brief he will be he says, 'She will only be able to get one letter from me at La Palisse.' That's how he treats an acquaintance of one week. He is no less good to old ones, but it does seem singular.

M. and Mme de Coulanges have so far come to no decision about their affair. 'We shall see'; that is useless.

I was forgetting to say that I had thought like you of divers ways of depicting the human heart, some white, others in blackest black. Mine for you is a lovely colour. A thousand embraces and real love, my lovely dear.

From Charles de Sévigné

I am not at all in a good temper. I have just had a serious conversation with the *Bien Bon* on the woes of our age, and you know how painful that subject is. I did however smile at the tale of the innocence of the girl at Lambesc; imagine what I would have done if I had been in my normal state. She was as anxious to have absolution as the reverend father to know the song, and apparently they satisfied each other.

As for the *Essais de Morale*, I humbly beg pardon if I say that the treatise 'Concerning Knowledge of Oneself' seems difficult to understand, over-subtle, jargon in some places and above all boring almost everywhere. I honour with my approval 'Manners of Tempting God', but, my dear sister, you who love good style and appreciate it so well, at least to judge by your own, can you compare that of the Port-Royal of today with that of M. Pascal? It is precisely the latter style that puts one off everybody else's, and M. Nicole puts lots of fine words into his which tire you out and sicken you in the end. It is like eating too much blancmange, that's what I think. To soothe your mind I will tell you that Montaigne and I are reconciled in many respects. Some things I find admirable and inimitable, others childish and even extravagant, and I won't retract over those. Please, when you have finished Josephus, do try an old treatise in the *Moral Works* of Plutarch entitled 'How one can distinguish a friend from a flatterer'. I have re-read it this year and was more impressed by it than the first time.

Let me know whether the question you raise about people who expend their resentment in impetuous speeches or those who keep it hidden under fine externals, concerns Mme de La Fayette; we have no idea because we probably don't know as much as you do. She has criticized the funeral oration of Monsieur de Tulle, and I challenge this because I think this oration is very fine. She does the same for the *Essais de Morale*; this upsets me rather less. She is very hard on the libretto of the new opera,[2] and I willingly agree without having seen it. Good-bye, beautiful little sister. Everybody greets and embraces M. de Grignan. I kiss little *Dague* on the forehead.

To Madame de Grignan

[Les Rochers, Wednesday 15 January 1676]

By dint of talking to me about a stiff neck you have given me one. I can't move my right side; my dear child, I get those little pains nobody else pities although one never stops moaning. My son falls about with laughter; I shall give him one on the nose as soon as I am able. Meanwhile, dear child, I embrace you with my left arm and with all my heart. The *frater* will be telling you a lot of tall stories. Your Queen of Hungary's water will have cured me before this letter gets to Paris. Good-bye, dear child.

From Charles de Sévigné

No, I am not laughing, as Mother tells you I am, but as her complaint is nothing that can give the slightest anxiety, one commiserates with her pains and amuses her in bed, in fact does one's best to give her relief. I think you will rely on me and the good Abbé over anything

2. *Atys*, by Lully, libretto by Quinault.

to do with a health so precious to us all. So set your mind at rest about this, little sister, for we shall certainly be better by the time you begin to worry.

Here is the history of our province. You have been told how M. de Coëtquen stood with M. de Chaulnes. He was openly at daggers drawn with him, and had presented to the King memoranda against his conduct since he has been governor of this province. M. de Coëtquen returned from the Court in order to go to his governorship[1] by the King's order. He came to Rennes, went to see M. de Pommereuil and spent from his arrival at Rennes at eight in the morning until nine at night without going to call on M. de Chaulnes. He hadn't even any intention of going there, as he said to M. de Coëtlogon, and made it a point of honour to flout M. de Chaulnes in his capital city. At nine o'clock at night, when he was at his inn with nothing more to do but go to bed, he heard a carriage arrive and saw coming up to his room a man bearing an Exempt's stick; he was M. de Chaulnes's captain of the guard, who requested him in his master's name to come to the Bishop's Palace (where M. de Chaulnes stays). M. de Coëtquen went downstairs and saw twenty-four guards surrounding the carriage, who escorted him noiselessly and in an orderly fashion to the Bishop's Palace. He entered the antechamber and waited some minutes with men under orders to hold him there. M. de Chaulnes appeared at length and told him he had sent for him to tell him to pay the dues of his governorship. After telling him that he knew what he had told the King, but that he had to prove it, he turned his back on him and went back into his office. Coëtquen stood there nonplussed, then returned in a rage and went back to bed at his inn.

To Madame de Grignan

[Les Rochers, Sunday 26 January 1676]

My hands are still swollen, dear child, but let that convince you of the end of all the rheumatism, which has steadily diminished since the attack we mentioned on the ninth day of my illness.

1. Saint-Malo.

So it is true that since that sweating following the other little ones, I have been free of fever and pain except what comes from exhaustion from the rheumatism. You know what it means to me to be lying on my back for sixteen days without being able to change my position. I am tucked away in my little alcove where I have been very snug and perfectly looked after. I wish my secretary were not my own son at this moment so that I could tell you what he has been up to in all this. This complaint has been very rife hereabouts, and those who have avoided pneumonia have been victims, but to tell you the truth I didn't think this universal law applied to me; never was woman more humiliated or treated more out of keeping with her temperament. If I had made good use of all I have gone through I wouldn't have lost everything (I ought perhaps to be envied), but I am impatient and don't see how one can exist with no feet, no legs, no hamstrings and no hands. You must forgive this letter and put it down to the natural self-centredness of a sick person. I shan't go over it again and in a few days we shall be in a state to write just like anybody else.

I seem to have heard, while I was delirious, that your Cardinal de Grimaldi had died; if so I should be very upset.

Good-bye, dear child. In spite of all this my illness has merely been painful, and all who take an interest in me have never for a moment had any reason for anxiety. Even the temperature was necessary to burn up the rheumatic humour, and now it is gone I have only to wait in patience for my strength to come back and the swelling to go down. I embrace M. de Grignan. The princess has done wonders during my illness.

Added by Charles de Sévigné

I have nothing to add, dear sister, except that the good Abbé and I have had an argument. He says that Mother's writing, such as it is, was necessary to reassure you. I maintain that it is more likely to scare you to death, and that you would have paid us the honour of relying on us for news of Mother's health, and our account would have dispelled your anxieties. That is what I think about it, for I don't imagine you would suspect me of being so hardened as to write witticisms when I was upset by something terrible. Let me know what you think so as to settle our argument. Greetings to M. de Grignan and kisses on *La Dague*'s brow.

To Madame de Grignan

[Les Rochers, Wednesday 29 January 1676]

Dictated to Charles de Sévigné by his mother

You will think it funny, my dear, that I am cured, with no temperature or pain left, and that nevertheless I shall not write to you myself, but it is for that very reason that I can't write. My pains have given way to swelling, so that this poor right hand of mine is no use for scribbling as in days past. It is just a bit more inconvenience that won't last long. I am at present getting over the aches caused by a fortnight in bed and am beginning to walk about in my room. I am gaining strength. This is no unpleasant state of affairs, so please don't worry yourself just when we are feeling appreciably happier. I have read your two letters, which are heavenly. You paint me delightful pictures, and if ever I can get my hand to work I shall answer. Meanwhile you know that with me you lose nothing either of the charm of your correspondence or of the affection you show. One of the greatest joys of my recovery has been the anxiety it will relieve you of. You ought not to have any more now, as we have told you everything with exact truth, and at present we are enjoying the delights of convalescence. I embrace you, dear child, with all my heart. So does the *Bien Bon*.

From Charles de Sévigné

And for me, little sister, you know I am sparing no pains. I have nothing to say today of my own, apart from the extreme joy I feel that we have done with complications.

From Charles de Sévigné, dictated by his mother

Guess, my child, what is the one thing in the world which comes quickest and goes away slowest, which brings you nearest to convalescence and takes you furthest away, which takes you within a touch of the most pleasant state in the world and does the most to prevent your enjoying it, which gives you the highest hopes in the world and defers them longest. Can't you guess? You give in? It's rheumatism. For twenty-three days I have been laid up with it and since the fourteenth I have had no temperature or pain; and then in this blessed state, thinking I am able to walk, which is all I wish, I find myself swollen in every quarter, feet, legs, hands, arms; and this swelling, which is called my recovery, and it is indeed, is the whole cause of my impatience and would be of my virtue if I were good. However, I think that it's now all right and that I shall be able to walk in two days' time. Larmechin gives me to hope: *O che spero!* I am getting from all sides letters from Paris rejoicing in my good health and rightly. I purged myself once with M. Delorme's powder, which worked wonders, and I'm going to take some more; it is the proper remedy for all these sorts of afflictions. After that I am promised eternal health, God willing! The first step I shall take will be to go to Paris. So please, my dear child, calm your worries, you know well we have always written truthfully. Before sealing this packet I shall ask my clumsy hand whether it will kindly permit me to write you a couple of words. I don't think it will, perhaps it will in two hours' time.

Good-bye, my beautiful beloved. I urge you all to respect with fear and trembling what is called rheumatism – it seems to me that at present I have nothing more important to recommend. Here comes your *frater*, who has been cursing you for a week because in Paris you were against M. Delorme's remedy.

From Charles de Sévigné

If Mother had followed this fellow's treatment and had taken his powder once a month as he wanted her to, she would not have developed this illness, which is only due to a frightful excess of humours. But it was like wanting to murder Mother to advise her to try a pinch of it. And yet this most dreadful remedy, the very mention of which makes people tremble, which is made of antimony, a kind of emetic, purges much more gently than a glass of water from a spring, doesn't give the slightest griping or pain and has no other effect than to make your head clear and alert, capable of composing verse if you put yourself to it. Yet she mustn't take any: 'Can you be serious, brother, to administer antimony to Mother? All she needs is a diet and a little senna tea once a month.' That's what you said.

Good-bye, little sister. I am furious when I think that we could have avoided this illness with this remedy, which restores health so quickly whatever Mother's impatience may make her say. Mother exclaims, 'Ah, my children, how foolish you are to imagine that an illness can be driven out! Must not God's Providence run its course? Can we do anything but obey it?' That is very Christian, but let us always take a little of M. Delorme's powder just in case.

To Madame de Grignan

[Paris, Wednesday 29 April 1676]

I must begin by telling you that Condé was taken by storm during the night of Saturday to Sunday. At first this news makes your heart beat faster; you think we must have paid dearly for this victory. Not at all, my dear, it cost only a few soldiers, and not one with a name. That is what you call real good fortune. Larrey, son of M. Lenet, the one who was killed in Candia, or his brother, is seriously wounded. You see how we can get on without the old heroes.

Mme de Brinvilliers is not as happy as I am, she is in prison. She is managing pretty well. Yesterday she asked if she could play piquet because she was bored. Her confession has been found. She tells us that at seven she was no longer a virgin, that she went on in the same way, that she had poisoned her father, her brothers, one of her own children and herself, but this was only in order to try out an antidote. Medea had not done as much. She admitted that this confession was in her own hand (a very silly thing to do), but says she was in a high fever when she wrote it, that it was an act of lunacy, an extravagance that could not be taken seriously.

The Queen has been twice to the Carmelites with *Quanto*, where the latter took it into her head to run a lottery. She got together all sorts of things that would appeal to nuns, and it made a fine entertainment in the community. She talked a lot to Sister Louise de la Miséricorde,[1] asked her whether she was really as happy as she was said to be. 'No,' she said, 'I am not happy, but I am content.' She spoke to her about Monsieur's brother[2] and asked if she wanted to send him a message and what she could say on her behalf. The other, with a charming tone and expression, and perhaps stung by this manner of speaking, said, 'Anything you like, Madame, anything you like.' Put into that all the grace, wit and modesty you can imagine. After that *Quanto* wanted something to eat; she gave a four pistole piece to buy the ingredients for a sauce which she made herself and ate with a commendable appetite. I am telling you the facts with no beating about the bush. When I think of a certain letter you wrote last year about M. de Vivonne I take all I am sending you to be a satire. Just think how far the silliness can go of a man who could think himself worthy of such exaggerated praises.

To Monsieur de Grignan

I assure you, Monsieur le Comte, that I would infinitely prefer the grace you speak of than that of His Majesty. I think you share my opinion and understand too my desire to see Madame your wife. Without being the *charcoal-burner* in your household, I think that in a quite different style you are more so than all the *charcoal-burners* in the world.[3] Nothing can have preference over you in any state one can be in, but be generous, and when she has been a good wife a little longer bring her here yourself to be a good daughter. That is the way one carries out all one's duties, and the only way to give me life again and persuade me that you love me as much as I love you.

1. La Vallière.
2. The King.
3. *charcoal-burners* refers to a proverbial expression: *le charbonnier est maître dans sa maison* (*a charcoal-burner is master in his own house*).

Well, well, how funny you are to talk about Cambrai! We shall have taken yet another town before you have heard about the capture of Condé. What do you say about our luck which brings our friend the Turk into Hungary? Corbinelli is overjoyed, we are going to have a good old argue.

I admire the devoutness of the Coadjutor; he should send a little of it to our fine Abbé. I am feeling the separation from my little girl; is she sorry to be in a convent?

I don't know whether Vardes will take it into his head to sell his office once again like the marshal. I pity the poor fellow; you misinterpret all his sentiments. In vain does he speak sincerely, you don't believe a word he says; you are unkind. He has just sent me a most affectionate letter. I believe it all literally, but then I am kind. Mme de Louvigny came to see me today; she sends kindest regards. I embrace the poor mites and my little girl, whom I shall not see for a long time.

I come back to you, my dear, and embrace you with all my heart.

Here is M. de Coulanges to tell you how Mme de Brinvilliers tried to kill herself.

From Coulanges

She had shoved a stick, guess where? Not in her eye, not in her mouth, not in her ear, not in her nose, not in the Turkish place – guess where? Anyway, she would certainly have died had not help come promptly.

I am very glad, Madame, that you like the works I have sent you.[4] I am impatient to hear whether M. de Bandols has returned, as I would like to know what he felt about the poem 'Tobias'; he will apparently have been clever enough to pass it on to you without wounding this pure soul that you have just washed in the healing waters of the jubilee. Madame your Mother is off to Vichy, but I shall not follow her because my health has been rather better for some time. I don't even think I shall go to Lyons. So, Madame la Comtesse, come home to Paris and bring your beautiful face if you want me to kiss you. Greetings to M.

4. Some songs.

de Grignan and tell him that today I have been instrumental in winning a very important suit for M. de Lussan, so that he can thank me if he thinks fit.

From Madame de Sévigné

Really it would be unpleasant if Pommier were convicted of having any part in this business. My dear child, I am all yours.

To Madame de Grignan

[Paris, Friday 1 May 1676]

To begin with, my dear, I must thank M. de Grignan a thousand times for the pretty dressing-gown he has given me. I have never seen a nicer one. I am going to have it altered so as to adorn myself next winter and sit in my corner in your room. I often think like you of our evenings last year; we may have yet more, but the best item in our bag won't be there.[1] The gentleman who brought me this gown nearly fell over with astonishment at the beauty and fidelity of your portrait. It is certain that it has even improved, for the canvas has matured and it is now in perfect condition. If you doubt this, my dear, come and see it.

There is a rumour running round here and everybody sends for me to ask about it. It is said that M. de Grignan has been ordered to go and shoulder the Vice-Legate out of Avignon, but I shan't believe it until you tell me. The Grignans would have the honour of being the first to be excommunicated if this war began, for the Abbé de Grignan here has orders from His Majesty to forbid prelates to go and see the Nuncio.

This little gentleman says you are very beautiful. He believes M. de Grignan will stay longer at Aix than you think. I am in no hurry to leave, for I know that the month of June is better than May for taking the waters. So I shall set off on the 10th or 11th of this month. Mme de Montespan has left for Bourbon. Mme de Thianges has gone with her as far as Nevers, where M. and Mme de Nevers are to receive her.

1. Retz.

My son writes that they are going to besiege Bouchain with part of the army while the King, with greater numbers, will hold himself in readiness to confront and beat the Prince of Orange. The Chevalier d'Humières has been out of the Bastille for five or six days; his brother obtained this favour.

Here people are talking of nothing but the speeches and doings of the Brinvilliers woman. Have you ever heard of being afraid of forgetting in confession that one has killed one's father? The peccadilloes she is afraid of forgetting are remarkable. She was in love with that Sainte-Croix and wanted to marry him, so she frequently poisoned her husband to that end. Sainte-Croix, who didn't want to have anything to do with a woman as evil as himself, gave an antidote to the wretched husband, so that having been tossed to and fro five or six times, now poisoned, now unpoisoned, he has remained alive and is now by way of interceding in favour of his better half. These absurdities might go on and on for ever.

I went to Vincennes yesterday with the Villars. His Excellency leaves for Savoy tomorrow and has asked me to kiss your left hand on his behalf. The ladies are very fond of you; mention them when you write so as to return their love.

We await your letters-patent for the marquisate and the signed form so that your pension can be paid. Good-bye, my dearest and sweetest, I shall say no more for today.

Mme de Coulanges is coming back this evening from Saint-Germain. She has told me she will be writing. You need only put your address as usual until I know what you will have to do. I am afraid our correspondence will be all at sixes and sevens during this journey. I hear much good about the little ones. There is no talk I like better than that of these gentlemen who tell me all about you and have just been looking at you. M. de Monaco called to see me but I was out.

To Madame de Grignan

[Nevers, Saturday 16 May 1676]

This is a journey, my dear, on which one is tempted to write to you even when one doesn't want to; so think what it is like when one is as well disposed to it as I am. The weather is superb, that heavy heat has gone without a storm. I have finished with those attacks I told you about. I think the countryside is very beautiful, and my river Loire looked to me pretty well as lovely as at Orléans; it is a pleasure to meet old friends on the way. I have brought my big carriage, so we are in no hurry and we are enjoying the beautiful views which spring surprises at every turn. My only concern is that in winter the roads are a very different matter, and you will have as many fatigues as we have few.

We are following in the footsteps of Mme de Montespan, and everywhere we ask for details of what she says, what she does, what she eats, and how she sleeps. She is in a barouche with six horses, with the Thianges girl. She has a coach following, harnessed in the same way, with six maids. Also she has two wagons, six mules, ten or a dozen men on horseback, excluding her officers. Her party consists of forty-five persons. She finds her room and bed all prepared; on arrival she retires to bed and eats very well. She stayed here at the château, where M. de Nevers had been to give orders, but didn't remain to welcome her. If someone comes to ask for alms for the churches she throws handfuls of gold about very charitably and graciously. Every single day she gets letters from the army. She is now at Bourbon. Tarente, who will be there in two days' time, will let me know the rest and I will write to you. Did I tell you that the Danish favourite, romantically in love with the princess, is a prisoner and has been tried? He had only a tiny plan, which was to make himself king and dethrone his master and benefactor. You observe that this man had no mediocre ideas. M. de Pomponne referred to him the other day as a real Cromwell.

The good Abbé will have told you how the Chevalier obtained from the King, with no trouble, the transfer rights of Entrecasteaux for M. de Grignan. We were astonished that he agreed to send your fine bosom[1] through the post to the Abbé de Grignan, and we said a lot of silly things the other day in that Montceau and Rochecourbière tone. My dear, as long as I don't die too soon I feel I shan't spend my life without seeing your château again with all its appurtenances; I treasure this hope, and would love to have an earlier hope of having you with me this winter. To tell you the truth, I have no small desires

1. French *gorge* (bosom), hence pun on *seing* (seal on document) and *sein* (bust or bosom).

in that respect; I hope you will judge by your own, and that no impossible circumstance will stand in your way.

The little Marquis is very much in my mind. I have been told about cauteries in the back, but I haven't deigned to send you such an abominable remedy. I think you should stick to the iron supports and the little diet tips of Mme de Pomponne.

Good-bye, dearest, until tomorrow. I am sure I shall write from Moulins. I even hope to get some letters there from you, sent on from Paris, which will be very pleasant. I am completely ignorant of any news. News of the war is very near my heart. That is not very good for taking the waters, but what can you do when you have someone in the army? At that rate one should only take the cure in January. In the carriage I am reading a little story about viziers and intrigues of sultanas in the harem. It is very pleasant reading, and this book is quite in the fashion. Good night, my dear. The worthy d'Escars adores you. Kisses to Grignan and kindest regards to M. de La Garde; tell me by what mischance our ensign's sale has gone wrong. You are very lucky to have each other. Tell me about Pauline, I am forgetting all about her. Not the big one, I love her. How is *Montgo*?

[At Moulins, on the day of the Visitation, in the room in which my grandmother died; surrounded by the two little de Valençays, Sunday after Vespers, 17 May 1676]

I reached here last night, my dear, in six days, very pleasantly. Mme Foucquet, her brother-in-law and son came to meet me and I am staying with them.[2] I have had dinner here and leave tomorrow for Vichy.

The mausoleum struck me as admirable; the good Abbé would have been delighted to see it. The young girls are pretty and charming; you have seen them. They remember that you fetched deep sighs in this church; I think I played some part in it, at least I know that I also fetched very sad ones. They say that Mme de Guénégaud said to you, 'Go on sighing, Madame, I have accustomed Moulins to sighs brought from Paris.'

I am very surprised at your having thought about a marriage for your brother; you have dealt with it very well and I value the

2. The Foucquets, Mme Foucquet and her son, lived near Moulins.

negotiator. I will follow it up when I am back in Paris. Write about it to d'Hacqueville. My son's money can be very well estimated from my daughter's. It would be worthy of you to bring off this marriage, and I will work at it as well.

So you feel you weren't sufficiently upset by my illness; good Lord, what could you have done? You were more worried than I was in danger. As the temperature I had for twenty-two days was caused by the pain, it didn't frighten anyone. As for my delirium, that came from my only taking four cups of broth per day and the fact that some people always get delirious in a fever. Your brother played me tricks which would make you die of laughing, and he has made a note of all my wild talk and will regale you with it. So set your mind at rest, my dear, you have been much too worried and upset about my illness.

M. de La Garde must really have good reasons for going to the length of harnessing himself to someone. I thought he was free and leaping and running in a meadow, but in the end one must go into the shafts and take on the yoke like the others.

I am sick at heart about the little girl. Poor child, so there she is! She has concealed her little trouble very well. I pity her if you love her and she loves you as much as we used to love each other, but you have courage to serve you when need arises. God would have been very good to me had he given me as much.

Mme de Montespan is at Bourbon, where M. de La Vallière had given orders for all the towns in his jurisdiction to deliver addresses to her, but she did not wish it. She has given twelve beds to the hospital, donated large sums of money, enriched the Capuchins. She receives visits very civilly. M. Foucquet[3] and his niece, who were taking the waters at Bourbon, went to see her; she talked to him for an hour on the most delicate subjects. Mme Foucquet went on the following day. Mme de Montespan was very pleasant, listened to her very kindly and with an admirable semblance of compassion. God inspired Mme Foucquet to say the best things possible, both on her urgent plea to be imprisoned with her husband and on the hope that Providence would give Mme de Montespan, should occasion arise, some remembrance and pity in her woes. In fine, without asking for anything positive, she used considerable art in showing the horrors of her plight

---

3. Gilles Foucquet, brother of Nicolas.

and the confidence she had in her kindness which could only come from God; her words seemed to me perfectly chosen to touch a heart, and with no grovelling or importunity. I can tell you that you would have been touched by the story.

Mme de Montespan's son[4] is with Mme Foucquet in the country, whence she came to see me. He is ten, good-looking and amusing. His father left him with these ladies on his way to Paris. D'Escars is very well and is taking very great care of my health. Tell me all about the witchcraft of Mme de Rus.[5] Good-bye, beloved, I love you as one ought to love one's own salvation.

To Madame de Grignan

[Vichy, Monday 8 June 1676]

Alas, my dearest and best, be assured that I am very much upset to find myself preferring something else to you, who are so dear to me and whom I love so perfectly. My great consolation is that you cannot have any doubt about my feelings and that you will find a good subject on which to base your reflection of the other day on preference for duty over inclination. This is a good example, dear, and I urge you and M. de Grignan to be kind enough to console me for this violent effort which costs me so dear. This is what is called virtue and gratitude, and I am not surprised that no great crowds of people are found exercising these virtues. I daren't dwell on these thoughts; they upset the peace of mind prescribed in this place. So please, once and for all, consider yourself quite settled in my home as you used to be, and do believe it is just the very thing I most ardently wish for.

You are worried about my baths. I have taken a bath for eight mornings now, as I have already told you. This has made me sweat profusely, which is just what was desired, and far from finding it weakening, I feel the better for it. It is true that your presence would have cheered me up a lot, but I doubt whether I would have wanted you to stay in all this steam. My sweating would have distressed you a little. But at all events I am the paragon of Vichy for having borne

4. Duc d'Antin, Mme de Montespan's legitimate son.
5. Mme de Rus, notorious adventuress.

the baths courageously. My legs have been cured, and if I could close my hands there would be no sign left. I shall take the waters until Saturday, my sixteenth day. They purge me and do me a great deal of good.

My one regret is that you can't see them dance bourrées in this part of the country. They are the most amazing thing in the world: peasants with a truer ear than yours, agility and natural aptitude – in fact I rave about them. Every evening I give a little concert with a violin and basque drum that costs only four sous, and in these meadows and pretty glades it is a joy to watch the last of the shepherds and shepherdesses of the Lignon dancing.[1] Sensible though you are, it is impossible not to wish you were at this sort of jollification.

We have the *Cumaean Sybil* here, all got up and dressed as a young person. She thinks she is being cured and is pitiful to behold. I think that it might be possible were this the Fountain of Youth. What you say about the liberty death takes in interrupting fortune is admirable. It must console one for not being numbered among her favourites: we find death less bitter.

You ask me whether I am religious; alas, no, and I am very sorry about it, but it does seem that I am turning my back somewhat on what is called the world. Age and a touch of illness give one time for much reflection. But, my dear, what I save on the general public I seem to give to you, so I am not making much progress in the land of detachment, and you know that by rights I should begin by putting *Sychaeus* out of my mind; you know the fable.

Mme de Montespan set off from Moulins on Thursday in a painted and gilded boat, furnished inside in red damask, all supplied by the Intendant, with quantities of devices and streamers in the colours of France and Navarre; there never was anything more romantic. This expense runs into more than a thousand écus, but he was reimbursed for it all by the letter the beauty wrote to the King which was full, she told him, of nothing but praise for this magnificence. She would not show herself to the women, but the men saw her in the shadow of M. Morant, the Intendant. She embarked on the Allier, to meet the Loire at Nevers, which should take her to Tours, whence to Fontevrault, where she will wait for the King's return, which is postponed owing

1. In *L'Astrée*, the pastoral novel of Honoré d'Urfé.

194

to the enjoyment he is getting from the business of war. I don't know whether this preference is very popular.

I shall easily get over the death of Ruyter because it seems to me to facilitate your journey – is that true, dear Comte? You ask me to love you both. Well, what else am I doing? Be assured, and you, my dear, that I always speak sincerely, and that in the arrangements of my poor little household the only thing that could put me out would be your refusal to come.

You deserve to be told about the goings-on of the duchess; they are far and away beyond anything I have told you. Bayard has given me an account of the stay she made at his place. She got him to the point at which he thought he could not decently get out of what is called tormenting her in her bed, and look at the fine opinion everyone has of her virtue. He was persuaded of the truth of all that is said about quagmires by the fine defence she put up. Don't you think it's funny to get oneself into that position? But this between ourselves, my dear, as you can imagine. I have told you what our friend Coulanges says about his cure, which consists of not bringing up the waters of Vichy; that is funny. You have seen how I know about Guenani[2] on the occasion you speak of.

I have taken my waters and brought up half of them. It is Tuesday at ten in the morning. As I am well aware that in order to please you I must put down my pen, I am doing so, dear one, embracing you with all my love and assuring you that the waters here are doing me a lot of good. Mme d'Escars adores you. I kiss Montgobert; I am delighted about her health and that she is with you. I can see from here that our little mite is very pretty. I suspected that all the child's perfections would come back, but I advise you not to neglect a little corded bodice and the harness recommended by Mme de Pomponne, and to stretch him in the mornings; it is very good. I have given instructions to Roujoux at Lyons so as to get your letters at Bayard's and at Moulins.

2. *Guenani*: a not very exact anagram on Enghien.

To Madame de Grignan

[Paris, Friday 17 July 1676]

Well, it's all over and done with, Brinvilliers is in the air. Her poor little body was thrown after the execution into a very big fire and the ashes to the winds, so that we shall breathe her, and through the communication of the subtle spirits we shall develop some poisoning urge which will astonish us all. She was tried yesterday and this morning the sentence was read to her; it was to make a public confession at Notre-Dame and to have her head cut off, her body burnt and the ashes scattered to the winds. She was taken to the torture but she said there was no need and that she would tell all. And indeed until five in the evening she recounted her life, even more appalling than people thought. She poisoned her father ten times running (she couldn't finish it off), her brothers and several others, and always love and confidential matters mixed up with it. She said nothing against Pennautier. This confession notwithstanding, they put her to the torture first thing in the morning, both ordinary and extraordinary, but she said nothing more. She asked to speak to the Public Prosecutor and was with him for an hour, but so far nobody knows the subject of this conversation. At six o'clock she was taken, with only a shift on and a rope round her neck, to make the public confession at Notre-Dame. Then she was put back into the tumbril in which I saw her, thrown on her back on to the straw, wearing a low cornet and her shift, having on one side a priest and on the other the executioner; it really made me shudder. Those who saw the execution say that she mounted the scaffold with great courage. As for me, I was on the Pont Notre-Dame with the good d'Escars; never has such a crowd been seen, nor Paris so excited and attentive. If you ask me what I saw, it was nothing but a cornet, but the day was given up to this tragedy. I shall know more tomorrow and it will reach you.

It is said that the siege of Maestricht has begun and that that of Philippsburg is still going on; it is sad for the onlookers. Our little friend[1] made me laugh a lot this morning; she says that Mme de Rochefort, in the depths of her grief, has kept an extreme affection for

1. Mme de Coulanges.

Mme de Montespan, and she imitated the sobs through which she told her that she had loved her all through her life with a quite special devotion. Are you wicked enough to find that as funny as I do?

Here is another silly story, but I don't want M. de Grignan to read it. *Petit-Bon*, who hasn't the wit to invent the slightest thing, artlessly told how, after he had been in bed in a casual way with the *Mousetrap* for two or three hours, she had said to him, '*Petit-Bon*, I've a bone to pick with you.' 'What, Madame?' 'You don't revere the Virgin, oh, you don't revere the Virgin, and that hurts me very much.' I hope you are more virtuous than I am and that this ridiculous story doesn't strike you as it has me.

It is said that Louvigny found his dear wife writing a letter he didn't approve of; it has been a sensation. D'Hacqueville is busy putting things right. You can imagine it is not from him that I learned this little matter, but it is no less true for that, my dear.

I am very anxious to know how you put all your visitors up. These rooms all upset and smelling of paint annoy me. I do beg you, my dear one, to stick to the plan of showing me by your journey the proof of your affection that I expect and of which you owe me a little, and at the time I have said. My health is still the same. My love to M. de Grignan.

To Madame de Grignan

[Paris, Wednesday 22 July 1676]

Yes, my dear, that's just what I want; I am satisfied and consoled for the time I miss seeing you by the happy concurrence of M. de Grignan's sentiments and my own. He will be very glad to have you at Grignan this summer. I have considered his interests at the expense of what I hold dearest in the world, which is seeing you, and he in his turn thought how he could please me by preventing your going back to Provence and making you come a month or six weeks earlier, which pleases me very much and relieves you of all the fatigue of winter and bad roads. There is nothing so right as this arrangement; it makes me feel all that pleasing hope we love and value so much. So that is settled, my dear, we shall discuss it again more than once, and more than once

I shall bless you for this kindness. My carriage will not fail you at Briare, provided it can get out of the water in the river; we ford our river every day and have no use for all the bridges on to the island.

I have quite lost your letter of 20 June, the only one since your departure and of course the one in which you had put the measurements of the little boy. That would happen! Send me them again, and I will see to it.

I have just written to the Chevalier, who was worried about my health. I have told him that I am very well apart from not being able to squeeze my hand tightly or dance the jig (two things I find it very hard to be deprived of), but that you will finish my cure. It is true that I still have a bit of pain in my knees, but it doesn't prevent walking; on the contrary I am bad if I stay sitting too long. Did I tell you that I went the other day to dinner at Sucy with the Présidente Amelot, and the d'Hacquevilles, Corbinelli, Coulanges, *Bien Bon* were there? I was delighted to see that house again, where I spent the lovely days of my youth – I hadn't got rheumatism in those days. My hands won't quite close, but I can use them for everything just the same. I like my present state, and my only terror is putting on weight again so that you can't see my straight back. In a word, dear, forget your anxieties and think only of coming to see me. Our Corbinelli will tell you all about it.

Villebrune says he has cured me. Ah well, I'm very glad it does him good; he is not in a position to neglect what brings him the Vardes and the Moulceaus *in ogni modo*. Vardes writes to Corbinelli that on that account he reveres him like the god of medicine. He may well amuse them in this matter as in others – he is a scared bird that doesn't know where to perch.

Another little word about Brinvilliers. She died as she lived, resolutely. She went into the place where they were going to put her to the torture, and seeing three pails of water: 'That must surely be to drown me, for given my size they can't suppose I can drink all that.' She listened to her sentence in the morning with no fear or weakness, and at the end had it read over again, saying that the tumbril had seized her attention at the beginning and she had not followed the rest. On the way she asked her confessor to put the executioner in front of her 'so as not to see,' she said, 'that villain Desgrez who arrested me'. He was riding in front of the tumbril. Her confessor reproved her for this sentiment and she said, 'Ah well, I beg your forgiveness; then let them

198

leave me that strange sight.' She went alone and barefoot up the ladder and on to the scaffold and for a quarter of an hour was prepared, had her hair cut, was placed in position and then placed in a different position by the executioner; a great murmur went up at this extreme cruelty. Next day people were searching for her bones because the populace said she was a saint. She had two confessors, she said. One said that everything must be told, the other not, and she laughed at this difference of opinion, saying, 'I can do what I like with a clear conscience.' It pleased her to say nothing at all. Pennautier will emerge rather whiter than snow. The public is not happy about it and says it all looks suspicious. Think what ill luck: this creature refused to give the information that was wanted and said what was not asked for. For example, she said that M. Foucquet had sent Glaser, their chemist-poisoner, to Italy to get a herb used for poison; she had heard that fine tale told by Sainte-Croix. Think of that for hitting a man when he is down and a pretext for finishing a poor devil off. It is all very suspicious. Much more is being said, but that is enough for today.

It is thought that M. de Luxembourg proposes to attempt a big action to relieve Philippsburg, which is a dangerous undertaking. The siege of Maestricht still goes on, but Maréchal d'Humières is going to take Aire, to play chess, as I said the other day. He has taken all the troops intended for Maréchal de Créquy, and the officers intended for that army have gone back to Germany, like La Trousse, the Chevalier du Plessis and others. Our boys[1] have stayed with M. de Schomberg; I would much rather have them there than with Maréchal d'Humières. M. de Schomberg will favour our siege and the fortifications of Condé, like Villa Hermosa, Maestricht and the Prince of Orange. It is all warming up.

Meanwhile jollifications go on at Versailles. Every day pleasures, plays, concerts, suppers on the water. Gaming every day in the apartments of the King, the Queen and all the ladies and courtiers; they play at *reversis*. The King and Mme de Montespan preside at one game, the Queen and Mme de Soubise, who plays when Her Majesty is at prayers (she is at two pistoles a hundred), Monsieur and M. de Créquy, Dangeau and his croupiers, Langlée and his. You can see two or three thousand louis lost or won there every day.

1. *Our boys*: Charles de Sévigné and Chevalier de Grignan.

Mme de Montespan's lady friend is more in favour than she has ever been – favour she had never been near before. Such is the way of the world, and our little friend seems none the more eager for that. Mme de Nevers is as beautiful as the light of day and shines very bright, not that anybody bothers much about it. Mlle de Thianges[2] is tall, wears black and looks altogether grown up. The Hôtel de Grancey is just as it was, nothing changes. The Chevalier[3] is very boorish and sickly looking; it would have looked as if he had been poisoned had Mme de Brinvilliers been his heiress. Monsieur le Duc is making this neighbourhood his summer quarters, but Mme de Rohan is off to Lorges, which is a bit embarrassing. Wouldn't you like to know something of the news from Denmark? This is what I have had from the good princess. I think this king's pardon will please you; that is the way to mitigate punishments instead of making them worse.

I have had your letter of the 15th. What is said is said about your trip; you always talk about it with so much affection and love that I am touched to the very heart and am astonished to have been able to find enough reason and consideration for your Grignan relations to leave you with them until October. I sadly contemplate the loss of time without seeing you when I could do so, and I have regrets and silly moods about it that the great d'Hacqueville teases me about.

I will send you a corset and frame for the little one. I wish he had it already; I think his poor little body is very weak and inclined to twist. You should have asked me in Lent when you first noticed. What a shame if his body doesn't get any stronger! I think about it as often as you. I will do what you say with regard to Parère and Rambouillet. I can see that you are doing your duty to perfection towards the Archbishop; aren't you very glad to be doing all that reason requires? I can see that you now know more about it than I do.

What are you saying about young de Castries and one of your girls? The elder boy isn't ten.[4] I haven't thought about seeing Mme de Castries, I confess, but the Cardinal pays me so many visits and is so kind that I think I shall go.

2. *Mlle de Thianges*: niece of Mme de Montespan. Wearing black was then a sign of having grown up.

3. Chevalier de Lorraine.

4. Actually he was thirteen.

Yesterday I was saying about Pennautier what you are saying about the very small company I foresee at his table.

Mme de Rochebonne has sent me a case of bottles of the Queen of Hungary's water. The Abbé de Rochebonne is said to have sent it here. It is addressed to me, but I have had no notification of it. If it is what Spinola was to give my son, it has been delivered in spite of all his comings and goings, and you can set your mind at rest.

I don't know how Monaco has treated her husband, but I haven't heard that she had changed her lover for a new one. Dear old d'Hacqueville could tell us a few tales if he wanted.

Bien Bon doesn't like you to forget him in your letters. He wants to know the width of your beams and joists so as to send you a drawing. I am disturbed not to see a bed in your room. It looks as if you lie on the bare floor with a cushion on your nose.

As for the waters of Vichy, my dear, I am very pleased with them, they have given me fresh strength by purging me and making me sweat. My body is fit. What I've got left of it is not very impressive. When you are here I shall try all the remedies you like. But for the summer I need none of them. I must be thinking of Livry, for I feel a bit stuffy here. I need air and exercise. You will recognize me from all that. As far as I can see, dear, you are going to talk with great candour about a certain marriage;[5] write me what you do really think so as not to forget the other style. I am being taken to task about it and Mme de Noailles is going for me; she said I shouldn't have let him leave Paris. But does he think the pension will be paid so regularly when he is at Montélimar?

What you say about your reason for being delighted that Monsieur de Marseille is a Cardinal is my sentiment exactly. It will be a fact, and he won't now have the joy or hope of becoming one.

I will tell Mme de Villars what you write and that you have something important to say to her. I think she will wait to hear from you. Do you know I am tempted to go with them tomorrow to Versailles? They will return in the evening if the weather is fine. I will speak to M. de Pomponne and to Parère.

I am told wonders about Germany. Those German rascals let a little stream drown them because they haven't the wit to divert it. I am sure

5. La Garde.

M. de Luxembourg will beat them and that they won't take Philippsburg. It isn't our fault if they are unworthy to be our enemies.

My very dear and charming girl, I am all yours, never doubt it. My son is in M. de Schomberg's army; it is the safest at the moment. What have you to say about the Grignans who have just come? I embrace as many as there are, and greet the Archbishop with all due respect.

To Madame de Grignan

[Paris, Wednesday 29 July 1676]

Here, my dear, is a change of scene that you will enjoy as much as everybody else. I went on Saturday with the Villars couple to Versailles; this is how things go. You know about the Queen's toilet, Mass, dinner; but there is no longer any need to be crushed to death while Their Majesties are at table, for at three the King, the Queen, Monsieur, Madame, Mademoiselle, all the princes and princesses, Mme de Montespan and all her suite, all the courtiers, all the ladies, in fact the whole French court is in the fine King's Room that you know. Everything is divinely furnished, everything is magnificent. To be too hot is unknown here – you pass from one place to another without there being a crowd anywhere. A game of *reversis* sets the tone and settles everything. There are the King (Mme de Montespan holds the card), Monsieur, the Queen and Mme de Soubise; M. Dangeau and company, Langlée and company. A thousand louis are scattered on the table, and there are no other counters. I watched Dangeau playing and was staggered at how silly we are compared with him. He concentrates on his game and wins when others lose. Nothing is neglected, he takes advantage of everything, keeps his mind on it; in a word, his skilful strategy defies fortune. So sums like 200,000 francs in ten days or 100,000 écus in a month go down in his book. He said I was joining in his play, so that I sat down very pleasantly and conveniently.

I bowed to the King as you taught me to, and he returned my bow as though I were young and beautiful. The Queen talked as long about my illness as if it had been childbirth. She also said a few words about you. M. le Duc bestowed on me a thousand of those absent-minded caresses of his. The Maréchal de Lorges tackled me in the name of the

Chevalier de Grignan, in fine *tutti quanti*: you know what it is like to catch a word from everybody you meet on the way. Mme de Montespan spoke to me about Bourbon, and asked me to tell her about Vichy and how I got on there. She said that Bourbon, instead of curing her knee, had given her a toothache. I thought her back very straight, as the Maréchale de La Meilleraye said, but seriously, her beauty is amazing, and her figure is not half as heavy as it was, while her complexion, eyes, lips, have lost none of their beauty. She was dressed from head to foot in *point de France*, her hair done in a thousand curls. From each temple they hung down low over her cheeks. Black ribbons on her head, the pearls of the Maréchale de l'Hôpital,[1] embellished with diamond festoons and pendants of exquisite beauty, three or four pins, no headdress – in a word a triumphant beauty to make all the ambassadors admire. She knew that there were complaints that she prevented the whole of France from seeing the King; she has given him back, as you see, and you wouldn't believe the joy this gives everybody and how lovely this makes the Court. This pleasant confusion without confusion, made up of all the most select people, goes on from three until six o'clock. If messengers arrive the King retires to read his letters and then comes back. There is always some music he listens to, and this makes a fine effect. He speaks to all the ladies who normally have that honour. Finally they finish play at the hour I have said, and there is no difficulty at all about settling accounts as there are no tokens or scores. The stakes are at least five, six or seven hundred louis, the large ones a thousand or twelve hundred. At the outset each player puts down twenty, that makes a hundred, and then the one who takes most tricks puts down ten. Each gives four louis to the one who has the knave of hearts, then passes. And when you play and don't take the stakes you add sixteen to the stakes to teach you to play badly. They all chatter all the time and nothing stays in their heads: 'How many hearts have you got?' 'I've got two, three, one, four.' So he only has three or four, and in all this cackling Dangeau revels, for he finds out people's play, he draws his conclusions, he sees what is to be done. In fine, I was delighted to see such remarkable cunning; he is indeed the man who sees what lies underneath the cards, for he knows all the other colours.

1. The second wife of the Maréchal de l'Hôpital married later, and secretly, the King of Poland, who later abdicated and died in 1672. Hence the wonderful jewels.

Well, at six o'clock they climb into the barouche, the King, Mme de Montespan, Monsieur, Mme de Thianges and the worthy d'Heudicourt on the tip-up seat, that is to say as if up in the gods or in *la gloire de Niquée*. You know how these barouches are made; you don't face each other, but are facing the same way. The Queen was in another carriage with the princesses, and then everybody arranged themselves as they liked. They go in gondolas on the canal, where there is music. The return is at ten and then there is a play. At midnight there is a *medianoche*. That is how Saturday was spent. We came home when they entered the barouches.

If I told you how many times people spoke to me about you, how many times I was asked for news of you, how many questions people asked without waiting for the answers, how many answers I spared them, how little anyone bothered about them and how much less I bothered myself, you would recognize perfectly the *iniqua corte*.* Yet it was never more enjoyable, and I very much want it to go on. Mme de Nevers is very pretty, very modest, very simple; her beauty reminds one of you. M. de Nevers is still the perfect yokel; his wife loves him passionately. Mlle de Thianges's beauty is more regular than her sister's. M. du Maine is incomparable; he is astonishingly intelligent and says things you can't imagine. Mme de Maintenon, Mme de Thianges, *Guelphs* and *Ghibellines*, everything is mixed up. Madame paid me many compliments because of the Princesse de Tarante. Mme de Monaco was in Paris.

Monsieur le Prince went the other day to see Mme de La Fayette, this prince *alla cui spada ogni vittoria è certa*.† How could one be anything but flattered by such a mark of esteem, the more so because he doesn't throw it at ladies' heads? He spoke about war; he is waiting for news like the rest of us. We all tremble somewhat about news from Germany. But it is said that the Rhine is so swollen by snow melting in the mountains that the enemy is more hampered by it than we are. Rambures has been killed by a soldier who was quite innocently firing his musket. The siege of Aire still goes on; we have lost a few lieutenants in the guards and a few soldiers. Schomberg's army is perfectly safe. Mme de Schomberg has begun to like me again; the Baron

* 'The evil court.'
† '[This prince] to whose sword every victory is assured.' Tasso.

benefits from this by the great affection of his general. The *conceited little man* is no busier than anybody else, he may get bored, but if he wants a bruise he will have to inflict it upon himself. God preserve them in this idleness! Here, my dear, are some appalling details: they will bore you terribly or amuse you terribly, but they cannot just have no effect. I hope you are in that mood when you sometimes say, 'But you won't talk to me; yet I am surprised at my mother, who would rather die than say a single word to me.' Oh, if you are not satisfied it isn't my fault any more than it's yours if I wasn't satisfied with the death of Ruyter. There are some wonderful passages in your letters.

What you say about marriage is excellently said. Judgement prevails, but it is a little late in the day. Remember me kindly to M. de La Garde, and love from me to M. de Grignan, as always. The rightness of our thoughts about your leaving keeps our affection fresh.

You think that my quill is always sharpened to write wonders about the Grand Master. I don't deny that altogether, but I thought I was laughing at him when telling you about his determination to get on, and that he wants to be a Marshal of France if possible, as of yore. But you don't agree with me on this subject; the world is very unjust.

It has also been unjust to Brinvilliers. Never have so many crimes been treated so leniently; she was not put to the torture. She was given a glimpse of a pardon, and such a clear glimpse that she did not think she would die, and said as she climbed the scaffold, 'So it's serious?' Anyway, she is being blown about by the wind and her confessor declares she is a saint. M. le Premier Président had chosen this reverend gentleman for her as a marvel: he was the one they wanted her to have. Have you not seen those people who perform card tricks? They keep on shuffling them and tell you to take any one you like, they don't mind. You take one, you think you have taken it, and it happens to be just the one they want you to take. The application of this is obvious. Maréchal de Villeroy said the other day, 'Pennautier will be ruined by this business.' Maréchal de Gramont answered, 'He'll have to cut down his table.' All that is so many epigrams. I suppose you know that it is thought that a hundred thousand écus are being laid out to facilitate things; innocence hardly goes in for such lavish gestures. I can't write all I know – it will be for an evening session. Nothing is so amusing as all you say about that horrible woman. I think you are

205

satisfied, for it is not possible for her to be in paradise; her dreadful soul must be kept apart from others. *Assassiner est le plus sûr*: we agree, it is a trifle compared with taking eight months to kill one's father while receiving all his caresses and all his presents, to which her only reply was doubling the dose.

Tell Monsieur the Archbishop what instructions Monsieur le Premier Président has sent me about my health. I have shown my hands and almost my knees to Longeron so that he can report to you. I have a sort of ointment that will cure me, so I am assured. I shall not be so cruel as to plunge into the blood of an ox until the scorching heat is over. You are the one, my child, who will cure me of all my ills. If M. de Grignan could realize the pleasure he is giving me by approving of your journey he would be consoled in advance for the six weeks he will be without you.

Mme de La Fayette is not getting on too badly with Mme de Schomberg. The latter is doing wonders for me, likewise her husband for my son. Mme de Villars is thinking seriously about going off to Savoy; she will meet you on the road. Corbinelli worships you, nothing less. He is full of wonderful kindnesses to me. *Bien Bon* asks you to be in no doubt about the joy he will have at seeing you; he is persuaded that this remedy is what I need, and you know how concerned he is about me. Livry keeps coming into my mind, and I say that I am beginning to be stifled so that my journey will be approved.

Good-bye, my most lovable and loved. You ask me to love you. Very well, I don't mind if I do – it won't be said that I refuse you anything.

To Madame de Grignan

[Paris, Wednesday 30 September 1676]

I am lying, it's only Tuesday, but all the same I am beginning my letter to reply to yours and tell you about Mme de Coulanges, and I shall finish tomorrow, which really will be Wednesday.

It is the fourteenth day of Mme de Coulanges's illness. The doctors won't answer for her yet because she still has a temperature, and in her continual delirium they have reason to fear moving her; also she hasn't been purged because of the haemorrhoids that are extremely painful.

However, as the recurrences get less serious there is every hope that all will be well. This morning they wanted to get her to take an emetic, but she was so unreasonable that she wouldn't pay attention to the pleadings of her doctors and all her friends on the necessity for this remedy. She was forced to swallow five or six miserable sips, which didn't do half what was wanted, and these wretched haemorrhoids prevent their going on tomorrow. As for Beaujeu, she was really dead and the emetic resuscitated her; it is not as easy to die as you think. It looks to me, my dear, as if you want to be anxious about my being in the feverish air of this house. So I tell you that I am perfectly well and that Mme de Coulanges is extremely glad and desirous of my presence. I am in the sickroom or in the garden, I come and go and talk to all sorts of people. I walk about and don't breathe in feverish air. So don't worry at all about me.

I have looked into the nice little remedy you suggest: it is admirable. Could you have been cruel enough not to use it until I had? Could you have written it down without laughing? I laughed most heartily. The convenience, suitability, simplicity and familiar nature of this remedy, the number of ladies who use it without one's knowing, all that part, my dear, is priceless. I love the cause with all my heart but will spare you from reading about it when you realize how little I need it. I was advised also to suggest that you use four of them along the child's back; when you approve of this advice for him I will begin to see what I shall have to do.

Mme de Villars's house remains for her son the Abbé, for young Bellefonds and something of hers for furniture. As for Saint-Géran, I have told you how she is: much about the same. But, my dear, let me know clearly about a house; I do understand that you must have a different one from mine if you want to have your girls with you. You know quite well that I can never go against your wishes either in what is useful or in what is agreeable to you.

On Saturday I made the nicest little excursion in the world. I went to see Parère and found him all hot and bothered, having, he said, turned his study upside down looking for our extracts. I thought he was going to say he hadn't found them. I was mistaken; there they were on the table, and I was delighted. I went hotfoot and took them to M. de Pomponne, who welcomed me affectionately. I showed him our papers and we discussed this business. He said he was very pleased with my health, found me quite my usual self and not at all changed. On Provence affairs, he said in a word that he found your claims justified and that since I wished it he would bring it up on Friday *without considering Monsieur de Marseille*. He received at the same time M. de Grignan's letter, which he read aloud and thought very well written. Mme de Vins came in. She didn't upset in any way what M. de Pomponne had promised, and her conversation became very animated. We looked forward to your return, they teased me about the joy I should feel at embracing you, and then I came home very pleased with my evening. D'Hacqueville came shortly afterwards, to whom M. de Pomponne retailed what he had promised me; I shall remind him of it. Parère has promised me the utmost speed. If I am not here d'Hacqueville will look after everything. So your business will be completed before the opening of the Assembly. I shall also take care to get back from Parère our letters patent to the marquisate. What a lot of detail! You will see from this reply of La Troche whether she has received your letter.

Poor Amonio is no longer at Chelles; he had to yield place to the Visitor.[1] The Mother Superior cannot get over this affront and by way of revenge she has forbidden anyone to enter her house, so that the de Biron sister, the de Biron nieces, the La Meilleraye sister, the de Cossé sister-in-law, all the friends, cousins, neighbours, everyone is barred. All the parlours are shut. All fast days are observed. All matins are sung without mercy. Lots of little relaxations have been tightened up. And when anyone complains: 'Alas,' she says, 'I am having the rule observed.' 'But you used not to be so severe.' 'I was wrong, and I repent.' In fact it can be said that Amonio has reformed Chelles. This little affair would have amused you, and in fact although you may say the silliest things in the world about it I am very much persuaded of Madame's wisdom, but it is for that reason that the thing is more painful. Amonio is with M. de Nevers, he is dressed like a prince and a most charming fellow. He sat up five or six nights with Mme de Coulanges. He is as fly as anybody, I can tell you, but his beard didn't dare show itself in front of M. Brayer's.

They all tell me that this year's vintage would have made me drunk and that I am very fortunate to have been warned off it. You will say,

1. *the Visitor*: the Inspector of Religious Houses.

'Who told you about this vintage?' Everybody, and Vesou as well, but he has thought better of it and I am very glad.

Everybody thinks that the King is no longer in love, and that Mme de Montespan is torn between the consequences that might follow the return of his favours and the danger of their not doing so, and the fear that he might turn elsewhere. Apart from that, the line of friendship has not been clearly adopted, and such great beauty still and so much pride cannot easily come down to second place. Jealousies are rife, but have they ever prevented anything? It is certain that there have been eyes and gestures for the *good woman*,[2] but although all you say is perfectly true, she is *another*, and that is a great deal. Many people think she has too much good advice to raise the standard of such perfidy with so little prospect of enjoying it for long. She would be exposed to the fury of Mme de Montespan, she would open the way to infidelity and would only act as a transition to others younger and more attractive. That is what we think about it, and yet everyone is on the watch and it is thought that time will reveal something. However, the *good woman* has asked for leave to be granted to her husband, and since his return she no longer appears all dolled up or any different from usual.

Have I told you that the dear Marquise d'Huxelles has smallpox? It is hoped she will recover – a great miracle at her age and mine.

I am glad you like the box, which I really think is lovely. D'Escars says that your letter is a thousand times more valuable than all she has done. I wouldn't take much notice of M. de La Garde, with all his fine compliments.

I have written to the Archbishops as you wished and as I feel, for nothing is happier for you than what they are doing for the child. I am so glad that his posture is improving; you'll see he will be as hunch-backed as the beauteous Rochebonne! I thank you for remembering me and my impertinences with her. It is true that I was more impressed with M. Dupuy's nose than the sight of the Pont du Gard. I like your memory and commemorations!

That fine Abbé has gone off without leaving me M. de Grignan's signed form for having the pension, although he had promised it. I am going to write to him for it, for perhaps we shall do something in his absence. The thought occurs to me not to go back before I have sent

2. *the good woman*: Mme de Soubise.

off your payment on Friday, thanked M. de Pomponne on Saturday and recovered, if I can, your letters patent. M. d'Hacqueville would undertake all these bothers, but I like to relieve him of them.

Your political arguments are just like those of Corbinelli; we have pretty well thought and talked like you while strolling in M. de Coulanges's little garden. Write to this little man. He has been terribly upset and is worn out with weeping.

It is Wednesday evening. Our poor sick friend is out of danger unless some unforeseen relapse occurs.

Bien Bon is all yours. I embrace the lovely, charming, pretty Rochebonne. And greetings to the Comte and the little ones. Much love to my very dear one.

To Madame de Grignan

[Paris, 2 October 1676]

From M. l'Abbé de Pontcarré

Following my ancient and praiseworthy custom, I hied myself this morning to the room of Madame la Marquise. Even as I presented my beaming face she suspected my object and gave me this sheet of paper; but this liberality is not total, for she also intends to utilize it, which I heartily approve of. So I will tell you briefly, and *in poche parole*, Madame la Comtesse, that we don't know yet what they will do during the rest of the campaign and whether M. de Lorraine will stay with his arms folded. *Ecco il punto.* We are also worried about M. de Zell, who is marching towards the Moselle. M. de Schomberg must have crossed the Sambre by the 27th and be marching towards Philippeville; it will be easy for him to send troops to M. le Maréchal de Créquy.

You know all the intrigues that have gone on in the conclaves. If it came to his Sovereign Eminence it would not be a bad idea to get you to Rome to offer him your arm; if it is a fact that the election won't be just yet you will have time. I went yesterday for part of the day to the Porte de Richelieu, where the ladies are much intrigued about their adornment for Villers-Cotterets. What I am able to tell you is that the

Angel will be one of the most splendid. As is my wont I jibbed at the expense, but was treated as an old dodderer and *Pantaloon*. I bore all these insults patiently because they cost me nothing. They would have liked to discuss some borrowing of jewels, but I was not to be lured into that proposition, having always strongly condemned this familiarity. On Monday we shall have Mme de Verneuil who is coming to make her preparations for departure to Languedoc. *La Manierosa*[1] is coming with her to stay a few days with us, and then she will take the road for the Loire. I am yours, Madame, with all the respect I owe, and to M. le Comte.

You know the fat Abbé and the joy he experiences in saving every scrap of paper; fortunately we find even more joy in giving him some. He has had a great misfortune which has made him very sad and inconsolable. He has given away a coat to his manservant which has only been worn for one year. He thought it was two. This miscalculation is serious; he is very funny about it. I find him odd about economy, just as the Abbé de la Victoire is about avarice.

Here is some news from Mme de Castries, who writes that Odescalchi is Pope; you know that earlier than we do. However, it therefore means that if our returning Cardinals come through Provence it will happen so soon that you will see them before you leave. Do you know that young Amonio is at present in the coach on the way to Rome? His uncle, that is to say a different one from the one attached to the late Pope, is Chamberlain to the new Pope Odescalchi. So you see his fortune is made, and he doesn't need Mme de Chelles or all the nuns any more.

It is Friday, and I would already have been back at Livry, because the weather is wonderful and Mme de Coulanges is out of all danger and in all the happiness of convalescence, were it not that I wanted to know at once whether M. de Pomponne has completed our business this morning so that I could send his letter on to you this evening. Also I want to thank him and speak to Parère, and after that my mind will be at rest and I shall go to Livry tomorrow or Sunday. I shall write another little note this evening in that neighbourhood, independently of this urgent one.

1. *La Manierosa*: the Duchesse de Sully.

Mme de Maintenon came yesterday to see Mme de Coulanges. She showed great affection for this poor invalid and much pleasure at her recovery. The lover and the beloved had been together all day yesterday; the wife had been to Paris. They dined together and there was no public card-playing. In fact joy has returned and all jealous airs have vanished. How everything can change from one moment to the next! The *great woman* returned by water, relationships are now as friendly with the beauty as they were hostile – all humours are sweetened.[2] Anyhow, what one writes today is no longer true tomorrow; it is a region quite unfavourable to immutability. But I beg you, my dear, not to imitate this in the matter of your departure, and remember that we have now reached 2 October. There is already some wood in your cellar. *Bien Bon* is devoted to you.

Don't be at all uneasy, my dear, about my health. Livry, whatever you say, will do me a world of good for the rest of the good weather.

Don't, please, say anything to Taubin, but I love him for having wanted to please you *in ogni modo* by saying he has seen me. That little fib comes from an admirable source; my dear, I haven't seen him and didn't even think it was he who was in Paris. Don't say anything to him, for goodness sake.

Langlade has nearly died at Fresnes of the same disease as Mme de Coulanges, except that he was even worse and was given extreme unction. Mme Le Tellier will atone for them all; she is very bad.

Good-bye, dearest Comtesse. I embrace the Comte and the pretty youngsters; oh dear, how I love them all! This is enough for the hour it is. I will write some more this evening. Read, do read, Père Le Bossu; he has written a little treatise of poetic art that Corbinelli ranks miles above that of Despréaux.

Love and kisses.

To Madame de Grignan

[Paris, 6 November 1676]

This is a letter, my dear, begun at Livry after having yours of 28 October, which I shall finish on Friday in Paris, where I want to go

2. Lover, beloved, wife, *great woman* – King, Mme de Montespan, Queen, Mme de Maintenon.

to speak to M. Colbert either in Paris or at Versailles. I shall see whether he will refuse me that pension. My son will stay a bit longer here, where I may well come back for him, for I think he will soon be free, either because of the return of his men-at-arms, who will come back without having seen any sign of the enemy, or because of a leave resulting from a dozen certificates I have in my pocket which he received at Charleville.

But what about you, my dearest, what can I hope from my decisions in which I so clearly explained myself? Have you still got scruples to overcome about appearances? You are too well acquainted with everything not to see that that can't serve as a reason. I leave you to examine the others with M. de Grignan, and I do urge you to think of the love I have for you and my longing to see and embrace you, founded on all the reasons and hopes in the world. If M. de La Garde has a little regard for me, couldn't he help to give me that joy, since he wants to come to Páris? I had resolved not to say any more, my dear, but my heart is full and I can't help it. I shall tremble when I open your first letter; it is a thing that often happens to me.

I don't like the sound of your stiff neck; it is always a perceptible and nagging pain although a slight one. Last year you had it too, and while answering that letter I was overcome by my own, and from that day you lost sight of my poor writing. The Queen of Hungary's water did me a great deal of harm, so I warn you against it, not that I won't ask you for some when you come, for it is still a craze with lots of people, including me sometimes.

I have never seen such a brilliant letter as your last. I nearly sent it back to you to give you the pleasure of reading it, and while reading it I was amazed that anyone could wish so vehemently not to receive any more. Yet that is the insult I mete out to them. I think you treat mine much better.

That Raymond woman is certainly *hem! hem!* with that head-dress you know of. She was drawn, as you say, by the desire to hear the music of paradise, and our Sisters by the desire for 7,000 francs in cash and an income of 1,000 francs, in consideration of which she goes out when she wants to and she wants to frequently. We had not yet had such bargains, but the beauty of our house makes us overlook everything. I am delighted, for her room and her voice are charming, *hem! hem!* I think you see what I mean.

The dates you think of when mentioning Mme de Soubise are, thank God, among those I don't recall.[1] There must have been some very rough usage at those Versailles fêtes, for Mme de Coulanges has just written that yesterday the tooth had appeared to be out; if that is so you will have guessed rightly that there will be no grudge against her.[2] You speak very amusingly about my friend Mme de Coulanges's illness, and all you say is true. The quartan ague of my friend in the Faubourg[3] has fortunately passed off.

I have just sent on your letter to the *chevalier sans peur et sans reproche*, whom I like very much.[4] And my little one? A kiss for him. I can picture him, but don't know whether I am right. Some day I shall see all these young persons. I can hardly visualize the eight-month-old; is she still determined to live a hundred years? I think those gentlemen who fought in the street will live as long. This would be a very satisfactory and just penalty for an encounter on the pavement in the summer. I wish there were one also for those who have the affliction that La Vallière had; for a long time this affliction has shocked me as much as you. Good-bye, dear love; I shall finish this in the great city.

[Paris, Friday]

So here I am. I dined with the good Bagnols and found Mme de Coulanges in that lovely room full of sunshine, where I have seen you so often, nearly as brilliant as the sun. The poor convalescent welcomed me warmly. She wants to write a few words to you, – it may be some news from the other world that you will be very glad to know. She told me about the transparents. Have you heard about transparents? They are complete dresses of the finest gold and azure brocade you could ever see and over them transparent black dresses, either of fine English lace or chenille velvet on gauze, like that winter lace you have seen. That is what a transparent is, a black garment, and one all of gold or silver or any colour you like. That is today's fashion. Thus attired they had a dance on St Hubert's day, a dance that lasted half an hour, for nobody would dance. The King pushed Mme d'Heudicourt

1. She was expecting a baby by the King?
2. Pun on *la dent*, tooth, and *avoir une dent contre quelqu'un*, have (bear) a grudge.
3. *my friend in the Faubourg*: Mme de La Fayette.
4. Bayard, here applied to the Chevalier de Grignan.

into it by main force. She obeyed, *Mais le combat finit, faute de combattants.** The grand jerkins intended for Villers-Cotterets are worn for evening walks and have come in for St Hubert.[5] Monsieur le Prince wrote from Chantilly to the ladies that their transparents would be a thousand times nicer if they would wear them on their lovely bare skin; I doubt whether they would look any better. The Granceys and Monacos did not appear at these pleasures because the latter is ill and the mother of the *Angels* was dying. It is said that the Marquise de La Ferté has been in painful labour ever since Sunday, in which Boucher's skill is defeated.

M. de Langlée has given Mme de Montespan a dress of gold on gold, all embroidered with gold, all edged with gold, and on top of that a sort of gold pile stitched with gold mixed with a certain gold, which makes the most divine stuff ever imagined. The fairies have secretly devised this work; no living soul knew anything about it. The way of delivering it was as mysterious as its making. Mme de Montespan's dressmaker brought her the dress she had ordered. He had made the bodice to ridiculous measurements, hence cries and complaints as you can imagine. The dressmaker said, all of a tremble, 'Madame, as time presses, see whether this other dress might possibly suit you instead.' The dress is displayed. 'Oh, what a lovely thing! What material! Has it come from heaven? There is nothing like it in the world.' The bodice is tried on; it is a picture. The King arrives; the dressmaker says, 'Madame, it is made for you.' It is realized that it must be a present, but who can have given it? 'Langlée,' said the King. 'It must be Langlée,' said Mme de Montespan, 'nobody else can have imagined such magnificence.' 'It's Langlée, it's Langlée,' everyone repeats. The echoes are all in agreement and say, 'It's Langlée!' So I, my dear, so as to be in the fashion, say, 'It's Langlée.'

From Mme de Coulanges

I am glad not to be dead, Madame, as you are coming back this winter. I am in your house; I couldn't bear the room or the bed in which I died any longer. Why don't you come here and wear transparents like

* 'But the fight ended for want of fighters.' Corneille, *Le Cid*.

5. The house party at Villers-Cotterets was cancelled.

everyone else? You could very well spare the brocade and nobody seems better qualified to believe Monsieur le Prince than you. What do you think? You are the first person I have written to in my own hand; there is some link between us, I am not quite sure what. The Abbé Têtu is not yet in his winter quarters. Good-bye, Madame, I do indeed wish very much for your return.

There is a style very similar to that of the late lamented. We laughed at what you said about her and La Garde concerning the extremity they both reached and from which they have come back; it shows that wisdom, like youth, comes back from afar.

I am expecting d'Hacqueville and the Chevalier de Grignan to make up my council of war, and to know what will happen to the poor Baron, whom I left at Livry quite maimed.

I have now seen M. d'Hacqueville. I couldn't help, though it was quite pointless, showing him my grief over your uncertainty and the endless time I envisage without seeing you unless God takes pity on me. He showed me your letter. I await your decision with very great trepidation. I will tell you what I have done at Versailles and about your brother's leave. Good-bye, dearest and too much loved – far too much for my peace of mind. I pray that this letter may find you already on the way. If you have made the decision we hope you have, you must have set off by now. My dear one, don't you feel a little pity for me, spending my days without seeing you?

To Madame de Grignan

[Livry, Monday 26 July 1677]

So M. de Sévigné will learn from M. de Grignan the necessity of having several mistresses because of the drawbacks which arise from having only two or three. But M. de Grignan must learn from M. de Sévigné the pains of separation when it happens that one of them is going away in a coach. On the day of departure he receives a note that is most embarrassing because it is extremely tender; it upsets the gaiety and freedom he is supposed to be enjoying. Yet another letter comes from the first stop, which infuriates him. What the devil? Is it going on at this pressure? He tells me about this trouble, he pins his only hope on the journey her husband must undertake, which apparently will interrupt this extreme regularity; otherwise he could not keep up an exchange three times a week. He drags out replies and tendernesses by dint of cogitation. The letter is frozen stiff, as I said, before the lyrical page is filled – the spring has quite dried up. He laughs his head off with me about the style and spelling. Here are a few examples you will recognize.

I set off at last; what a journey! For whom am I in so deplorable a state? I would answer: for an ingrate. *I have had a letter from my sister as affectionate as you ought to write; she has been softened by my departure. All day long I have been sad and dreamy, my heart weighed down, sighs, a languor, a misery beyond my control.* It seems to me a most incongruous thing that, in this coach, going along hell for leather, one should feel an amorous languor, a languishing amour. How on earth can one imagine that a condition so suitable for a day spent in a shadowy glade, seated by a fountain or at the foot of a beech tree, can suit the tearing speed of this vehicle? I think that anger, fury, jealousy, revenge would go better with this mode of travel.

But then, she says, *I am confident enough to believe that you are thinking of me. Alas, if you only knew the state I am in you would think I deserved well of you and would treat me as I deserve. Already I begin to wish I could retrace my steps. I defy you to think it is not for you. I shall scarcely feel the joy and peace of a journey's end. Think at any rate a little about the life I am going to lead. Farewell; if you love me you do not love an ingrate.*

This is what I happened to come upon and that is the sort of style your poor brother is condemned to write answers to three times a week. My dear, it's cruel, believe me. Think of the sort of pledge those poor creatures have committed themselves to respect. It's a martyrdom, and they fill me with compassion. The poor boy would collapse under it were it not for the consolation he finds in me. It is your loss that you are not within reach of such confidence. My sweet, I am writing this by way of a sideline to amuse you by giving you an idea of this delightful correspondence. I do beg of you to burn these two pages, which are of no consequence, for fear of some mischance. Remember that this is the sincere and natural creature that you will have; just one slip is all that is needed.

To Madame de Grignan

[Paris, Tuesday 12 October 1677]

Oh yes, dear,

> Quand octobre prend sa fin,
> La Toussaint est au matin.*

I had already thought of that more than four times, and I was going to convey this news to you, had you not forestalled me. So this month is eaten into and finished, I agree. You are well acquainted with a lady who doesn't like changing a gold piece because she finds the same inconvenience with the change. This lady has more bags full of a thousand francs than we have louis; let us follow her economical example. So, dear, I'm going to gossip a bit with you although this letter won't go off today.

We are moving, my pet, and as the servants will manage better than me I am leaving them all here and running away from the muddle and from the infernal racket of Mme Bernard, who wakes me up at six with her carpenters; these adieux console me for the separation. Gargan is near Blois with Fieubet and d'Escars at Vaux, so that I am enchanted to be leaving La Courtaude. I shall return when everything is taken out.

My dear, d'Hacqueville and I are having a dispute. He wants you to be with me in the main apartment, I wanted to put you downstairs below me, where all the rooms are the same, so that you would be less hemmed in and not so near me. Here are his reasons set against mine. He says that upstairs is much lighter and more cheerful than down, and he is right. There is a big room in common which I shall furnish, then a passage, then another big room – that is yours. From this room you pass into that of Mme de Lillebonne – that is mine. And from this big room you go into a small one that you don't know, which is your *pussy-basket*, which I shall furnish for you and where you can sleep if

---

* 'When October's at its end All Saints is tomorrow morning.' (A proverb.)

218

you like. The big room will also have your bed in it; I shall have enough tapestry. The small room is pretty. He says that people who want to see us both won't upset you much by going through your large room. Those whom I shall want to take off your hands so as to skim your pot, will come by a quite separate staircase straight into my little room. This will also be the morning staircase for my servants, workmen, creditors. Near this staircase there are two rooms for my maids. You have accommodation for yours, too, and Montgobert upstairs with Mlles de Grignan, where at the moment there are two princesses; it is called *the princesses' room*. M. de Grignan will be at the end of the hall, my son below and the great hall will not be furnished. *Bien Bon* will be in a very pretty little wing. That is how the great d'Hacqueville has worked it all out. If you prefer downstairs you have only to say so and it can be arranged. A few bigger and cleaner windows; furniture for the big room can be found. At all events, your decision will settle our arrangement, for this house is so large that it is no trouble to put my son up as well. There are four coach-houses and a fifth can be made; stabling for eighteen horses. I think we shall be comfortable. From now on address your letters there: *Hôtel de Carnavalet, rue des Filles-Bleues*. We don't think you will need to bring tapestries, but rather house-linen, if you don't want to buy any here. The garden is very nice and well kept; I thought it was a riding-school, so dirty are M. and Mme de Lillebonne, but I was mistaken. Let me know what you think about all this.

Monsieur de Marseille came to see me the very next day after my arrival; I had gone over to his house for a moment. Mmes de Pomponne et de Vins came here yesterday, full of affection for you and me. Mme de Vins answered for Monsieur de Marseille's changed behaviour and his genuinely peaceful intentions. As you say, he has another cope in view than that of Aix, and as a sign of that he doesn't want to go to the Assembly. That is why he has been brought forward, which I think will annoy you. He received the provost de Laurens very coolly, who turned up all bright and cheerful, thinking he was interested only in Provence. Mme de Vins was there; he behaved very frigidly to her.

I have told you how little hope there is for your curé de Saint-Esprit.

I approve of all your plans for the boy. When I think I am going to see him it is impossible not to give myself up to that joy. When you think it over and change your mind, I must enter into your sentiments. I miss the charms of Pauline, of which I shall never see anything.

M. de Guitaut is here and has strongly recommended the poor exile.[1] But to express it better, he has taken him under his patronage. He is very hard put to it to deceive his wife, who thinks her son is hale and hearty at Epoisses, whereas he is dead. He is afraid of the scenes she will make when she hears the news. It is a real business. Those sisters are a strange lot; although Mme de Guitaut has many good things about her there is always the stamp of the artisan.

I have been to see Mme de La Fayette at Saint-Maur. I have had enough of her affliction about the loss of poor Bayard; she can't stop talking about it or get used to it. She is now taking nothing but milk, and her health is uncannily delicate. That is what I am afraid of for you, my dear, for you can't look after yourself like she does. Oh dear, how glad I shall be to see with my own eyes this good health everybody promises and about which you have so successfully deceived me when you've wanted to! Oh, there's a lot of roguery in this world! Still long letters! I don't understand how you could manage. You get annoyed when you get three of mine together. But, my dear, are they written in that way? Don't you see that they have sometimes taken twelve days?

I have seen Malclerc. I am not at all reassured about the Cardinal's health. I am sure he won't last long if he stays there; he is wearing himself out with overwork. I feel strongly about it.

I can understand your sadness about the death of that young canon. I can't recall him at all. Like you, I can see the hand of Providence in the obstinate refusal to give him what might have cured him. He took good care not to take the emetic which might have cured him; the Scriptures must be fulfilled. We always believe we could have done this or that, and can never be convinced, for example, of the impossibility of giving that emetic, because we don't do what we don't do and people think it could have been done. So the argument will go on until the valley where we all shall meet.

I greatly approve of all your dinners at the various fountains; changes of basket[2] are admirable. Does M. de Grignan agree? Does he need this procedure so as to eat his consecrated bread? Never within living memory has such lovely weather gone on so long. Rain has been

---

1. *the poor exile*: the curé of Saint-Esprit at Aix, mentioned earlier.
2. *changes of basket*: proverbial expression.

forgotten. A few aged folk say they saw some long ago, but nobody believes them. My dear, don't ever scruple about talking to me about the Gospels for the day when your head is full of them; well, why not talk about them? What is the difficulty, and what is the point of this coyness among friends? I don't agree that it is a fault, but if it is, I consent to being guilty of it all my life.

M. de Saint-Hérem was worshipped at Fontainebleau – he did the honours so well, but his wife had taken it into her head to doll herself up and be in everything. She had diamonds and pearls; one day she sent somebody to borrow all Mme de Soubise's jewels, feeling quite sure she would be like her as soon as she had put them on. It was a great laugh. Don't friends or mirrors exist in the world? The lovely Ludres is still at the *Poucet*[3] with her divine beauty. There are murmurings about some extraordinary cold, as last year about *Quanto*.

[Continued at Livry, Tuesday evening]

I have come here to sleep, my dear, on Mme de Coulanges's back. Abbé Têtu is here, and good Corbinelli. *Bien Bon* has stayed in Paris with all my household for the moving. He has a cold. All that together made up his mind for him. I shall go back on Thursday with Mme de Coulanges and probably sleep at her home that night until I get straight. I am here with Marie and Louison and bear Mme de Coulanges company, who has been established here for five weeks. You mentioned her *throat being cut* the other day. It was only so to the extent that you wanted, and I even assure you that for some time it has been a question of speaking about you. She did more good and useful things than could be wished for, and did them so naturally that none of your friends could do better. You will do as you feel best this winter, but I think that reason should oblige you to behave differently towards her than last year.

My dear, the hope of seeing you, expecting you, giving you a good welcome means so much more to me than all the waters of Vichy, although I am perfectly satisfied with them. I am waiting for one of your letters, but I shan't wait for it before sealing this one; I shall answer it on Friday.

3. For Le Bouchet.

221

I went to see M. de Pomponne yesterday. I found the place full of the joy of his daughter's forthcoming marriage to the son of the Marquis de Molac. He is making over the reversion of his estate and a warrant for deduction of two hundred thousand livres, together with six years' keep for them personally and three or four servants; that's what it is costing him to marry his daughter. You will get here in plenty of time for the wedding.[4]

I saw Monsieur de Marseille, who was full of kind remarks and admirable protestations about his conduct regarding you. I found him just as he used to be, with that awful treacherous cough that I hated so much; I think the heart is better.

The news about *Quanto* is false, and the fair Ludres is at Versailles with Monsieur and Madame. Everybody here sends kindest regards. My dear, I am all yours, this is a great truth that I feel at every moment of my life.

I embrace the Comte and M. de La Garde.

To Bussy-Rabutin

[Paris, Friday 18 March 1678]

What do you think of the capture of Ghent? It was a long time since a king of France had been seen there. Truly our King is admirable and deserves to have other historians than two poets.[1] You know as well as I do what we mean when we say *poets*; he should have no need of such. There should be no need for fable or fiction to place him above others; only a straightforward, pure, clean style, and I know such exists. I am always thinking of this and I shall take up the thread of the conversation again with the minister, as a good Frenchwoman should.

So these two poet-historians are following the Court, more flabbergasted than you can imagine, on foot, on horseback, up to their ears in mud, sleeping poetically in the rays of Endymion's lovely mistress. But they must have good eyesight to notice exactly all the actions of the prince they want to describe. They act the courtier by the amazement they show at such numerous legions and fatigues all too real; they look

4. *for the wedding*: this marriage did not come off.
1. Boileau and Racine were appointed Historiographers Royal.

quite like the two *Jean Doucets*.[2] They said to the King the other day that they were no longer so astonished at the extraordinary valour of the soldiers, and that they were right to wish to be killed so as to put an end to such a dreadful life. That causes laughter and thus they pay their court. They also said that although the King dislikes smells this *gant d'Espagne* won't give him a headache.[3] I add to that that somebody less wise than His Majesty might well have his head affected by this without having the vapours. All this is very silly, my dear cousin; I don't know how Racine and Despréaux have landed me into it without thinking; my pen has put all this down without my consent.

They are now at Ypres and I am worried about it,[4] for the place is crammed with soldiery although two thousand men have left to go to Bruges, because you never know where the King will strike. All the towns are a-tremble. I think that out of all this we shall have either peace or Flanders.

But let us speak of Mme de Seignelay, who died the morning before last before she could give birth to a boy. Fortune has struck a very daring blow to venture to anger M. Colbert. He and all the family are inconsolable. This is a subject worthy of meditation. This great heiress, so wished for and captured at last with so much pomp and circumstance, has died at eighteen.

The Princesse de Clèves lived scarcely longer; she will not be forgotten so soon. This is a little book that Barbin gave us two days ago and it seems to me one of the most enthralling things I have ever read. I think our Canoness will send it to you soon. I will ask your opinion of it when you have read it with the charming widow.[5]

It still seems very early to me to have gone to Chaseu. Aren't your meadows and pretty stream still frozen? You have taken five or six sunny March days for the summer, and they will soon show you, as they have us, that they were only deceivers.

You date your last letter 3rd February. You were dreaming, cousin, it's March, and that being so I am answering quite promptly. I don't know how you can like my letters; they have a slovenliness I am

2. *Jean Doucets*: stage naïfs.

3. A very involved pun. *Gants d'Espagne*, Spanish scented skins for gloves; the town of *Gand* (Ghent) then a Spanish possession.

4. Her son Charles was there.

5. Mme de Coligny – Bussy-Rabutin's daughter.

conscious of without being able to remedy it. But it all dates further back, and it is me you like. You do very well to do so, and I beg you to continue without fearing you are loving an ingrate.

And I say the same to you, my dear niece. Tell me about your amusements and reading; it is the consolation for all the boredom and loneliness. But can one pity both of you? Certainly not, for you are in very good company.

I like La Hire and his speech to his master. It is up to date and well turned. I think you would have said the same thing to Charles VII, and that you could say to the King: One couldn't take Flanders more agreeably than does Your Majesty.

My daughter is a little better, she sends love to you and to my dear niece.

Extract from Bussy-Rabutin's reply, 22 March 1678

Canoness Rabutin has not written to me about *La Princesse de Clèves*, but this last winter one of my friends wrote that M. de La Rochefoucauld and Mme de La Fayette were going to give us something very fine, and it is clear that he was referring to *La Princesse de Clèves*. I am ordering it to be sent and will tell you what I think of it when I have read it, and with as much detachment as though I didn't know its parents.*

To Bussy-Rabutin

[Paris, Wednesday 12 October 1678]

I have had two of your letters, cousin. In one you tell me about your way of life and how you amuse yourself. I feel that you are in very good company and are making excellent use of everything that can contribute towards a peaceful and enjoyable society. I hoped that M. and Mme Guitaut were there, but you develop a lot of reasons to which I give way. Neither of you two has yet made the first move; you cannot be in a hurry to break this ice. So I think a little silence in this regard is called for from me, but I shall not behave in the same way over all the

---

* It is noteworthy that the circle of their close friends took it that La Rochefoucauld had a hand in the composition of the novel.

friendship you and Mme de Coligny promise me. I am delighted to please both of you and to deserve your respect. Recently my daughter, M. de Corbinelli and I began talking about her. In fact she was worthily celebrated, and one of the finest things we found about her was the affection and attachment she has for you and the pleasure she finds in sweetening your exile; that comes from a heroic character. Mlle de Scudéry says that the true measure of merit must be calculated from the extent of one's capacity for loving; judge from that the worth of your daughter. One should also praise those who are worthy of love, and this concerns you, cousin. Anyhow, I can answer for your *incorruptibility* so long as you are together.

M. de Luxembourg's army is not yet disengaged; the orderlies even talk of the siege of Trèves or Juliers. I shall be in despair if I have to start thinking about war all over again. I very much wish that my son and my property were no longer exposed to their *glorious sufferings*. It is wretched to be moving on into the land of misery, which is inevitable in your trade.

You do know, I believe, that Mme de Mecklenburg, on her way to Germany, passed through her brother's army.[1] She spent three days there, like Armida, amid all these military honours which don't give in without a lot of noise. I can't understand how she could think of me in those conditions. She did more, she wrote me a very nice letter, which surprised me very much indeed, for I have no contact with her and she could do ten campaigns and ten journeys in Germany without my having any cause for complaint. I wrote to her that I had often read about princesses in armies being adored and admired by all the princes, who were so many lovers, but that I had never come across one who in the midst of such a triumph thought of writing to an old friend who was not in the princess's confidence. People are trying to read things into her journey. It is not, so they say, to see her husband, whom she doesn't love at all, and it is not that she hates Paris. It is, then, to find a wife for Monsieur le Dauphin. There are some people who are so mysterious that you can never believe that their actions are not equally so.

Monsieur de Brandenburg and the Danes have so thoroughly cleared the Swedes out of Germany that that Elector has nothing left to do but join our enemies. It is feared that that will delay peace for the Germans.

---

1. That of M. de Luxembourg.

The Court is at Saint-Cloud. The King wants to go to Versailles on Saturday, but it seems that God is not willing because it will be impossible for the buildings to be in a fit state to receive him and because of the enormous mortality of workmen of whom, as from the Hospital, they take away cartloads of dead every night. This mournful procession is concealed so as not to put fear into the work force and not to spoil the look of this *unworthy favourite*. You know that joke about Versailles.

I haven't seen anyone who is not certain that it is Père Bouhours who has written the criticism of *La Princesse de Clèves*. I don't doubt that he will deny it, but it is not a piece to disavow from the point of view of wit.

The Jesuits are more powerful and fanatical than ever. They have forbidden the Oratorian fathers to teach the philosophy of Descartes, and consequently the blood to circulate. They have also revived the five propositions. What they have wanted has had to be promised and then disavowed; *lettres de cachet* are powerful arguments of persuasion. God will judge all these questions in the Valley of Jehoshaphat; meanwhile let us live with the living.

We have come back from Livry earlier than we meant to because of a fever that stupidly attacked one of the Mlles de Grignan. We have gradually got used to this fine city again. We nearly wept when we left our forest. The worthy Corbinelli has a cold and keeps to his room. My daughter's health, which bade fair to improve, has become poor again, that is to say extremely delicate, not that that prevents her from loving and honouring you, Monsieur and Madame. I am sure Corbinelli would say the same of himself if he were here. Good-bye, dear relations and friends. I often think of you with great affection.

To Guitaut

[Paris, Friday 25 August 1679]

Alas, my dear Monsieur, what a piece of news you are about to learn, and what grief I have to bear! Cardinal de Retz died yesterday after seven days in a continual fever. God did not permit that he should be given the Englishman's medicine[1] although he asked for it and the experience of our good Abbé de Coulanges was quite recent, and it was this very Eminence who, to get us out of the clutches of the cruel Faculty, had made up our minds for us by declaring that if ever he himself had a single rise of temperature he would send for the English doctor. Thereupon he falls ill. He asks for this medicine, he has a temperature, he is full of humours which bring on attacks of giddiness and hiccup showing the presence of bile in the stomach. All this is precisely the sort of thing that can be cured and ended by the hot and alcoholic remedy of this Englishman. Mme de La Fayette, my daughter and I all cry mercy on us and produce our Abbé restored to life, but God will not let anybody decide. And by saying, 'I don't want to take responsibility for anything,' people become responsible for everything. Finally M. Petit, supported by M. Belay, first had him bled four times in three days, then given two little glasses of cassia which killed him off in the process, for cassia is no harmless remedy when the fever is malignant. When the poor Cardinal was in his agony they consented for the Englishman to be summoned; he came and said he could not raise the dead. So perished before our eyes this man, so charming and so illustrious that you could not meet him without loving him. I am writing all this to you out of the grief of my heart, with that confidence that makes me tell you more than I would others, for, please, this must not go any further. The dreadful outcome has justified only too well what we said, and one cannot go back over this conduct without making a great deal of fuss. That is all that is in my mind.

My daughter is grieved as she must indeed be. I daren't dwell on her departure, but it does seem as though everything is deserting me, and that the worst thing that can happen to me, namely her absence, will soon overwhelm me. Monsieur and Madame, don't you think I deserve a little pity? These various griefs have prevented my appreciating sufficiently the convalescence of our good Abbé, who has come back from death's door.

I will pass on all your offers to my daughter. Can one have any doubt about your very great kindness? You are both so worthy of being loved that anyone who felt the opposite would have nothing to be proud of.

1. *the Englishman's medicine*: Dr Talbot, or Tabor, had effected spectacular cures on the Dauphin and Dauphine with a secret remedy (quinine in wine). The King bought it and it was made available publicly and became very fashionable.

I am very far removed from that and nobody could be more sincerely devoted to you than I am. I ought to have a hundred things to tell you. But how can one when one's heart is so full?

To Madame de Grignan

[Paris, Wednesday 22 November 1679]

My dear, I am going to surprise and shock you: M. de Pomponne is disgraced. On Saturday night, as he was about to return from Pomponne, he was ordered to resign his appointment and was told that he would be paid 700,000 francs, that his salary of 20,000 francs as a minister would be continued and that the King had arranged all these things to show him that he was satisfied as to his loyalty. It was M. Colbert who paid him that compliment, assuring him the while that he was desperately sorry to be obliged to, etc. M. de Pomponne asked whether he might not have the honour of speaking to the King and learning from his own lips what shortcoming had brought this bolt from the blue; he was told that he could not speak to the King. He wrote to him and indicated his extreme grief and ignorance of what could have brought this disgrace upon him. He mentioned his large family, implored him to consider his eight children. Then he immediately had his horses harnessed to the carriage and returned to Paris, where he arrived at midnight.

I told you that we had been to Pomponne on Friday, that is M. de Chaulnes, Caumartin and I. We found him and the ladies there and they welcomed us gaily. We talked all the evening. We played chess. Oh, what a checkmate was being prepared at Saint-Germain! He went there the very next morning because a courier was waiting for him, so that M. Colbert, who thought he would find him on Saturday evening as usual, realizing that he had gone straight to Saint-Germain, retraced his steps, nearly killing his horses. We didn't leave Pomponne until after dinner, leaving the ladies there, Mme de Vins having sent much love to you by me. So we had to send them this dreadful news. One of M. de Pomponne's manservants reached Mme de Vins soon after nine on Sunday, after such an extraordinary journey and looking so terribly upset that Mme de Vins felt sure he had come to tell them of M. de Pomponne's death, so that when she realized he was only disgraced she breathed again. But she felt it very badly when she got over the shock. She went and told her sister.[1] They set off at once, leaving all those little boys in tears, and reached Paris, sick with grief, at two in the afternoon, where they found M. de Pomponne. You can imagine their conversation and what they felt like as they saw each other in such a different state from what they thought they were in the day before. I learned this from the Abbé de Grignan, and I confess it touched me to the very heart.

I went to see them towards evening; they were not appearing in public, but I went in and found all three. M. de Pomponne embraced me, but couldn't say a single word. The ladies couldn't hold back their tears, nor could I, nor, my dear, could you have held back yours. It was a painful sight. The circumstance of our having separated at Pomponne in such a different way added to our emotion. But I cannot make you realize the state we were in. Poor Mme de Vins, whom I had left looking so blooming with health, was not recognizable – I mean really not recognizable – fifteen days of fever wouldn't have changed her so much. She spoke of you and said she was sure you would feel her grief and the state of M. de Pomponne, and I assured her you would. We spoke of the repercussions of this disgrace that she felt conscious of. They are dreadful both for her business affairs and for the comfort of her daily life as well as the position of her husband. She can see all this and feels it very grievously, I can tell you. M. de Pomponne was not a favourite at Court, but he was in a position to obtain certain ordinary things which all the same do keep up the standing of people; there are many degrees below the favoured position of others[2] which still mean good fortune for individuals. It was moreover a very pleasant thing to find oneself naturally established at Court. Oh Lord, what a change – what retrenchment! what economies in that household! Eight children! Not to have time to obtain the slightest easement! They pay out 30,000 livres annually; think what they will have left! They will cut down miserably in Paris and at Pomponne. People say that so much travelling, sometimes with couriers in attendance, and even the one from Bavaria who had come on Friday and whom the King was impatiently waiting for, has contributed something towards this misfortune. You will easily understand the workings of Providence when you know that it is M. le Président Colbert who has his post. He is in

1. Mme de Vins, sister of Mme de Pomponne.
2. Colbert and Louvois.

Bavaria, and Monsieur his brother meanwhile does the necessary and has written joyfully to him as a surprise, and as though he had made a mistake in addressing the letter: *To Monsieur, Monsieur Colbert, Minister and Secretary of State*. I referred to it in the afflicted home; nothing could be better. Reflect a little on all the power of that family, adding foreign countries to all the rest, and you will see that everything on the other side, the marrying side, fails to come up to that.[3]

My poor dear, what a lot of details and circumstances, but I feel they are not unwelcome on such occasions. I feel that you always want to be told, but I have told all too much. When your courier arrives I shall no longer have to inform you, and it is one of my sorrows that I shall then be quite useless to you. It is true that I already was to Mme de Vins, but we all stood together. Anyhow that's that and such is the world. M. de Pomponne is better able than anybody to bear this misfortune with courage, resignation and in a very Christian spirit.

Yet, my dear, I must say a little word about your little letter. It was a considerable consolation to see that the child's health is so much improved, and your own, of which you tell me wonders. You assure me that I would be very pleased if I saw you; you are right to think so. How delightful to see you concerned with your own health and with resting and building yourself up again. This is a pleasure you have never given me before. You can see that it is not in vain that you are going to this trouble, for the results are obvious. And when I fuss about wanting to inspire in you that same attention, you can see I am right and you are very cruel to treat yourself so harshly. What an obligation I am under to make you calm my worries by the care you take of yourself! Nothing can be more pleasing to me or convince me more of your affection for me. It is such that I would give up your long letters for the satisfaction of thinking I hadn't tired you out or inflamed that poor chest of yours. Ah, my dear, for me there is no comparison between the pleasures of reading your nice letters and the displeasure of thinking what they have cost you.

Please don't lose that Capuchin water that your cook brought you; it is miraculous for all the pains of the body, headaches, bruises and even wounds when one is brave enough to bear the pain. These poor folk have left for Egypt. The doctors are cruel and have deprived the public

3. Louvois marrying his daughter to a grandson of La Rochefoucauld.

of these admirable and disinterested people who really worked prodigious cures. I said farewell to them at Pomponne. Lock up that little phial; there are occasions when one would give a lot of money for it.

I have received your little letter by an extra post. It is wonderful; you haven't realized it. Mlle de Méri is still bothered about her little household; I do my best about it, I can assure you, and I have reliable witnesses to it. All the friends of my grandson have come here quite scared of her illness, M. de Sape, M. de Barillon, MM. de Sanzei. Mesdemoiselles de Grignan, I have lots of kisses to send you on behalf of Mlle de Vauvineux. I embrace you, my dears, and Monsieur your father. And for you, my dearest, I have no words that can make you understand properly how perfectly and solely I am yours. The good Abbé sends his kindest regards.

All these pages have made a fine old muddle; I can't make anything out. I think M. de Grignan will be as astonished as you by this day's news.

To Madame de Grignan

[Paris, Wednesday 27 December 1679]

The whole Pomponne household has been here for the holiday. Mme de Vins came first; I saw her twice. I found M. de Pomponne, the M. Pomponne of Fresnes, now merely the finest gentleman in the world; as his position in the Ministry had not changed him, disgrace doesn't change him either. He is very good company. He spoke most affectionately about you; this subject lasted us a long time as I had to tell him on my side how you wrote about him. Mme de Vins was touched as she spoke of the kindness of your heart, and all our eyes were moist. They are going back to Pomponne, as they are still uncertain about what to do. They have not handed in their resignation and have not received any money. He asked if he could have the honour of seeing the King, but has had no answer. He can't be better off than at Pomponne, inspiring real virtue into his children and talking to the solitaries there.

Mme de Vins and I have been paying calls all day today. She is now without Mme de Villars and you, so I mean quite a lot to her. I am happy to be able to give her these little pleasures. We went to see

Mmes de Richelieu, de Chaulnes, de Créquy, de Rochefort and then back to M. de Pomponne, whom I am finding more and more likeable; I have never seen such a level-headed man. They are off tomorrow. Mme de Vins is off to Saint-Germain; how painful for her to see that place where she was at home and now is a stranger! I fear this journey for her. After this duty visit she will go back to join the unhappy people whose joy and consolation she is; she is more upset than they are. She seems very affectionately disposed towards you; an old misery is the very last thing she is.

The Court is very happy about the marriage of M. le Prince de Conti and Mlle de Blois.[1] They are in love like characters in a novel. The King has made great play of their mutual inclination. He spoke to his daughter tenderly and said he loved her so dearly that he hadn't wanted to let her go away. The young thing was so deeply affected and happy that she shed tears, and the King said he could see clearly that she disliked M. le Prince de Conti. Whereupon she redoubled her tears; her little heart could not contain so much joy. The King described this little scene, which everyone thought was delightful. As for M. le Prince de Conti, he was transported. He didn't know what he was saying or doing, he ignored everybody he found in his path to reach Mlle de Blois. Mme Colbert didn't want him to see her until evening. He stormed the doors and threw himself at her feet and kissed her hand; without more ado she kissed him and off she went into tears again. This nice little princess is so tender and pretty that you want to eat her. The Comte de Gramont complimented the Prince de Conti like everybody else: 'Monsieur, I rejoice at your marriage. Take my advice and watch your step with your father-in-law, don't haggle with him and don't take umbrage about little things, live on good terms with this family and I guarantee that you will benefit very greatly from this alliance.' The King is very happy about it all and is giving his daughter in marriage just like anybody else, and paying compliments to Monsieur le Prince, Monsieur le Duc and Madame La Duchesse, asking the last to be kind to Mlle de Blois who, he says, will be only too happy to be with her often and follow such a good example. He is amusing himself by scaring the Prince de Conti to death, letting him be informed that the articles are not quite in order, that the whole thing must be put off until next winter. Whereupon the prince falls into a

1. *Mlle de Blois*: daughter of the King and Louise de La Vallière.

faint, the princess swears that she will never have anyone else. This conclusion smacks somewhat of a novel, but certainly there never was a prettier one. You can imagine how this marriage and the way the King is managing it gives pleasure in certain quarters.[2] There, my dear, are lots of details to amuse Mlle de Grignan.

The portrait of Madame la Dauphine has come; it is very mediocre. People praise her intelligence, her teeth, her figure, which is just where De Troy had no chance to practise his art. I gave your thanks to M. de La Rochefoucauld; he takes very kind interest in M. de Grignan and yourself. Mme de La Fayette sends you her love; the Cardinals d'Estrées and de Bouillon and the widows; I can find nothing but people who ask me to remember them to you.

Mme d'Effiat has spoilt nothing yet and is not spoilt herself. The Maréchale de Clérambault is here. She is bearing her disgrace stoically and is not going to open her veins, but she lost a thousand louis to young d'Harouys while travelling, on the day before her arrival. That is sufficient explanation of what is happening to her at the Palais-Royal. Good-bye, sweet child.

To Madame de Grignan

[Paris, Wednesday 17 January 1680]

The time is no more, my dear daughter, when it was a great consolation for me to have a long letter from you, but now it is a real distress, and when I think that writing gives you trouble and considerable pain, you can't write little enough. If you find it burdensome you mustn't write; if you don't, you mustn't write. Anyhow, if you care for yourself at all and have any affection for me you must, whether of necessity or by way of precaution, follow that line. If you are ill, rest; if you are well, take care of yourself. And since this precious health, the joy of which one only knows after losing it, forces you to spare yourself, remember it must be your sole concern and the one that will oblige me most.

You sound overwhelmed by the expense of Aix; it is cruel to ruin your affairs in Provence still more instead of improving them. You wish you were at Grignan. It is the only place, you say, where you don't spend anything; I realize that a bit of a stay in your château

2. To Mme de Montespan, by opening up prospects for her children.

would not be amiss in that respect, but you are no longer in a position to put that consideration first. Your health must come first, and that surely should be your guide. And why should those who love you have to leave you in an atmosphere that visibly makes you wilt? You are so upset by the cold winds at Aix and Salon that you should expect those of Grignan to be much worse. So, my dear, you must make a sensible resolve and no longer be poised for flight as you always are; there is no good in this unquiet mind. You should change your style of life since you are changing in health and temperament. You should say, 'I can't travel any more, I must recover; rest and good air are essential,' and not say, 'I am perfectly well,' when you are perfectly ill. Why not let yourself be influenced, don't hide anything from M. de Grignan, who loves you and doesn't want to lose you, but it looks as though you are deceiving him as well as yourself. At all events, my dearest, you must rectify all these goings-on, which so far have done nothing but a lot of harm. We shall have more to say about it, but I can't help saying all this, and you can think it over.

I think you find the Court a very stormy place. You are right to be surprised at Mme de Soubise; nobody knows the truth about this disgrace. It doesn't look as though she were a victim. She coveted a place that the King prevented her getting; many an epigram could be said about that. When she saw that all this distinction only amounted to an increase in pension she spoke up, complained and came to Paris. *J'y vins, j'y suis encore*, etc.;[1] it would not be impossible to bend the meaning of the rest of those lines. Nobody sees her at all, neither brother, sister, aunt nor cousin; she only has Mme de R— to act as the lot. She won't be made to say what she is not saying, for she is a recluse. Yet her interests are being well served there and she hopes to go back soon. It is thought she may be mistaken; if so she will have to change her way of life, for her withdrawal cannot be maintained. Mme de Schomberg doesn't go near her at Charenton; apparently it is a case of plague other than measles. Mme de R— is not to be seen either. It makes one beautiful woman the less in the celebrations going on for the grand wedding.

So Mlle de Blois is Mme la Princesse de Conti. She was affianced on Monday with great ceremony, married yesterday in broad daylight in the chapel at Saint-Germain. A great celebration like the day before,

---

1. *J'y vins, j'y suis encore, etc.*: Racine, *Andromaque*, IV, 5.

a play after dinner, put to bed in the evening and their night clothes presented by the King and Queen. If I see anyone who has come back from Court before I have sent this letter off, I will tell you more. But think how profitable it is to put oneself out a bit to get positions. It is certain that those who had been appointed maids of honour to this princess had worked for it. As chance had it the name of Mme de Bury, who is fifty leagues from here, came into Mme Colbert's mind; she saw her some time ago. She mentioned it to M. de Lavardin, her nephew, and she talked about it to the King. It was found that she was just the right person. She was told by letter that she would have 6,000 francs in emoluments and sit in the Queen's carriage. They get Père Bourdaloue to write. He is her confessor, for she is no Jansenist like Mme de Vibraye, and it is that word that has put the latter out of the race, although she is directed by Saint-Sulpice.[2] So the post goes off and is expected tomorrow. Mme de Lavardin is presenting Mme de Bury with a black dress, a skirt, a lace kerchief and cuffs, all ready to wear. It has been all very well for the Senneterre to dance round the Bourdaloue – nothing doing. You are astonished that the crowd was so great; you are not the only one, but the rage is now to be there *in ogni modo*. So there is a friend of Monsieur le Coadjuteur placed once again. She is a jawbag as you know, she speaks *Bury* (that's the name of a language!), but at any rate she hasn't used it to get to this position.

That of the Maréchale de Clérambault is most extraordinary. She is under the patronage of Madame, who would like to see her one of the Queen's ladies. She attends Court as though nothing had happened, and doesn't seem to remember that she has been but is no longer Governess,

> *Et trouve le chagrin que Monsieur lui prescrit*
> *Trop digne de mépris pour y prêter l'esprit.*[*]

You can adapt those lines yourself, but they come into my head as I am scribbling, and they will have to do.

I think you are a most jealous person, and M. de Grignan extremely in love.[3] Montgobert talks of a ball at which I can see my little Marquis

* 'And finds the sorrow the gentleman prescribes Too far beneath him to lend it an ear.' Adaptation of: '*Et tient la trahison que le Roi leur prescrit/Trop au-dessous de lui pour y prêter l'esprit.*' Corneille, *La Mort de Pompée*, II, 2.

2. *Saint-Sulpice*: i.e. the Jesuits.
3. With Mme d'Oppède?

dancing very prettily. Has Pauline the same inclination for dancing as her sister d'Adhémar? That attraction would put the finishing touch to her charms. Ah, my girl, enjoy that pretty child and don't put her in a place where she can be spoilt. I am very anxious to see her.

I am going to tell you a funny thing, to which Corbinelli will bear witness. I told him on Monday morning that I had been dreaming all night about Mme de Rus, that I didn't understand where such an idea had come from and that I wanted to ask you for news of this witch. Thereupon I had your letter, and lo! you refer to her as if you had heard me; it seems a funny coincidence. So now I know what I wanted to ask you. It is a strange thing to see a man sufficiently in love with this creature to lose his fortune over her. I can't write anything so extra-ordinary to you, but it is thus that she can inspire love.

I have not forgotten the Comte de Suze. His brother, Monsieur de Saint-Omer, was at the point of death and had received all the sacra-ments. He obstinately refused to be bled, even with a high fever and inflammation. The English doctor forced him to be bled, so you can tell whether he needed it.[4] Then with his own remedy he brought him back to life, and in three days' time *il jouera à la fossette*.[5] Alas, the poor Lieutenant's lady, who was so much in love with M. de Vins and was so afraid he would never know it, is dead, and very young. What did she die of? Do let me know. I am always surprised by the death of young people. You are right to complain that I have brought you up badly; if you had learned to take things as they come and not to neglect bowings and scrapings in Provence, this would have amused you very much.

Haven't you noticed the *Gazette de Hollande*? It details those who have positions in Madame la Dauphine's household: M. de Richelieu, gentleman in attendance, M. le Maréchal de Bellefonds, first equerry, M. de Saint-Géran, *nothing*. You must admit that that is funny. So this folly has reached Holland.

My son is still the delight of Quimper. I hope, however, that by now he is in Nantes and will be here at the end of the month – I have brought him up better than you, as you observe. I hope that in a fortnight's time he will not be seen there and be prepared to go off with the others. I will give him your love. Don't write back, and take care not to answer all this gossip. Alas, dear child, in three weeks' time I

---

4. The English doctor was anti-bleeding.
5. Molière, *Le Médecin malgré lui*, I, 5.

shall have forgotten all about it myself. If Montgobert's state of health can run to writing for you she will relieve you altogether, without your even having the trouble of dictating. She writes just like us.

I am very glad you are now having supper; it's better for you than a dozen spoonfuls of milk. Oh dear, I change every hour; I don't know what I do want. I really want you to regain your health. You must forgive me if I dart for whatever I think best, and if I change my mind it is always between the good and the better. You mustn't change your mind about the good opinion you should have of yourself in spite of the unkind shafts of fortune, for indeed, if she allowed, M. and Mme de Grignan might well enjoy their place at Court. You know where all that is ordained and the fruitlessness of the disappointment one can't help feeling.

I still don't know any news about the wedding and whether it was indeed in broad daylight or by the light of the moon. Mme de Vins has sent me this package and I will go and make up mine at her place and send on to you what I have found out. Meanwhile there is one piece of news I will tell you and it is the greatest and most extraordinary you can imagine: Monsieur le Prince had himself shaved yesterday. He was shaved. This was no illusion, nor one of those things you just say without thinking; it is a truth. The whole Court witnessed it, and Mme de Langeron, seizing her moment when he had his paws crossed like a lion, made them put him into a jacket with diamonds on the lapels. A valet, taking advantage of his patience, curled his hair and powdered it, and so at length reduced him to a courtier of the most handsome kind, with a head that eclipsed all the wigs. This was the miracle of the wedding. M. le Prince de Conti's coat was beyond price, embroidered with very big diamonds which edged the sections of black velvet on a background of straw colour. They say that the straw colour was not a success, and that it made Mme de Langeron, who is the life and soul of all the adornments of the House of Condé, quite ill, and indeed things like that can't be got over. Monsieur le Duc, Madame la Duchesse and Mlle de Bourbon had three outfits with different precious stones for the three days. But I was forgetting the best: Monsieur le Prince's sword was ornamented with diamonds,

> *La famosa spada,*
> *Al cui valore ogni vittoria è certa.**

* 'The famous sword to whose valiance every victory is assured.' Tasso.

The Prince de Conti's cloak was lined with black satin with a sort of flecked effect in diamonds. The princess was romantically beautiful, adorned and happy:

> Qu'il est doux de trouver dans un amant qu'on aime
> Un époux qu'on doit aimer!*

I don't know any more. I will tell you what I learn this evening. I advise you to have the gazettes read to you, they are very well done.

M. Courtin is back from Saint-Germain; he has seen everything. The noonday sun lit up the wedding; the moon has been witness to the rest. The King kissed her tenderly when she was in bed and urged her not to resist the Prince de Conti, but be meek and obedient; we think she has been.

To Madame de Grignan

[Paris, Tuesday 30 January 1680]

You write too much. Now I can't see much of your writing without sorrow, for I know, my dear, the pain it gives you, and although you write me the nicest and most loving things in the world, I feel upset at having this pleasure at the expense of your chest. I can see, my dearest, that it still hurts you. This is a long attack, and with no other cause than your illness itself, for you are not tiring yourself at all and you say that the weather is mild and you write less than usual. So whence this obstinacy? You don't say a word about it, and Montgobert is cruel enough to have pen in hand and be writing for you, yet not telling me a word. Good Lord, what does all the rest matter? And what interest can I take in all the joys of your town of Aix when I know that you are not there but go to bed at eight o'clock? You will say, 'So you want me to stay up and get tired?' No, my dear, God save me from such deplorable wishes! But when you were here you were not unable to take some part in social life.

---

* 'How sweet to find in a lover one loves A husband one is obliged to love!' *Bellérophon*, opera by Th. Corneille/Lully.

I have seen M. de Gordes. He told me quite honestly that in the heat you were very exhausted and listless and that you were much better at Aix, but with the same naïvety he claims that the air of Provence is all too rarefied, too keen and dry for the state you are in. When you are healthy anything is all right, but when you have chest trouble and are thin and delicate that kind of air reduces you to a state impossible to recover from. And believe me, if you insist on trying to do it and make your illness worse and feel worse, it will really be a very cruel thing and no return for the affection M. de Grignan must feel for you. So I address myself to him in such an important matter in which lost time is irrecoverable; I beg him to keep watch on you. I know the state of your affairs, and I don't think a winter at Aix will set them to rights; I know how much it costs. But I do know too that nothing is preferable to life itself, and everything gives way to that consideration. I urge you both to treat this matter without self-deception or complacency. He astonished me when he told me how bad for you that air is. You move me deeply when you say that your delicate chest makes us seem the same age. Oh, I hope that God will not have upset such a natural order so pleasant and delightful for me. My dear, what I feel about this fits exactly my tenderness and attachment for you; there is nothing so easy to understand.

You ask about my health. How can you think about it? In its present state it is as unworthy of your anxiety as yours is worthy to be the object of all mine. And you are ingenious enough to write me a long letter without saying a word about that! Such a silence says much more than I would like but much less than I think.

I must take up the thread of my letter again. I always leave it to rest awhile when I have to deal with the subject of your health. So as not to bore you I must follow out the pitiful adventures of these poor folk.

M. de Luxembourg has gone two days without food. He has asked for several Jesuit fathers, but this was refused. He asked for the *Lives of the Saints* and that was vouchsafed. As you see, he doesn't know *to which saint to dedicate himself*. He was interrogated for four hours on Friday or Saturday, I don't remember which, and afterwards he seemed relieved and had a meal. People think he would have done better to state his innocence quite clearly and say he would come back when his natural judges, that is Parlement, summoned him. He has done great harm to the Dukedom by recognizing this Chamber, but he was determined to obey the King blindly. M. de Saissac followed the example of Mme la Comtesse. Mmes de Bouillon and de Tingry were interrogated on Monday in this chamber at the Arsenal; their noble families accompanied them to the door. So far there does not appear to be anything black in their follies, not even dark grey. If nothing more transpires these are still serious scandals that might have been spared people of this rank. Maréchal de Villeroy says that these ladies and gentlemen don't believe in God but in the devil. They really do say a lot of absurdly silly things about everything that went on among those wretched women. The Maréchale de la Ferté, so well-named,[1] went out of kindness with Mme la Comtesse, but did not go upstairs; Monsieur de Langres was with her. All that looks very black. This business affords her a pleasure she doesn't normally enjoy – to hear it said that she is innocent.

The Duchesse de Bouillon went to ask the Voisin for a little poison to kill off an old husband who was killing her with boredom, and for some scheme for marrying a young man who was leading her on without anybody's knowledge. This young man was M. de Vendôme, who was leading her on with one hand and M. de Bouillon with the other. It was a real laugh. When a Mancini is only guilty of a folly like that, it's a gift! And those witches serve all this up seriously and terrify Europe with a mere bagatelle.

Mme la Comtesse de Soissons asked if she could bring back a lover who had left her. This lover was a great prince, and it is reported that she said that if he didn't come back he would rue it; this is understood to mean the King, and everything is important on such a subject, but look at the sequel. If she has committed great crimes she hasn't mentioned them to these creatures. One of our friends says that there is a senior branch of the poisoning business which one can never reach because it is not French. All these are lesser fry, juniors without any shoe leather.

Tingry suggests something more important because she has been a novice mistress. She says, 'People really are funny. They believe I have slept with M. de Luxembourg and had children by him. Alas, God knows.' Anyhow, the line at present is the innocence of the women who

---

1. *La Ferté, so well-named*: pun on *fierté*, pride.

have been named and horror of scandal; maybe tomorrow it will be the opposite. You know these kinds of general moods. I will keep you faithfully informed. It is the sole topic at all gatherings. And indeed there are few examples of such a scandal in any Christian court. They say that this Voisin woman put all the children aborted by her into an oven, and Mme de Coulanges, as you might think, never fails to say, when on the subject of Tingry, that the oven was heated up for her.

I had a long talk yesterday with M. de La Rochefoucauld on a subject we had already discussed.[2] There is no hurry for you to write, but he urges you to believe that the thing he has most at heart in the world would be to help you to change places if there were the least sign of a change you would like. I have never seen a man so obliging and pleasant in his desire to say agreeable things.

This is what I have heard from a reliable source. Mme de Bouillon sailed like a petty queen into this Chamber.[3] She took her seat on a chair specially provided, and instead of answering the first question she requested that what she wished to say should be written down. This was that she had only come because of her respect for the King's order, and not for the Chamber, which she did not recognize, and that she didn't mean to belittle the privilege of the dukes. She did not say a word that wasn't taken down in writing. Then she took off her glove, displaying a very beautiful hand. She answered truthfully, even about her age. 'Do you know the Vigoureux woman?' 'Yes.' 'Why did you want to get rid of your husband?' 'Get rid of him! What, me? You only need ask him whether he believes that; he has just given me his hand to the door of this place.' 'Then why did you go so often to see this Voisin?' 'Because I wanted to see those Sibyls she had promised me, a company well worth the journeys.' Had she not shown this woman a bag of money? She said no, and for more reasons than one, and all this in a very sneering and scornful voice. 'Well, gentlemen, is that all you have to say to me?' 'Yes, Madame.' She rose, and on her way out said in a loud voice, 'Really, I would never have believed that wise men could ask so many silly questions.' She was welcomed with adoration by all her family and male and female friends, so pretty, simple, natural

2. A post for M. de Grignan.
3. *Chambre Ardente*, inquired into cases of poisoning.

241

and spirited was she, as well as straightforward and cool. As for Tingry, she was not so saucy.

M. de Luxembourg has quite gone to pieces; he isn't a man, nor a mannikin, not even a woman, but a little old woman. 'Shut that window. Light a fire. Give me some chocolate. Give me that book. I have given up God and He has given me up.' This is the behaviour he has shown Besmaus and his commissaries, with a mortal pallor. When that is all you have to take to the Bastille, it is much better to clear off, as the King most kindly gave him ample opportunity to do until the moment he shut himself up, for a fortnight has elapsed since he knew that the decree would be against him. But one must come back to Providence in spite of oneself; it was not natural to behave as he has done, being as weak as he appears to be. I was wrong, Mme de Meckelbourg has not seen him. And such a thought never occurred to Tingry, who returned from Saint-Germain with him, nor did it either to him, to give the slightest warning to Mme de Meckelbourg. There was time, moreover, but she obsessed him so completely that he knew nobody but her, and she kept everybody else away from him. I have seen this Meckelbourg at the Daughters of the Blessed Sacrament, where she has retired. She is very distressed and complains bitterly about Tingry, whom she accuses of all her brother's misfortunes. I told her that I gave her all your compliments in advance and that you would be very concerned about her troubles; she said many kind things for your intention.

At present one could do whatever one liked in Paris and nobody would think anything of it. They have forgotten Mme de Soubise and the agony of poor Bartillat; indeed I don't know how things will turn out.

However, I must think of my poor little d'Adhémar. Poor child, how I sympathize with her for being jealous! Alas, dear, take pity on her; I feel for her. It's that naughty Pauline who is causing all this upset.[4] She is already having her hair curled with her sisters and the excited little boy. Yes, dear, I can see all that and M. de Grignan beating time. *Pythie* should make quite an effect. M. d'Oppède is giving up his dear wife wholly to you. Do give him a little compliment from me. The only thing I am sorry about is the idea of you in bed while your children

4. Pauline was the beauty of the family, hence the jealousy.

enjoy themselves. I understand that you would not have been displeased to watch them dance awhile. You are no longer fit, and nobody could be sorrier than I. The other day I had a dream that the milk diet had cured you. On waking up I found it was only a dream, and my heart was very heavy.

Don't write more than half a page, my dear. Let me tell you everything that comes into my head; Montgobert will send me a word back. That's all I want, and for you to be better than you are. I write on and off, and only to you, I tell you everything I learn; I must write volumes, you three words.

My son is still at Nantes, although I have told him to abandon our affairs.

From Corbinelli

Sentiments of Monsieur Descartes touching the essence and properties of the body, opposed to the doctrine of the Church and in agreement with the errors of Calvin on the subject of the Eucharist, addressed to their Lordships the Bishops. That is the title of a book just printed. The style is very good, order perfect, the arguments equivocal; all the cabal is on the alert! I will give you an account, my dear Madame, of the success either of the book or the replies to it. Meanwhile I protest that my dialectics and myself are devoted to your opinions and to your mind.

From Bussy-Rabutin

Oh, when will you come back to us, Madame? I have five more months to wait for you here. I assure you that I should be very glad to see you back, but if you don't come within that time, you will certainly want me to write about some prodigious event, for this winter we write about nothing else.

So good-day, Madame. Please do believe that I hold you in very great honour and even love you. Mme de Coligny will certainly not disagree when I tell you that she is your very humble servant.

I say farewell once more and embrace you with all my heart, my very lovely and very dear girl.

My dear Montgobert, I beseech you to write a short answer to all this volume, and do prevent my daughter from writing. Her writing distresses me, but the cause of this distress is quite serious. Let me know, dear, some news of her health and whether it is still keeping up, and if her diet is as I advised.

I am the very humble servant of the curl-papers of Mlles de Grignan.

To Madame de Grignan

[Paris, 15 March 1680]

I am very much afraid that this time we are going to lose M. de La Rochefoucauld. He still has a high temperature and yesterday he received Our Lord. But his state of mind is worth admiring. He is quite at peace with his conscience; that is all done with. The question is the illness and death of his neighbour. He is hardly affected by it and not upset. He hears the arguments of the doctors in front of him, Frère Ange and the Englishman, in quite a detached manner, without so to speak condescending to express his own opinion. I come back to the line: *Trop au-dessous de lui pour y prêter l'esprit.** He did not see Mme de La Fayette yesterday morning because she was crying and he was receiving the Sacrament, but he sent for news of her at noon. Believe me, my dear, he hasn't written reflections all his life to no purpose. So he has drawn near to his last moments, and there is nothing new or strange in them for him.

M. de Marsillac arrived at midnight the day before yesterday, so overwhelmed with grief that you couldn't be more so if it were for me. He was a long time composing his face and expression, then he went in and found M. de La Rochefoucauld in that chair, hardly any different from what he always is. As of all his children this one is the closest to him we were persuaded that he was troubled within, but nothing showed and he forgot to mention his illness. His son went out to let

* 'Too far beneath him to give it a thought.' Corneille, *La Mort de Pompée*, II, 2. Typical seventeenth-century attitude.

his grief burst forth. After several upsets and intrigues, Gourville against the Englishman, Langlade for him, each supported by several members of the family, and the two principal parties keeping all the bitterness they feel for each other, M. de Marsillac decided for the Englishman. And yesterday, at five in the evening, M. de La Rochefoucauld took his medicine, and again at eight. As nobody at all can enter this house it is difficult to know the truth but I am assured that, having at one moment in the night been at the point of death because of the struggle between the remedy and the gouty tendency, he had such a considerable evacuation that although the fever has not yet gone down there is reason for great hope. For my part I feel sure he will come through. M. de Marsillac doesn't yet open his soul to hope; in his tenderness and grief he can only be compared with you, my dear child, who don't want me to die. You can understand that in his present state I am not giving him M. de Grignan's letter, but it will go with the others that will come, for I am convinced with Langlade, from whom I have heard all this, that this remedy will work a complete miracle.

I wonder, my dear, how you are after your journey to Marseilles. I blame M. de Grignan for taking you there; I can't approve of this pointless rushing about. Won't it also be necessary for you to show Toulon, Hyères, la Sainte-Baume, Saint-Maximin and La Fontaine de Vaucluse to Mlles de Grignan?

I am more or less all the time with Mme de La Fayette. If she were less afflicted she would be a stranger to the delights of friendship and tenderness of the heart. I am sending this off from her home at nine o'clock at night. She has read your little note, for in spite of her anxieties she still is hopeful enough to have cast an eye down it.

M. de La Rochefoucauld is still in the same condition. His legs are swollen, and that worries the Englishman, but he believes his treatment will overcome it all. If that is so I shall marvel at the doctors' goodness in not killing, murdering, tearing to pieces and massacring him, for they will be quite undone, as to take fever out of their domain is to take away their livelihood. Duchesne doesn't worry overmuch, but the others are furious.

To Madame de Grignan

[Paris, Sunday 17 March 1680]

Although this letter won't go until Wednesday, I can't help starting today to tell you, my dear, that M. de La Rochefoucauld died last night. My head is so full of this calamity and of our poor friend's overwhelming grief, that I must talk to you about it. Yesterday, Saturday, the Englishman's remedy had worked wonders; all Friday's hopes that I wrote to you about had improved, we sang hymns of victory, his chest was uncongested, his head clear, his temperature down, his motions normal. In that state yesterday at six o'clock he suddenly turned towards death. The fever redoubled, suffocation, delirium, in a word gout treacherously seized him, and although he was very strong and the bleedings had not weakened him, four or five hours were all it needed to carry him off, and at midnight he gave up the ghost in the care of Monsieur de Condom. M. de Marsillac never left him for a moment; he died in his arms, in that chair you know so well, and courageously spoke to him of God. His affliction cannot be imagined, but he will still have the King and the Court and his own family will still be in its place. But where will Mme de La Fayette find such a friend, such society, so much gentleness, enjoyment, confidence and consideration for her and her son? She is infirm, she is confined to her room, cannot get about. M. de La Rochefoucauld was infirm too, and this state of affairs made them necessary to each other. Nothing could be compared to the confidence and charm of their friendship. Just think, and you will see that it is impossible to sustain a more cruel loss which time can do less to heal. I have remained by her side all these days. She was not going to add to the family throng, so she needed someone to take pity on her. Mme de Coulanges has been very good too, and we shall be going on for some time at the expense of our spleen, which is full of melancholy.

That is the sort of climate in which your nice letters have come, and another note by way of replying to the first from M. de Marsillac. Such is their fate! So far they have only been admired by me and Mme de Coulanges, who found the Arnoton girls very amusing and the scene very elegant. M. de Grignan writes to perfection. When the Chevalier arrives I will hand them over; perhaps, after the first griefs are over, he will find a suitable time to say, 'There they are!' Meanwhile I have to write a sad one. He does honour to family affection and shows that you are not the only one, though, truth to tell, not many will be found to imitate you. All this sadness has stirred me and shown me the horror of separations. My heart is full of heaviness, and more than ever I beg you on my knees and in tears not to keep putting off the remedies M. de La Rouvière wants you to take and without which you can't get better. You are satisfied just to know about them, they are a standby, they are kept in a box, but your blood is getting no better and you often have pains in the chest. Yet you are content to know about the remedies and won't take them. And when you do decide to, my dearest, alas, perhaps your illness will be too far advanced. How can you possibly give me this bitter and continual grief? Are you afraid of getting well? Don't M. de La Rouvière and M. de Grignan mean anything to you?

And as for you, M. de Grignan, aren't you being cruel to take her to Marseilles and perhaps further still? Can you calmly make her rush about with you? Alas, you know how she needs rest, so how can you let her risk such fatigues? I beg you, through your affection for me, to explain this behaviour. Are you perfectly happy about her health, and wish for nothing better? Would to God it were so! I have noticed that you used to talk about her dear health; now you have given up mentioning it and I see you are taking her about.

And yet, my darling, M. le Coadjuteur, whom I have seen for a moment, has not satisfied me. He says that you are still writing and sometimes come out of your room so exhausted that you are un-recognizable. Good heavens, when I think that you are killing yourself for the people who love you most dearly in the world and would give their lives to save yours, and it is all for the sake of trivialities or correct answers that you are inflicting on us the cruellest worry one can experience, I declare you fill me with a strange trouble when you write more than a single page. Your last letter is too long, you are overdoing things for yourself and me, and as soon as you are a little better you do everything to make yourself ill again. Hold back that pen that runs so fast and so easily – it is a dagger. I don't want any more of it, for I am horrified at the harm it is doing you. The Coadjutor has told me that if somebody would cut off your right hand you would be bonny. Don't give yourself the treat of answering these bits of news, don't condescend to do so. I don't even remember them myself as soon as they have gone. My dearest, excuse the length of this topic; the Coadjutor has upset me and I am full of the awful grief of having lost someone I love. Alas, my dear, have pity on me.

To Madame de Grignan

[Paris, Friday 22 March 1680]

Well, my dear child, you have taken your delicate health to Marseilles, and M. de Grignan wanted you to. I am sure he will have taken you to Toulon and all the places Mlles de Grignan must be shown. He doesn't want to be separated from such good company, and he is right, I should certainly be of the same opinion. I am very glad my letters have not been taken to you at Marseilles. Lord, what would you have done with them? It is even quite a business to read them, and as for answering them – well, I forbid you to. I should very much begrudge the trouble you would take to hold forth about trifles I have already forgotten. I am sorry to have let you answer them even when you were well; the awful number of tomes has helped to make you thin. My dear child, I think of nothing but your health and your life. I know about life in Marseilles. Mlles de Grignan must have found that city pleasant; it is not at all like other towns. And the view as you approach from a certain height, weren't they charmed with that?

You mention a M. de Vivonne[1] very different from the other one. Aren't you amazed how people can change and how differently things come into one's head? So he was determined to do you the honours of his sea; I don't know whether the other mood, less good for him, might not have been healthier for you. I wish you enjoyed the same health as at that time or he the same fancy. You would have been on the sea; I hope that so much good nature hasn't hurt you. You were very surprised at this memory and all these names of bygone days, which brought back your earliest youth and first dances.

M. de Pomponne was here yesterday for part of the day. He studied your portrait attentively and recalled your beauty so tenderly, and your

1. M. de Vivonne, brother of Mme de Montespan.

wit and those lovely evenings at Fresnes, that it looked as though he would never stop. He gave me to believe that my eyes were reddening at the memory, but really he was as touched as I was, and I even think that a recollection of his present plight upset for a moment the tranquillity of his soul. He went to pay his respects to the King on the Court's return. It is a strange situation for him, and as he has always been either in exile or an ambassador or minister, he is not accustomed to the mob of courtiers. It would be somewhat more pleasant not to revisit that region, but a pension of 20,000 francs and hopes of some abbey tie him to these kinds of duties.

I gave up my place in Mme de Chaulnes's carriage to Mme de Vins. That duchess wanted me, but many reasons prevented my going. They are saying very nice things about Madame la Dauphine. She really is a personality with a real mind. She has charming and quite French manners, she is as at home in this Court as if she had been born there. She has sentiments which are entirely her own and doesn't accept those that are presented to her: 'Madame, do you not want to play cards?' 'No, I don't like gambling.' 'But you will go hunting?' 'By no means, that amusement is beyond my understanding.' What will she do, then? She is very fond of conversation, reading verse or prose, needlework, walking and above all pleasing the King. It is her one preoccupation, and she is also His Majesty's; he spends many hours in her room and none at all now in Mme de Montespan's. It makes for a very private Court, for nobody sees this princess while she has such good company. There is a circle there for only one hour of the day, and she will not be seen either at her toilet or on retiring to bed.

The favoured position of *the person with a cold* (which is what you called her last winter)[2] gains strength every day, as does the hatred between her and the sister of the man who received you so well. It has reached the point of no longer entering her room. Everything Madame la Dauphine says is right and well expressed. There is nothing to be desired in intelligence and humour – it is all so good that the rest is forgotten. The King instructed Monsieur le Dauphin about everything he had to do, and gave him a sort of geography lesson with which he highly diverted the courtiers.[3]

2. Mme de Maintenon.
3. The Dauphin was sexually backward and innocent.

Concerning M. le Prince de Conti, it is a strange thing what nasty rumours[4] are circulating about him; it is beginning to embarrass him. The young Prince de La Roche-sur-Yon upsets him. The other day Mme la Princesse de Conti was dancing and he said aloud, 'Indeed, there's a girl who dances well.' This sheer, ill-mannered silliness made the poor elder brother blush and took the stuffing out of him. What a lot of nonsense I'm telling you; it would be a fine undertaking to answer it all.

Dear old des Hameaux is *deceased*, as M. de Coulanges expresses it. She wanted her death to be reported in the *Gazette*, so that friends she still has abroad might pray for her, and she has requested that the main peal of bells be rung at Saint-Paul, and that a gentleman who lives in her house should not play cards on the day of her death. She leaves only a moderate fortune because she has spent it very honourably during her lifetime; and so our Blue Sisters are in mourning.

M. de Marsillac is overwhelmed with grief. His poor father is sadly on the road for Verteuil.[5] And as for Mme de La Fayette, the weather that is so lovely for others increases and will increase her melancholy.

I have not yet seen the Grignans, who are all scattered. My son has written me a long letter, still full of his reasons. I wanted to send it on to you, but if I had been able to copy the reply I wrote and show you how I rebut and laugh at all his arguments you really would have liked this letter.

To Guitaut

[Paris, Friday 5 April 1680]

There are two fell maladies, apart from the third, which is childbirth. Oh dear, how I pity you, my dear Sir, and how much better qualified I am than the next man to sympathize with your troubles! Alas, I spend my life worrying about my daughter's health. She had had a longish intermission and had tried some new remedies from a doctor at Aix whom she thinks very well of. She neglected these and has relapsed into discomforts which seem serious to me because they are internal. There

4. That he was impotent.
5. Verteuil was the country residence of the La Rochefoucauld family.

is heat and pain and heaviness in the left side which would be very dangerous if it went on all the time, but thank God she has times when she doesn't feel anything and that suggests that with a little perseverance in doing what is prescribed she would cool this blood that is being held responsible for all the pains. She has written to you. Oh, as you love her, beg her to stop writing in her own hand; it is the act of writing that is hurting her, quite obviously. Let her get Montgobert to write. I have got her to agree to write just one page herself and the rest by another hand. So I come back to assuring you that I do understand your troubles better than anybody else.

M. de La Rochefoucauld is dead, as you know, and it is a terrible loss. I have a friend who is inconsolable. You loved him, and you can imagine the tenderness and pleasure of an association filled with the greatest friendship and confidence possible between two people of quite uncommon merit. Add the circumstance of their ill-health, which made them so to speak indispensable to each other and gave them the leisure to savour each other's good qualities which is not found in other relationships. I think that at Court you haven't time to get fond of anybody. The whirlwind, so violent for everybody else, was calm for them and gave plenty of scope for enjoying such a delectable life together. I don't think any passion can be stronger than such a friendship. It was impossible to have been with him so often without being very attached to him, so that I have missed him both on my own account and on that of poor Mme de La Fayette, who would be thought lacking in friendship and gratitude were she less afflicted than she is. It is true that he has not long known the good fortune and wealth recently enjoyed by his family. He foresaw it all and spoke to me about it several times, for nothing escaped his wisdom and thought. He showed great courage in his death. We could talk about it for a long time.

And poor M. Foucquet, what do you think of his death? I believed that so many miracles for his preservation promised a happier end, but the *Essais de Morale*[1] condemn this profane talk and teach us that what we call riches are no such thing, and that if God has shown him mercy, and there is every appearance of it, that is true riches and the worthiest and happiest end one can hope for. That should be the object of all

---

1. By Nicole.

our desires if we were worthy to fathom these truths, and so we would correct our language as well as our ideas. That is another chapter, on which we could go on for a long time. This letter is becoming a list of chapters, and would be a volume if I said all I think. If the family of this poor man took my advice they would not bring him half out of prison. Since his soul has gone from Pignerol to Heaven I would leave his body there after nineteen years; it would go from there to the Valley of Jehoshaphat as easily as from a burial among his fathers. And as Providence has guided him in an extraordinary manner his tomb would be extraordinary too. I would find some piquancy in this thought, but Mme Foucquet will not share my opinion. The two brothers have become very close to each other; their hatred was the flaw in both of them, but more so in the Abbé, who carried it to insane lengths.

A fresh chapter: let us say a word about Madame la Dauphine, whom I have had the honour of seeing. True she has no beauty, but it is equally true that her intelligence suits her so perfectly that that is all you see, and you are solely concerned with the good grace and natural manner with which she finds her way through all her duties. No princess born in the Louvre could come through it better. It is a lot to have intelligence out of the common in this situation where usually one puts up with what politics gives one, and is fortunate indeed when one finds real worth. She is most obliging, but with dignity and without dullness. Her sentiments were all formed from her Munich days, and she does not adopt other people's. Somebody suggests playing cards: 'I don't care for cards.' A hunting expedition is proposed: 'I have never liked hunting.' 'What do you like, then?' 'I like conversation, I like being quiet in my room, I like my work.' All that is settled and can't be forced. What she really loves is to please the King. This desire is worthy of her intelligence, and she succeeds in this enterprise so well that the King gives her a big share of his time at the expense of his older lady friends, who are bearing this privation with a bad grace.

Just think, practically all the Fronde is dead. Many more will die. For my part the only consolation, if there is one, that I can find in losses one feels deeply is the thought that at any moment one may follow them, and that the very time you spend mourning them does not delay you for one moment; you are still moving along the road. What could not be said on that theme?

Good-bye, dear Sir. Let us always be very good friends. And you too, Madame, don't you want to join us? Let me know at once when you have enlarged the brood – it may be a little man. In fact, believe me, I take a great interest in the hen and her chicks. The good Abbé sends his kindest regards.

To Madame de Grignan

[Paris, Saturday evening, 6 April 1680]

You are about to learn some news that is no longer a secret, but you will have the pleasure of being one of the first to know it. Mme de Fontanges is a duchess with an income of 20,000 écus; today she was receiving compliments on her day-bed. The King went there openly. She takes her official stool tomorrow and then goes to spend Easter in an abbey the King has presented to one of her sisters. This is a kind of separation that will pay homage to his confessor's severity. Some people say that this establishment smacks of dismissal. I don't really believe it, but time will show.

Here is the present position: Mme de Montespan is furious. She wept a lot yesterday. You can imagine the tortures her pride is going through. It is even more outraged by the high favour of Mme de Maintenon. His Majesty often goes and spends a couple of hours after dinner in her room, chatting with a friendliness and free and easy air which make that place the most desirable in the world.

Mme de Richelieu is beginning to feel the effects of her dissipation; the machine is running down visibly. She presents everybody, but has stopped saying fitting words for each; the little business of lady in attendance, which she used to manage so well, is all at sixes and sevens. She presented La Trousse and my son to Monseigneur, omitting to name them. She said of the Duchesse de Sully, 'That's one of our dancers.' She did not name Mme de Verneuil. She nearly let the Dauphine kiss Mme de Louvois because she thought she was a duchess. In fine, this situation is dangerous and shows that little things do more harm than the study of philosophy. The search for truth does less to wear a poor brain out than all the compliments and nothings she is full of.

M. de Marsillac has appeared rather interested in the well-being of the lovely Fontanges; until then he had shown no sign of life.

Mme de Coulanges has just arrived at Court; I went purposely to see her before writing to you. She is charmed by Madame la Dauphine. She has good reason to be, for this princess has shown her very great affection. She knew her already from her letters and by the favourable way Mme de Maintenon had spoken of her. Mme de Coulanges went into a little room to which Madame la Dauphine retired after dinner with her ladies, and she had a delightful conversation. One could not have more wit and intelligence than this princess, she makes the whole Court love her. She is a person it is possible to please and on whom real worth can have a great effect.

Mme de Coulanges is still obsessed with our cousin. Her love no longer shows, but they are body and shadow. The Marquise de La Trousse is still crazy. Do you know she has changed in the matter of her daughter? She didn't want anything to do with her, now she does. And M. de La Trousse, who did, now doesn't. This antagonism settles the profession of the girl, who has no other. The father daren't bother about her or his wife because the lady treats it all with shocking contempt. So he has to stifle all natural feelings. *Pour qui? pour une ingrate* whom he no longer loves, as I know, but he is so miserable and abject that his weakness is like a passion. I have never seen less affection than in that love. My dear, that's all that comes into my head at the moment, but I feel I ought to have lots of things to say. Let me know when you get this letter, which is a bit like those of Cicero.[1]

To Madame de Grignan

[Rennes, Tuesday 6 August 1680]

I am wrong, dear, indeed I am the heretic. I offend the Jesuits, whereas you only attack baptism, so there's no comparison. Do you remember when *Tartuffe* was banned and *Le Festin de Pierre* was being played openly, what Monsieur le Prince said? That the one only aimed at overthrowing religion, but the other offended the zealots: *a l'applicazione, Signora*. But really I've many other things to say than

1. *those of Cicero*: i.e. dashed off at any time, not in usual routine of posts.

texts from St Paul; I have to tell you about the reception given yesterday in this town to Mme la Princesse de Tarente.

M. le Duc de Chaulnes first sent forty guards with the captain at their head to pay a compliment a good league away. A little later Mme de Marbeuf, two presidents, some friends of Mme la Princesse de Tarente, and finally M. de Chaulnes, Monsieur de Rennes, M. de Coëtlogon, de Tonquedec, de Beaucé, de Kercado, de *Crapodo*, de *Kenpart*, de *Keriquimini*; seriously, a *drapello eletto*. We all stop, kiss, sweat, don't know what we are saying. We advance, hear trumpets and drums, a crowd dying to shout something. Without vanity, I advise a brief call on Mme de Chaulnes. We found her with at least forty women and girls of quality, every one of whom was of good family. Most of them were the females of the men who had come out to meet us. I was forgetting to mention that there were six coaches with six, and more than ten with four horses. To come back to the ladies; I first found three or four of my *daughters-in-law*,[1] redder than fire, so frightened were they of me. I saw nothing to prevent my wishing them other husbands than Monsieur your brother. Everybody kissed, men and women alike. A strange performance. The princess showed me the way, and I followed her with admirable rhythm. Towards the end nobody could come away from the cheek he had got stuck to; it was a perfect union and the sweat ran down us. Eventually we climbed back into our carriage quite unrecognizable, and reached the home of Mme de Marbeuf, who has rearranged her house and had it furnished so suitably and all so tastefully and lavishly that she deserves all kinds of praises. We shut ourselves in our rooms and you can guess more or less what we did. I changed my underwear and other clothes, and without boasting I acquired a degree of beauty which quite outshone my *daughters-in-law*, so the honour of noble maternity was upheld with dignity.

We went back to Mme de Chaulnes's after she had returned with all her entourage, and we found the same arrangement, with lots of lights and two long tables set out with sixteen covers each, at which the whole company sat; it is the same set-up every evening. The time after supper was devoted to cards and conversation. But what really upset me was to see a pretty young madam, who certainly is no brighter than me, give

1. *my daughters-in-law*: Charles's lady friends.

two checkmates to M. le Duc de Chaulnes with an air of competence to make me die of envy. We came back here to sleep a delicious sleep, I woke up early and am writing to you, my dear, although my letter won't go until tomorrow. I am sure I shall describe to you the largest dinner, the largest supper and always the same things: noise, trumpets, violins, a parade of royalty, and you will conclude that the government of Brittany is very grand. And yet I have seen you in your little Provence accompanied by as many ladies, and M. de Grignan attended by as many gentlemen and received once at Lambesc as worthily as M. de Chaulnes can manage here. I reflected that you were receiving your court and that I have just paid mine; thus has Providence ordained.

I don't advise you to frame this painting of mine; I think it's hardly worth it. I only gauge their value by you. It can be said of this one as of Rubens: 'It is very realistic.' Moreover, my dear, if we want to put ourselves into frames, my room will be incomparably more beautiful than yours; I only scribble miserable narratives whereas you do finished reasonings and reflections with a brush I love and value. M. de La Garde writes bidding me farewell on his departure for Provence. He is off to look at a person I would very much like to see; I often examine and marvel how heartfelt my desire is. He has seen your apartment and likes it. He assures me that M. le Chancelier has similarly approved of the course M. de Grignan has taken about the First President, and that the Court will not hesitate about it. You are now on the very best of terms, and if he took advantage of this reconciliation I would advise you to fall out again so as to enjoy the one thing he can do well – be absent. You might even be wrong for a long time without his noticing it, so well has he established the bad opinion people have of him. I am anxious to know what upset he caused to the meal Montgobert had ordered.

You know well, my dear, that I share all your feelings, yet I want to teach you jealousy, at least in theory, and assure you (*credi a me pur che lo provato*)* that people sometimes say lots of things they don't think. And even if they did think them it would not be a sign of not loving; quite the reverse, if you dissect speeches of this kind, full of anger and resentment, you will find a great deal of real affection and attachment. There are delicate hearts, and when they are combined with over-

* 'Believe me, for I have experienced it.'

reasonable minds there is a marvellous progress in the land of jealousy. That is what my conscience obliges me to tell you; think it over. I won't go into any further detail at two hundred leagues distance.

[Wednesday morning, 7 August]

Dinner, grand supper with M. and Mme de Chaulnes, a thousand duty calls and convent ones, coming, going, paying compliments, wearing oneself out and going quite out of one's mind like a Maid of Honour, that's what we did yesterday, my dear. I long most passionately to be out of here, where they are doing me too much honour; I am totally famished for fasting and silence. I have not much intelligence, but here I seem to be spending what I have in small change, which I throw away and distribute in silly little things, and that is ruining me. Yesterday I saw men and women dancing very well, minuets and jigs couldn't be danced better. Just as I was thinking of you I heard a man behind me say quite loud, 'I have never seen anyone dance as well as Mme la Comtesse de Grignan.' I turned round and saw an unknown face. I asked him where he had seen this Mme de Grignan. He is a Chevalier de Cissé, brother of Mme Martel, and he saw you at Toulon with Mme de Sinturion. M. Martel gave you a reception in his ship; you danced and were as beautiful as an angel. I was delighted to meet this man but, my poor dear, I wish you could understand the emotion your name gave me, that the secret of my heart had been discovered when I expected it least.

I have found here part of a letter to a very fine gentleman from another very fine gentleman, who refers so amusingly to your funny little Monsieur d'Aleth that I wanted to send it to you, hoping it will amuse you as much as it did me.

Good-bye, child, good-bye, my unvarying taste, my inexhaustible affection. I shall finish on this note. I have to dine with Monsieur de Rennes; these feasts never stop. Oh Lord, when shall I be able to die of hunger and hold my tongue? I can't say another word: here come a thousand people. My dear, you say you aren't good-looking. If that is so, your thinness is continuing, you are deceiving me and are not well. I will write from Les Rochers, where I hope to be back tomorrow. I embrace everybody who is with you, my dearest.

To Madame de Grignan

[Les Rochers, 28 August 1680]

Yes indeed, my dear, I am very glad you are going to stay in bed, and however much fondness I have for your letters, you know that I care even more for your rest and health.

I am sure that baths, as you are now taking them, will do you as much good as the others did harm. This cold treatment was strange to imagine and even more to carry out, a little heat makes you perspire gently and can console all those poor subalterns without offending that most important person we put in the top rank.[1] Montgobert informs me that you are taking this remedy very seriously and seem to be anxious that it should benefit you. God grant it, my dear, and that so many pains and discomforts are ended by such gentle and elegant care! You can imagine my impatience to hear the outcome. By the time you get this letter it will be all over. That is the pleasure of being at a great distance, everything is different by the time you get letters and answers. For example, you advised me not to part company with M. le Chevalier de Cissé. I have not followed your advice, preferring the pleasure of thinking of you quite at my ease to that of talking about you with him.

You think that Pilois doesn't know your name? Make no mistake, my dear, he is too good a courtier, and often speaks to me about that pistole you gave him when he was in the depths of affliction about the death of his cow, and how but for that he would have been lost. So, my dear, wherever I am your name is celebrated; it flies, flies to the ends of the earth, since it is in this bit of country.

My son arrived a short time after my letters had gone; he brought Monsieur de Rennes and a very well-bred Marquis, a friend of M. de Lavardin, and one Abbé Charrier, son of our good friend at Lyons. The prelate was only here for one day, he left with the Marquis for Maine, where M. de Lavardin and his stout little wife have asked him to go. The Abbé has stayed here with your brother.

My child, there are some women who should be slain at public expense. Do you really grasp what I am saying? Yes, they should be

---

1. A rather feeble joke – the head *v.* the lower limbs.

slain. Perfidy, treachery, insolence, effrontery are the qualities they most normally make use of, and infamous dishonesty is the least of their faults. Moreover, not the slightest feeling, I don't say of love, for they don't know what it is, but I mean of the simplest friendship, natural charity, humanity. In fact they are monsters, but monsters who talk, who have intelligence and who present a front of brass, who are above all reproaches, enjoy triumphing over human weakness and abusing it, and who extend their tyranny over all sorts and conditions. Calculate how many there are in Brittany. We see clergy, nobility and the third estate all involved; that's just what I mean. Put a frame round all this pretty picture and you will have a portrait of a lady I will not name. Would it were the only such in the world! But there are people so sick that it will be a stroke of luck and a miracle if we are not obliged to go to extremes. People find consolation in moaning with me about these kinds of woes, and indeed I think I enter into them and understand them better than anybody.

My son has told me about a conversation he had with M. de La Trousse, thinking, taking Brancas's word for it, that he was *all sugar and honey*. But soon clouds covered the surface of the earth, and as soon as my son began to speak the weather worsened and from one thing to another it came to asking why he had taken up this rank. It reminded me of Hermione, when she asks Oreste after he has killed Pyrrhus on her orders, *Who told you to?* Whereupon Oreste goes out of his mind. My dear, I think your young brother would have gone mad like him had not his guardian angel supported him; anyhow, we shall see. It is certain that there is no hurry so long as he doesn't noise his plans abroad, for they are not really settled for Bouligneux. What one must try to do is have some opinion to present to M. de Louvois and get out of this position by having some other one that can be got out of more easily. Speak to M. de La Garde about it when you have him with you; we greatly respect your advice and his, and that of the Chevalier if he were there to take part in your discussions. That is what I can tell you about our affairs. I hope passionately that yours turn out in such a way as to mean that I can soon embrace you; that is the object of everything.

But isn't Mlle de Méri thinking of finding a house? When she had her own on her hands she said that there were a thousand to let; she doesn't need so many. It would be annoying if she made it awkward for you to come back, and if unfortunately you did not, one could put it to better use than leaving you with that little expense on your hands. My dear, I am always thinking of your interests, great and small; to you I can talk plainly about them.

I am told that the Queen is very happy with the Court and that she has shown so much kindness and interest on this journey, going to see all the fortifications without complaining of heat or fatigue, that this behaviour has called forth many kind attentions.[2] I don't know whether the others have done as well. Madame la Dauphine said the other day, admiring Pauline in *Polyeucte*, 'Well, that is the most virtuous woman in the world, who doesn't love her husband in the least.' How is yours, my dear, whom you do love and I love too? How is the *pinprick*?[3] Does he only embrace me today with his left arm? For my part I am using my two arms, but gently, for fear of hurting him.

From Charles de Sévigné

I have found one of your letters here, little sister, but at the same time I saw the one you wrote to Mother; it made me nearly die of laughter in spite of the terrors that have attacked me these two or three days. They are beginning to go off a bit, and I hope that if my illness hasn't a fine Greek name it can at least be named in French without making anyone blush, even Mlles de Grignan.[4] M. de Grignan's *pinpricks* and the tenderness with which you made him yell at the top of his voice for two nights, and this fine name *arthritis* with which they have baptized a very ordinary gout, seemed worthy of having a frame too. The picture Mother paints of women who ought to be suffocated between two mattresses is done to the life, but I beg you to keep this secret and not to mention it either to M. de La Garde or anyone else, still less to name Monsieur d'Evreux. You can easily guess why. This prelate's star has rid him of his old predecessor, and the Chevalier's is also beginning to be more favourable. I would begin to tremble if one of them had married you, but that of M. de Grignan reassures me and I hope to resist it myself for a bit longer. But they say that

2. *kind attentions*: from the King.
3. Grignan's rheumatism or gout.
4. *even Mlles de Grignan*: in fact he learned later that it was a venereal disease.

prosperity usually comes with gout. He is still only at the *arthritis* stage, and that sets my mind at rest. Thank you a thousand times for the real interest you are taking in my affairs. They are in a very parlous state; all or nothing. Providence will decide. And if they turn out ill you might lose more than me.

Good-bye, lovely young sister; I kiss and embrace you. At any rate I am very well. I also embrace M. de Grignan and continue my respectful bows to Mlles de Grignan. If M. de La Garde is with you please remember me kindly to him, and as to the worthy *Gobert*, please give her a bit of a wallop on my behalf.

So good-bye, dearest, for we must always return to our muttons. Your letters have been a great entertainment for us; we put your name back in its native air.[5]

We have found summer again these last two days. We must put on our summer clothes again without losing sight of our winter ones; such is France. Your hot weather is very suitable for your baths; I finish, dear, where I began, by hoping with all my heart that they do you good. The good Abbé sends a thousand fatherly words. My profound respects to Monsieur the Archbishop and my affection and esteem to Mlles de Grignan. I kiss my grandchildren and embrace my daughter, my dear, beloved daughter.

To Bussy-Rabutin

[Paris, Saturday 4 December 1683]

If, my poor cousin, you knew what it means to marry your son, you would forgive my having been so long without writing. I am in the middle of most lively dealings with mine, who is in Brittany and on the point of marrying a young lady of good family, whose father is a councillor in Parlement and worth more than sixty thousand francs a year. He is giving two hundred thousand to his daughter, and so it is a good marriage as times are now. There have been many things to sort out before being able to sign the articles, which we did four days ago. I wish you the same bothers, dear cousin, and I promise in that case

5. *its native air*: she was Breton by birth.

to accept your excuses for not having written to me for a long time as I beg you to accept mine. I have heard that Mme de Bussy is in Paris, although I had heard that she was going to Burgundy with you. Good-bye, cousin, good-bye, niece. I hand you both over to my dear Corbinelli after embracing you most affectionately. My daughter asks me to say the same for her.

From Corbinelli

I am so glad your health is back to its usual perfection, Monsieur. Go on taking care of it. The Spanish Council has resolved to declare war on us, from what the Queen of Spain has written to Monsieur. People are arguing furiously about the vainglorious pride of a nation we have insulted so many times with impunity, and which can show it again after the Prince of Orange has been turned down by the States when he asked them for commissions for sixteen thousand men. Politicians are saying that it is an act of desperation not without subtlety, and that they don't want to be burdened with looking after the rest of Flanders, which is no use to them and only brings them insults; that either the Dutch and Flemings will enter the war and defend their common interests, in which case they will have been right to start the war, or they will refuse to come in and Spain will be very glad to give them a master and be free of responsibility for the provinces which are reduced to skin and bone. That is how people are reasoning here about this unhoped-for audacity.

To Mauron[1]

[Paris, Wednesday 8 December 1683]

Monsieur, it is not possible that, by reflecting a little, not only on what has happened during the past two months, but also in four years, you can fail to be sure that I have never wished anything for my son more strongly than the honour of being connected with your family. This letter would go beyond all normal limits if I attempted to express all

1. Baron de Mauron, wealthy Breton nobleman. Charles married his daughter, Marguerite de Mauron.

my feelings about the sincere and genuine joy this hope gives me. I cannot help flattering myself that when you know me you will view me in a different way from that in which you have so far. We shall have conversations which will reveal my heart and the esteem and respect I have for your qualities.

I have sent you, Monsieur, some signed articles that are not strictly speaking in form, but merely to show you that we agree with everything you have wished, pending the authorizations that enable you to draw up the contract. Our own are of no importance, but that of M. de Grignan, who is in Provence and whom my daughter's letters have not found where she thought he was, is the sole cause of this delay, for I assure you, Monsieur, that there is nothing lacking in his goodwill. She will tell you herself how happy she is to send her consent. We understand that it will reach you as soon as possible, but we cannot hurry it up any more than we have done.

I very humbly beg you to believe, Monsieur, that I would go to Brittany with the greatest pleasure in the world to be a witness to the one thing in the world I have always wished for most, if I were not tied to my uncle the Abbé de Coulanges, whose age of over seventy-six does not allow him to make this journey at this time of year. I trust that you will find that this excuse is all too good and true, and that in spite of that you will believe me no less zealously, Monsieur, your most humble, obedient servant

M. de Rabutin-Chantal.

From Bussy-Rabutin

[Chaseu, Friday 10 December 1683]

As I have married off daughters, Madame, I do suspect what the bothers are of marrying a son, and bearing that in mind I forgive you for not having answered earlier. Two hundred thousand francs have at any time been a good marriage, but it is true that in this one the sum means more than it did twenty years ago. If it were only a matter of signing I wish you the same bothers you have had and that you wish me, but the implications make me nervous. Mme de Bussy has not left Paris; we had decided she would come with me to Burgundy, but when she realized I had to return so quickly her weight would not fit in with this haste.

Good-bye, dear cousin. My daughter and I love you with all our hearts and we both assure the fair *Madelonne* of our most humble service.

To Corbinelli

If the Council of Spain considers that it cannot endure any more outrages from us than it has so far without losing face, it will be right to congratulate itself on the break; it must save its reputation as well as its lands. The reasoning of the politicians seems very good to me, and it will certainly be justified by the outcome.

To Bussy-Rabutin

[Paris, Wednesday 15 December 1683]

At last, after so many tribulations, I shall marry my poor son. I am asking for your authorization to put a signature to his marriage contract. I enclose two little formal letters, which please hand to my aunt and my cousin. We must never despair of good fortune. I thought that my son had no hope left of a good match after so many storms and shipwrecks, with no position of his own or path to fortune. And while I was entertaining these gloomy thoughts Providence was holding in store, or had all along held in store for us, such an advantageous marriage that even when my son could most hope for it I could not have desired a better. Thus we live and move like the blind, not knowing where we are bound, taking for evil what is good, taking for good what is evil, and always in total ignorance.

Would you ever have believed, moreover, that Père Bourdaloue, carrying out the last wishes of President Perrault, had delivered six days ago at the Church of the Jesuits the most beautiful funeral oration for the late Monsieur le Prince it is possible to imagine? No action has been more rightly admired. He looked at the prince from the most advantageous points of view, and as his return to the faith made a great effect for Catholics, this aspect, as handled by Père Bourdaloue, made the finest and most Christian panegyric ever pronounced. If it is printed I will send you a copy. Good-bye, dear cousin, and your charming daughter. I embrace you both.

To Charles de Sévigné

[Paris, 5 August 1684]

While waiting to hear from you I must tell you a very pretty little story. You repined about Mlle de Garaud, you counted it as one of your misfortunes that you had not married her; your best female friends were outraged by your good fortune – Mme de Lavardin and Mme de La Fayette were by way of cutting your throat. A well-connected girl, good-looking and with a hundred thousand écus! A man must really be destined never to be established and to end his days like some poor wretch if he does not take advantage of matches of such consequence when they are within his grasp. The Marquis d'Alègre was not so hard to please, so she was well established. One must have a curse on one to have failed to pull that affair off – look at the life she leads. She is a saint, an example for all women. It is true, my dearest, that until you had married Mlle de Mauron you were ready to hang yourself; you could not have done anything better. But wait for the outcome. All those fine tendencies of her youth, which made Mme de La Fayette say that she would not have wanted her for her own son, even with a million, had turned, happily, towards God. He was her lover, the object of her love, everything had combined in this one passion. But as everything in this creature is extreme, her head was unable to stand up to this excess of zeal and burning charity with which she was possessed, and to satisfy this Magdalene's heart of hers she wished to benefit from the inspiring examples and uplifting reading of the *Lives of the Holy Fathers of the Desert* and pious penitent women. She wanted to be the Don Quixote of these admirable stories. So two weeks ago she set out at four in the morning with four or five pistoles and a young manservant. She found a post-chaise in the suburbs. In she climbs and off she goes to Rouen, dirty and dishevelled for fear of some unfortunate encounter. Having got to Rouen she makes arrangements to embark on a ship bound for the Indies. That is where God summons her, that is where she wishes to serve her penance, where she has seen on the map places calling her to end her days in sackcloth and ashes, where Abbé Zosime will come and administer the sacrament when she dies. She is pleased with her resolve, she sees that that is exactly what God requires of her. She discharges the young servant and sends him home. She waits impatiently for the vessel to sail, her guardian angel must console her for all the moments that delay her departure. She has piously forgotten husband, daughter, father and all the family. She says repeatedly, *Ça courage, mon coeur, point de faiblesse humaine.**

Her prayers seem to be answered, she is reaching the blessed moment separating her for ever from our continent. She is obeying the law of the Gospel, leaving all to follow Jesus. Meanwhile at home it is noticed that she is not back for dinner. They scour the nearby churches – no sign of her. They think she will come home in the evening – no news. They begin to be astonished, question the servants who know nothing. She has a young servant with her, no doubt she will be at Port-Royal des Champs – she is not. Where can she be? They run to the curé of Saint-Jacques-du-Haut-Pas. He says that for a long time now he has given up the care of her conscience, and that seeing her full of extraordinary thoughts and wild desires for a solitary retreat, and being himself a simple and sincere man he did not want to be involved with her behaviour. They don't know who else to seek help from. One day, two, three, six days go by, they send off to the various seaports, and by a strange chance find her at Rouen, on the point of leaving for Dieppe and from there to the ends of the earth. They catch her and bring her neatly back. She is a bit put out: *J'allais, j'étais . . . l'amour a sur moi tant d'empire.*†

Somebody in her confidence gives her plans away. In the family they are very upset and seek to hide this folly from her husband who is away from Paris and would much prefer an infidelity to such an escapade. The husband's mother weeps with Mme de Lavardin, who is helpless with laughter and says to my daughter, 'Will you forgive me now for having prevented your brother from marrying this Infanta?'

---

*Courage, my heart, no human weakness!' Adapted from: *'Allons, ferme, mon Coeur,/Point de faiblesse humaine!'* Molière, *Tartuffe*, IV, 3.

† 'I was going, I was . . . love holds such sway over me.' Rotrou, *Venceslas*, IV, 4.

This tragic story is also recounted to Mme de La Fayette, who has repeated it to me with relish and asks me to ask you whether you are still angry with her. She maintains that nobody could ever regret not having married a madwoman. Nobody dare say anything about it to Mlle de Grignan, her friend, who is muttering something about a pilgrimage, and, so as to get the business done with, enveloping herself in a profound silence. What do you think about this little tale? Were you bored with it? Aren't you glad?

Good-bye, my son. M. de Schomberg is on the march in Germany with twenty-five thousand men; it is to hurry up the Emperor's signature.[1] The *Gazette* will tell you the rest.

To Mademoiselle de Scudéry

[Monday, 11 September 1684]

In a hundred thousand words I could only tell you one truth, which comes down to assuring you, Mademoiselle, that I shall love and adore you all my life; there is no word but this to comprehend the idea I have of your extraordinary worth. I often make it a subject of wonderment and of my good fortune in having some share in the friendship and esteem of such a person. As constancy is a mark of perfection I tell myself that you will not change for me, and I venture to boast that I shall never be so God-forsaken as not to be always entirely devoted to you. In that confidence I am leaving for Brittany, where I have countless things to do. I say good-bye to you and embrace you with all my heart. I ask you to convey my best friendship to M. de Pellisson; you will answer to me for his feelings. I am taking your *Conversations* to my son; after being charmed myself I want him to be charmed with them too.

To Madame de Grignan

[Les Rochers, Wednesday 11 April 1685]

You really are too kind, my dear Comtesse, to send me just a word about Versailles. I marvel at you in this whirlwind; you make me die

1. The double treaty of Ratisbon between France and Spain and France and the Empire.

267

with laughing. I see you with your mouth full going to the sermon, then, all emotional from the sermon, straight to the play. This is all very fine, my dear, but come back and rest; when you have a pain in your side it is taking advantage of it and exasperating it to do too many things in one day. I am asking you to keep yourself fit just as you ask me to. It is so easy for you to judge my feelings by your own that you are guilty when you risk giving me endless worry. You must stop being worried about me. Just at the moment it is the weather that is preventing my exercising my new leg. I am still treating it as a visitor; it is not for everyday use. It is a stranger I want to get used to me very gradually. I am not expecting anything unusual or extravagant from it; when it has done a big walk I don't expect it to start again, as I would the other one. In fact I treat this newcomer with consideration.

I gave your compliments to the Aesculapean Fathers;[1] I tell you they receive them from all over Europe. You are not in the know about this affair, which is why you won't understand the force of my argument. These good Fathers, who were like people ready to retire stained with ignominy, have been delighted to be re-established in their good reputation by the judgement of Solomon, for that is what the King's decree looks like. It is believed that the Duc de Chaulnes has become First Minister because of it, and that is a great thing for them. The whole province has in its hands the statement of the Fathers and in its mind the certainty of their innocence, with joy at their triumph and all that precedes and follows it. In fact, Monsieur le Duc, I rejoice with you at the glory that comes to you from all this because I love and admire you; my daughter will answer for that.[2]

What do you mean, dear child, about your dreams? What are you up to, taking my poor person as object of your sick imagination? You see me in an awful state, and that upsets you and makes you feel a pain I haven't got. Ah, my dear, you would be quite reassured if you could see me at present; ask the princess. Won't you thank her for the celestial electuary she sends you? I would have done so myself were it not that she has often asked to see the part of your letters concerning her, and I should not like to be caught out.

1. The Capuchins of the Louvre. The King had granted some Capuchins, who had brought back some remedies from the East, permission to occupy premises in the Louvre for research.
2. Passage intended for the Duke.

I have just written to little Coulanges. The whim came over me to preach to him about his wicked little conscience, the number of sins on which he cuts down annually, being afraid of reaching the limit without ever losing the quality, for I am sure that by the end of the week at Bâville his only sin, which is *gaudeamus*, will be as deep-rooted as ever before. Everybody is more or less the same. The difference is that his habit is less shameful and wicked than that of many people, and so they are more prone to take the liberty of scolding him. I beg him to tell M. de Lamoignon that I accept with great pleasure the arrangement to meet you for the month of September at Bâville.

I wish that the abbés you have named were already named by His Majesty; their time will come. I think this arrangement is very praise-worthy and pleasant for people of quality no longer to sell the position of chaplain.[3] Oh, what a fine seminary that will make! Will you please ask the Abbé Bigorre to remind Cardinal de Bouillon of the little pittance given to me every year out of the King's bounty? It isn't much, but it means the livelihood of some poor person. I will tell you where this money should be sent.

To Madame de Grignan

[Les Rochers, Sunday 26 August 1685]

What do you think of the 26th, my dear child? It is even better than your 22nd, and you will see how all the rest will turn out well, God willing – God willing, for therein lies the whole business. Tell me the exact date when you go to Bâville so that I can come the following day. Don't come any further, just rest and let me arrive and don't tire yourself. If you had any doubts about my sincere and perfect joy I should doubt yours. Don't let us take offence, but let us do justice to each other. On my part, for fear of upsetting myself, I refuse to envisage anything unpleasant in the future. I want to see the wedding of Mlle d'Alérac at Livry in that same room;[1] it is a fête that should honour that forest yet again. I shall be delighted to be involved in it. Why have you been so seldom to Versailles? It's a lot of bother for a moment. I

3. The King had vetoed it in March 1685.
1. *in that same room*: i.e. where Mme de Grignan was married.

see you are still pleased with Mme d'Arpajon; if we had chosen a matron of honour I don't think we could have wished for any other. I like your Grignans for putting themselves out for me. I am their *bonne* as I am yours.

My son has come back from the States with M. de La Trémouille, who is received at Vitry like the most alien of the German princes. I think Les Rochers will go and dine at Vitry and Vitry will return to supper at Les Rochers. M. de Chaulnes will soon be able to tell you as many tales as my son is telling us here. I doubt whether you will be able to pay as much attention, but roughly: M. de Chaulnes has had troubles that at last have been relieved and set to rights, M. d'Harouys has reason to be satisfied with the States and all his friends, and that is enough to put your mind at rest. I don't know who will be in a position to let you have news from Paris when I am no longer here! I would be telling you a lot today if I wrote all I know, but I prefer to save it for Bâville.

I am astonished that our young Coulanges is not alarmed at Mme de Louvois's anger. He makes out that it will not be much bother to justify himself and doesn't want to write; he wants to talk. But meanwhile people are finding confirmation for all they believe, they are complaining and angry and saying harsh things and getting used to regarding us now simply as enemies. Aren't you amazed that there are people spiteful enough to heap on to this poor little man a thousand things he has probably never thought of? At least get him a chance to be heard and let them observe the rule not to condemn without hearing. He is at Chaulnes and will write to you.

I am not referring to my leg because there is nothing left to say about it, and I am enjoying the pleasure of being cured and going out for walks night and morning. You will see for yourself and you will love Charlotte. Meanwhile I embrace you heartily and shall dream of anything that can gently flatter my hopes. I feel that I am beginning to neglect my writing. I am aspiring to something better, although to tell the truth corresponding with you is the most pleasant thing in the world after you yourself.

I very much hope that what I have written about M. de La Trousse does not get back to its source nor into our neighbourhood. You can see perfectly well I am right and that this is for you only. We went yesterday to the Princesse de Tarente and saw her son. Oh, how well set up he is and how ugly! He is not the first to be like that. My son sends his very best love. He has been cured of his slight temperature, as I have, by taking an infusion. Good-bye, my lovely, I kiss you on both cheeks. Are you still beautiful and buxom? I hope to know very soon if God spares me.

To Bussy-Rabutin

[Livry, Sunday 28 October 1685]

Here I am, cousin, with my daughter, her son, her stepdaughter, the good Abbé and the loveliest weather in the world. We could do with our friend Corbinelli to warm up and enliven our society, but we can't always have him when we want. He has other friends, business, he loves his freedom, and yet we go on loving him. I shall send him this letter to put his answer to you at the end. He will probably let you know the hour and the moment of the death of the Chancellor.[1] Yesterday he was at death's door. His steadfastness is an example to all who want to die as Christians. To achieve that happy combination is all one could wish for. With time you will be avenged on all those you complain of. There is one in particular, whose youth is a little difficult to wear out, but what does time not destroy? You are very well, and *if God be for us who can be against us*?

You probably know that M. de Lamoignon has lost his brother-in-law. I have always heard you say that expectations stifled the feelings of nature. If that is so it must be all laughter in that household. Yet I saw tears there which seemed genuine to me. As well as being a brother he was still a friend. I am delighted to have met both the husband and wife. People very rightly love them when they get to know them.

I wish you could have swelled the good company at Bâville: it would then have been perfect. I always like Père Rapin, he is a good and cultured man. He was supported by Père Bourdaloue, whose mind is fascinating and delightfully agile. On the King's orders he is off to preach at Montpellier and in those provinces where so many have been converted without knowing why. Père Bourdaloue will teach them why and turn them into good Catholics. The dragoons have been very good

1. Le Tellier.

missionaries so far, and the preachers being sent now will make the work perfect. You will no doubt have seen the Edict by which the King revokes that of Nantes. Nothing is so fine as everything it contains, and no king has ever done nor will do anything more memorable.[2]

From Madame de Grignan

I accept you as handsome, Monsieur, and I treated you as such when I answered the letter you did me the kindness to write when you sent your *Genealogy*. Even had I wanted to look down on you that would have stopped me, but truly, Monsieur, I am far from that. I like your humour and respect your merit as I should. As for your person, I take such great interest in it that I insist on knowing what diet you have followed to make two chins out of the loose skin I saw. M. de Grignan has developed this superfluity and I should be very glad for him to become once more as handsome as you by following your advice.

I gladly gave up my pen to my daughter. She has told you herself how far she is from forgetting you or ever being able to forget you.

Good-bye, dear cousin. Good-bye, dear niece. You are in a state of peace if you await death as you say, *Sans la désirer ni la craindre.**

What wisdom! And what folly to worry about it except in connection with Christianity and the arrangements necessary for this final act!

Extract from Bussy-Rabutin's reply, 24.11.1685

I admire the King's measures to destroy the Huguenots. The wars against them in earlier times and the Saint Bartholomew massacres only multiplied and encouraged this sect. His Majesty has weakened it little by little, and the Edict he has just promulgated, helped by the dragoons and people like Bourdaloue, has put the finishing touch.

---

* 'Neither desiring nor fearing it.'

2. This paragraph on the Revocation of the Edict of Nantes is typical of the general attitude. Unmoved by atrocious cruelty, blind to political and economic folly, ordinary people felt that the different, the non-conforming, must be criminal or dangerous and should be converted or stamped out. Note also Bussy-Rabutin's reply.

To Bussy-Rabutin

[Paris, Monday 10 March 1687]

Once again here come death and sorrow, my dear cousin. But how can one avoid telling you about the finest, the most magnificent, most triumphal funeral pageantry ever known since mortals have existed? It is that of the late Monsieur le Prince, which took place today at Notre-Dame. All the great minds have worked themselves to exhaustion to celebrate all this great prince has done and all he has been. His forefathers, as far back as Saint Louis, are represented on medallions, all his victories on bas-reliefs, covered as if by tents with corners turned up and held by skeletons in admirable attitudes. The mausoleum, reaching almost to the vaulting, is covered by a canopy like a pavilion which reaches even higher, the four corners of which fall like tents. The whole choir area is adorned with these bas-reliefs, with devices beneath them telling of all the phases of his life. Then of his alliance with the Spaniards is represented by a dark night in which three Latin words say: *What happens far from the sun must be hidden*.[1] Everything is sown with fleurs-de-lys of a sombre hue, and beneath is a little lamp shining with ten thousand tiny stars. I forget the half of it, but you will have the book which will tell you all the details. If I hadn't been afraid it had been sent to you already I would have enclosed it in this letter, but you would not have liked this duplication. Everybody has been to see this grandiose decoration. It is costing the present Monsieur le Prince 100,000 francs, but this expense does him great honour. The funeral oration was pronounced by Monsieur de Meaux; it will appear in print. That, dear cousin, is very roughly the plot of the play. If I had dared to venture to make you pay double carriage you would be better pleased. So here we are back in sorrow.

But to enliven you a little I am about to pass from one extreme to another, that is to say from death to a marriage, from excess of ceremony to excess of intimacy, with both as original as possible. I am referring to the son of the Duc de Gramont, aged fifteen, and the daughter of M. de Noailles. They are to be married this evening at Versailles. This is how: nobody is invited, nobody is informed,

1. *Lateant quae sine sole.*

everyone will have supper or a collation at home. At midnight the bridal pair will be brought together to be taken to the parish church, without the mothers and fathers being present unless they are already at Versailles. They will be married. There will be no great display of clothes, they will not be officially put to bed; the duty of putting them together in the same bed will be left to the governess and tutor. Next morning it will be assumed that everything has passed off properly. There will be no teasing, no witticisms, no nasty jokes. They will get up, the boy will go to Mass and the King's dinner, the young person will dress as usual and go off to pay visits with her grandmother. She will not be lying on her bed like a village bride, exposed to all the tiresome visitors, and all this wedding (an affair usually marked by a lot of fuss) will merge in the prettiest and most natural way into all the other actions of life and has been worked so imperceptibly into normal routine that nobody has noticed that some celebration has happened in these two families. This is what I mean to fill up this letter with, dear cousin, and I maintain that this picture, in its way, is as singular as the other.

I have just seen a prelate who was at the funeral oration. He told us that Monsieur de Meaux had surpassed himself and that never has such a fine subject been so nobly brought out or expressed. I have seen Monsieur d'Autun here once or twice. He seems very friendlily disposed towards you; I find him very pleasant and from the gentleness and ease of his manner I can quite understand how attached one is to him when one gets to know him. He has had friends of such exalted position who have loved him so long and so dearly that that in itself is a reason for valuing him even if one did not know him personally. The Provençal lady sends you her best respects. She is involved in a lawsuit which makes her closely resemble the Countess of Pimbêche.[2]

I rejoice with you that you have to cultivate the body and mind of the Coligny boy.[3] It is a *fine name to have to medicate*, as Molière says, and it is a pleasure we have here every day with young Grignan. Good-bye, dear cousin, good-bye, dear niece. Keep your loves for us and we guarantee you ours. I don't know whether that plural is right, but whether it is or not I shan't alter it.

2. Countess of Pimpêche, litigious old lady in *Les Plaideurs* of Racine.
3. Bussy-Rabutin's grandson.

From Corbinelli

I shall not say anything today, Sir, except that I honour you totally. I have just finished a book entitled *The Truth of the Christian Religion*, which to my mind is a perfect book. I shall end by assuring you that I am devoted to you and to your wonderful daughter.

To Bussy-Rabutin

[Paris, Thursday 13 November 1687]

I have just received a letter from you, dear cousin, the kindest and most affectionate that ever was. I have never seen friendship explained so naturally and so persuasively. Anyway, you have persuaded me, and I believe that my life is essential to the preservation and enjoyment of yours. So I am going to give you an account of it to reassure you and show you my present state.

I take up my story from the last days of my dear uncle the Abbé, to whom, as you know, I was infinitely indebted. I owed him all the sweetness and repose of my life, and it is to him you owe the joy I brought into your society. Without him we should never have laughed together, you owe him all my gaiety, my good humour and vivacity, the gift I had of grasping what you said, the intelligence that made me understand what you had said and guess what you were about to say, in a word the good Abbé, rescuing me from the abyss in which M. de Sévigné had left me, restored me to what I was, to what you have seen me, worthy of your esteem and friendship. I draw the veil over your shortcomings, which are great, but I must forget them and tell you that I felt keenly the loss of this lovable source of all the peace and rest of my life. He died in seven days of a continuous fever, like a young man, with most Christian sentiments which touched me very deeply, for God has given me a foundation of religion which has made me look closely at this last act of life. His life lasted eighty-four years. He lived with honour and died a Christian. God show us the same mercy! It was at the end of August that I wept bitterly for him.

I would never have left him if he had lived until the day of my death.

But seeing by the 15th or 16th September that I was all too free, I decided to go to Vichy to cure at any rate my imagination about some kind of spasms in my left hand and suggestions of vapours which put fear into me about apoplexy. This proposed journey made Mme la Duchesse de Chaulnes want to do it too. I joined her, and as I rather wanted to go on to Bourbon I remained with her. She only wanted Bourbon, so I had Vichy water, which is excellent when warmed up in the wells of Bourbon. I took some and then Bourbon water to follow, a very good mixture. These two rivals made it up between them until they were but one heart and soul. Vichy rests in Bourbon's bosom and warms herself at her fireside, that is to say in the bubblings of her fountains. It did me a great deal of good, and when I asked for a douche it was refused and they derided my fears, treated them as vague imaginings and sent me away as a person in perfect health. They assured me of it so strongly that I believed it and now consider myself such. My daughter is delighted, for she loves me, as you know.

So that is how things are with me. As your health depends on mine you have a great store laid up. Look after your cold and by so doing do me good, too. We must always keep together and not let each other go.

I have been back from Bourbon three weeks now. Our pretty little abbey was not yet given away, and we spent twelve days there. Now it has been given to the former Bishop of Nîmes, a very devout prelate. I left there three days ago, very upset at having to say good-bye for ever to that pleasant solitude I loved so much. After mourning for the Abbé I mourned for the abbey.

I know you wrote to me during my journey to Bourbon. I have not taken time off today to answer you, but have given in to the temptation to talk about myself with no curb, no reticence, no measure. I beg forgiveness and assure you that next time I shan't take the same liberty, for I know, and Solomon says so, that the person who talks about himself is hateful. Our friend Corbinelli says that to realize how much we bore people by talking about ourselves we must think how others bore us when they talk about themselves.[1] This is a pretty general rule, but I think I can exempt myself today, for I should be delighted if your pen were as inconsiderate as mine and overjoyed if

1. Vital seventeenth-century classical idea, *le moi est haïssable*. Corbinelli's reasoning is pure La Rochefoucauld. cf. Molière.

you talked for a long time about yourself. That is what persuaded me to embark upon this terrible discourse, and with that confidence I will not make excuses, so I embrace you, dear cousin, and the charming Coligny.

Many thanks to Mme de Bussy for her compliments. I would let myself be slain rather than be made to write any more.

To Bussy-Rabutin

[Paris, Wednesday 3 November 1688]

I have been so taken up, dear cousin, with capturing Philippsburg that in truth I've not had a moment to write. I had waived everything else to such a degree that I was like those people whose concentration prevents their getting their breath back. So it is over, thank God. I sigh like M. de La Souche and breathe at my leisure. And do you know why I was so taken up? Because that little Grignan child was in it. Think of a youth of seventeen, just emerging from under his mother's wing, and still afraid he might be catching a cold. She suddenly has to leave him and send him to Philippsburg, and with unheard-of cruelty to herself has to set off with her husband for Provence and thus remove herself from news one can't want to be too close to, and in fact for fifteen days on end has to turn her back and never take a step that doesn't take her further from her boy and anything that can bring news of him. I am frightened myself as I write this, and am sure that loving the Comtesse as you do (for you know that you love her), you will be touched by the state she is in. It is true that God consoles her for her worries with the joy of knowing that at the moment her son is in good health. She will have been in a state of worry for six days longer than us; those are the disadvantages of distance.

So this stronghold is taken. Monseigneur has done miracles of firmness, skill, liberality, generosity and humanity, distributing money wisely, saying good things about people, doing kindnesses, asking for rewards and writing letters to the King that were the admiration of the Court. It has been a pretty good campaign, all the Palatinate and most of the Rhineland ours, good winter quarters and the wherewithal for quietly awaiting the decisions of the Emperor and the Prince of

Orange. It is believed that the latter has embarked, but the wind is such a good Catholic that so far he has been unable to set sail.[1] It is said that M. de Schomberg is with him, which is a great pity for that Marshal and for us. The affairs of Rome are still going badly.

But what is this that I have heard about 2,000 francs income for M. de Bussy and promise of a suitable place? I realize that that means your son, and pending my sorting out the rumour I congratulate you, dear cousin, and you, my niece, and rejoice at this beginning. He had not followed Monseigneur; this good fortune has befallen him when he was least expecting it.

Corbinelli is in Normandy with the Civil Lieutenant. I think you know that, so as to relieve Mme de Montataire of all worry, the *Canon* has been good enough to let herself die; that really is a kindness I didn't think her capable of, for she had assured me not long ago that she knew perfectly well she would never win anything against Montataire, but that she preferred to torment herself to the last degree rather than leave her in peace. I hope she hasn't taken that sentiment into the other world.

You know the news about the killed and wounded at Philippsburg, but I can inform you of the natural deaths of Mmes de Mesmes and de Château-Gonthier. And then we shall depart after the others; I am always thinking of that, my friend.

To Madame de Grignan

[Paris, Friday 5 November 1688]

Yesterday I took a little dose as recommended by my Capuchins. It was to clear my system; all it did was to sweep through me with a big broom. It was their idea and it made me perfectly well. I was a little vexed at not seeing you take possession of this room first thing in the morning and question me, lecture me, examine and govern me, and help me at the slightest sign of the vapours. Ah, my dear child, how comforting and nice all that is! What sad sighs I have heaved at not

1. William of Orange did not sail until the 11th, and landed at Torbay on the 15th. For Schomberg, see List of Persons.

having any more of these very natural marks of your affection! And that coffee you drink, and the dress that comes for you, and your morning visitors hunting you down and following you about, against whom my curtain acts as a screen. Truly, my child, one loses everything when one loses you. Nobody has ever mingled such charms with affection as you do. I am always telling you, you spoil the job, for everything else is flat and insipid when one has experienced it. M. de La Garde talked to me some time ago along these lines and I had thought on certain occasions that you cruelly concealed all these treasures from me, but, my dear, you have uncovered them. I know your heart to be quite perfect and full of tenderness and affection for me. It is a consolation at the end of my life which would make me happy were it not for your absence; but, my child, that capital doesn't waste and absence will end.

M. le Chevalier has been to see me. He went off with that pain which affects his foot, and is a great trial to him and a great misfortune for you. How useful he might be to you at Versailles, both for your son and for your business affairs! We must not dwell on this; it is God's will. What would one do without that thought? Mlle de Méri wanted to come here and look after me. She had such a terrible attack of the vapours that she was obliged to fly; see how our poor house is sometimes a hospital. Abbé Bigorre really is the consolation of every apartment. I wanted to tell you all this pending your letters.

[The same day, at 5 o'clock in the evening]

The weather is appalling. Your letters have not come. I am in M. le Chevalier's room. Unworthy as I am, I am looking after him. He is in bed, but will write to you because his trouble is in his knee. At every moment he thinks he is free of it. We talked at one moment about your son and we expect him here. He doesn't think he should go to Provence, it would be rather a pointless expense. Better that he should take advantage this winter of his lovely country.

We also thought that M. du Plessis, with all his fine qualities, is going to be a bit of a strain on your resources as well as useless to the Marquis, for there is hardly any question of a tutor at Court and still less in the army. Tomorrow, my dear child, your heart will be full of joy and you will learn that *Philippsburg has fallen* and *your son is well*. Nobody doubts here that Mannheim will have surrendered without waiting to be asked and burnt up by our bombs. So sleep in peace and as soon as you can begin putting into practice all your good intentions.

It is reported that the Prince of Orange has embarked and that some gunfire has been heard, but they have been saying the same thing for so long that I don't yet report that as certain. M. de La Bazinière has died of gangrene in the leg.

· Good-bye, dearest and best. The more one sees of the sentiments of some people the more charmed one is by yours. I make no mention of Brittany; I am satisfied with it, but one day I will retail to you a little case of ingratitude that I have retailed to the Chevalier, and that I shan't think of any more now I have told it.

Mme de Castries is leaving. She sends you a hundred thousand compliments on the happy outcome at Philippsburg, and I embrace you with all my heart.

To Madame de Grignan

[Paris, Monday 8 November 1688]

It is today you set off, dear Comtesse; we always follow you step by step. The weather is very good and the Durance cannot be as terrible as it sometimes is. Indeed it seems as though you are moving further away from us again out of spite – you will end up by being on the coast. My dear, God wills that there must be in life some periods difficult to live through; one must try by submitting to His will to atone for an excessive regard for others than Him. Nobody could be more guilty of that than I am.

M. le Chevalier is much better. What is cruel is that his good days are just the ones that can be used to dethrone the King of England, whereas during these past days the Chevalier was groaning and suffering a great deal when the wind and storm dispersed the fleet of the Prince of Orange. He feels miserable not to be able to combine what is good for his health with the good of Europe, for joy is universal at the rout of this prince whose wife is a Tullia.[1] Oh, how gladly she would drive over her father's body! She has authorized her husband to take possession of the English realm, to which she says she is heiress, and if her husband is killed (for her imagination has no delicacy) she gives authorization to M. de Schomberg to take possession in her name. What do you think of this hero who is so cruelly spoiling the end of such a fine career? He witnessed the sinking of the *Amiral*, which he was to board, and as the Prince and he were the last to go, following the fleet which was sailing in perfect weather, when they suddenly saw a frightful storm they returned to port, the Prince with his asthma and very put out, and M. de Schomberg very sick at heart. Only twenty-six vessels got back with them; all the rest were blown off course towards Norway or Boulogne. M. d'Aumont sent a messenger to the King to tell him that vessels had been sighted at the mercy of the winds, with some signs of wreckage and sinking. A store ship went down before the Prince of Orange's eyes, with nine hundred men aboard. In fact the hand of God has clearly weighed heavily on this fleet. Many may come back, but for a long time to come they will be in no state to do any harm, and it is certain that it was a considerable rout, and at the moment when we had the least hope. It still looks like a miracle and act of God. I ought not to hold forth about this great news, for the gazettes are full of it, but as we are, too, and are not talking about anything else, it comes naturally off the pen.

Would you like another word about the wounds inflicted elsewhere than at the siege of Philippsburg? It is about the Chevalier de Longueville. The place was taken. Monseigneur came to inspect the garrison. This young Chevalier climbs on to the back of the trench to look at something. A soldier wants to shoot a snipe and shoots this boy. He dies the next day. That is a death as strange as his birth.[2]

I told you that Méli, a captain of Livry, wanted to fire a gun that had

1. *Tullia*: Tullia, daughter of Servius Tullius, sixth King of Rome. According to legend she connived at her father's murder by her husband Tarquinius, and later ordered his chariot to drive over his corpse. Mme de Sévigné's likening Queen Mary's treatment of her father James II to the behaviour of Tullia is typical of the French attitude.

2. *as his birth*: the Chevalier de Longueville, son of the Duc de Longueville and the Maréchale de La Ferté. Strange because although the boy was recognized by the Duc de Longueville, his mother, the Maréchale de La Ferté, had a large sum settled on her by another man unknown.

been loaded a long time, and the gun exploded in his hand, and they have had to amputate the arm as happened with Jarzé. He died of it near here, at Mme Sanguin's. That is some news for the Marquis in spite of the lack of interest he is showing nowadays in our poor Livry. I confess that all the memories you keep of it flatter the attachment I have had for that lovely place and the regrets I have for being without it.

M. de La Bazinière has died of gangrene in the leg, but he died like Mars. He has soon followed his daughter, whom he had not stopped bemoaning since her death.

I am anxious to know how you are feeling about moving still further away from me. You should not miss Grignan considering the state you have left it in. I have faith in the Coadjutor's desire to finish his building, but even more in the infinite slowness of Monsieur de Carcassonne's. You are putting up with all this with admirable patience; we could discuss that for a whole year. I have written to M. de La Garde and thanked him very much for the affectionate and true friendship he has for you. I have no fear he will change; people don't give you up, nor Pauline, for whom he seems to have a real attachment.

I have told you that coffee is quite out of fashion at our Court, but for the same reason it may come back. As for me, who am a companionable animal, you can appreciate that I have put it out of my mind. But I should be wrong to complain, for it has never given me any cause. Don't worry about my health, it is excellent, only pity me for not having my dear daughter who is such a sweet and charming preoccupation and without whom life is empty. Give my compliments to Monsieur d'Aix just to see how he remembers me. I think that as M. de Vendôme has settled the affair you must stop arguing and live in peace and enjoy his good, sparkling talk. Any other line of behaviour is just to amuse the Provençaux and will do you no good either at Court or in the province. Mme de La Fayette thinks that M. de Grignan did very well to treat this affair with the lofty indifference that was apparent. It means he has lost nothing. She urges him, and Monsieur d'Aix and you too, my dear, to live down there as Court people who have met, and will meet again, at Versailles. Love to the dear Comte and to our Coadjutor, and if you will kiss Pauline for me you will give her great pleasure, for I am sure she adores you, and that is the way to love you.

To Madame de Grignan

This is a day of worship, my dear Comtesse. I would like to be reassured that I shall not have on my conscience anything I shall take the liberty of doing between now and tomorrow morning. I am all of a tremble when I think of the consequences. You know what we shall be doing tonight with our good Blues. The Marquis and M. du Plessis want to go to Catherine, but they will come back and eat my soup and boiled fowl.

The Marquis has been to Versailles on his own; he behaved very well there; dined with M. du Maine and with M. de Montaussier, supped with Mme d'Armagnac, acted the courtier at every *lever* and every *coucher*, Monseigneur had him hold the candlestick. In fine, behold him launched into the world, doing very well in it, being quite in the fashion, and never was there such a promising beginning nor anybody so well spoken of by all. I should never end if I tried to name all who speak well of him. I can't get over your not having the pleasure of seeing and embracing him as I do every day.

But doesn't it look, by the way I'm calmly chattering to you, my dear, as though I had nothing to tell you? Listen, listen, here is a little piece of news hardly worth talking about. The Queen of England and the Prince of Wales, his nurse and one nursemaid only, will be here at any moment. The King sent his own carriages along the Calais road, where she arrived last Tuesday, 21st of this month, escorted by M. de Lauzun. Here are the details, told us yesterday at Mme de La Fayette's by M. Courtin, just back from Versailles.

You know how M. de Lauzun resolved five or six weeks ago to go to England. He could not put his leisure to a better use. He has never abandoned the King when everybody else betrayed and left him. Finally last Sunday, the 19th of this month, the King, having made up his mind, retired to bed with the Queen, dismissed everyone still in his service, and an hour later got up, told a footman to admit a man he would find at the door of the antechamber; it was M. de Lauzun. He said to him, 'Monsieur, I entrust the Queen and my son to your care; you must take every risk and try to get them to France.' M. de Lauzun thanked him, as you can imagine, but he wanted to take with him a gentleman from Avignon, named Saint-Victor, well known for great courage and ability. He came and concealed in his cloak the little Prince, who was said to be in Portsmouth but was hidden in the palace. M. de Lauzun gave his hand to the Queen (you can visualize her farewell to the King) and, followed by the two women I have mentioned, they went into the street and took a hired carriage. Then they embarked in a small boat and went down the river where the weather was so bad that they didn't know what to do. At last, at the mouth of the Thames they embarked on a yacht, M. de Lauzun staying by the ship's master in case he was a traitor, when he would have thrown him into the sea. But he thought he was only taking ordinary people who often cross that way, and all he was concerned about was threading his way between some fifty Dutch vessels, who didn't even look at this small craft. So, protected by heaven and disguised by its mean appearance, it landed safely at Calais, where M. de Charost received it with all the respect you can imagine. The news, with all these details, reached the King yesterday at noon, and at once orders were given to the royal carriages to go and meet the Queen and take her to Vincennes, which is being furnished. It is said that His Majesty will go and meet her. This ends part one of the story, and you will have the sequel very soon.

We have been told that, to put the finishing touch to the beauty of the adventure, M. de Lauzun, having handed the Queen and the Prince safely into the keeping of M. de Charost, wanted to go back to England with Saint-Victor to follow the sad and cruel fortunes of the King. I admire M. de Lauzun's star, which seeks to make his name glorious again when it seems as though it is quite dead and buried. He had taken 20,000 pistoles to the King of England. That is a fine action indeed, and a very brave one, and what makes it perfect is to have gone back into a country in which to all appearances he is bound to perish either with the King or at the hands of the English for the trick he has just played on them. I leave you to meditate on this great event and embrace you, my dearest, with a kind of affection and love quite out of the ordinary, and which you deserve.

I am in the room of M. le Chevalier. Would to God you were here instead of your portrait! The Chevalier will be writing to you and your boy too. As for me, I am off to my room for a while to commune with myself.

M. Coignet has the gout. I spent an hour with him yesterday, having a pleasant talk about you. I had taken M. du Plessis with me. I was afraid I would never be able to keep the conversation going; however it didn't falter. He asked me to pay you a hundred thousand compliments. I told him the news from England. He is determined to marry your boy to M. de Lamoignon's daughter and 100,000 écus; he's got it on the brain.

To Madame de Grignan

[Paris, Monday 3 January 1689]

Your dear boy returned this morning from Châlons, where he had been to see his company. We were delighted to see him and M. du Plessis. We were at table. They dined miraculously on our dinner, which was already somewhat eroded (anyway they will get a better supper). But why haven't you heard, my dear, all the boy told us about the beauty of his company? – as he was told when he inquired whether the company had arrived and if it was smart, 'Indeed, Sir, it is one of the finest, *it is an old company*, which is much better than *the new ones*.' You can imagine what such praise means to a man they didn't know was its captain. He was transported the next day to see this fine company mounted, these men specially selected by you, the true expert, and horses cast in the same mould. It was a real joy for him, in which Monsieur de Châlons and Mme de Noailles shared. He was welcomed by these pious persons as the son of M. de Grignan, and there is no kindness or friendship he didn't receive from them. But what folly to talk to you about all this; it is the Marquis's job and he will do it very well.

Now for your errands, my dear. Don't make any bones about asking me for anything you want done promptly; you will always be led astray by your hesitations. You ask me to send you a dress and a cornet; I am sending you a dress and a cornet. You say that if I approve I can't send them too soon. I shall go and choose the things on the morning after the holidays. I shall have the dress and cornet made. Mme de Bagnols, Mme de Coulanges choose and approve of everything. Mme de Bagnols does the trimming herself; she fits it on her own head. Just now it is called a *cabbage*, so this is a red cabbage. When it is made of green ribbon it is a green cabbage – anyway, it is the fashion. There is not a word to be said to this, and I give this fashion, for what it is worth, to Pauline as a New Year present and am very sorry not to be giving the whole consignment, which will go off on Wednesday. If you want to copy the cornet I will let you know just what it costs; they will be very glad to have it at Aix. You will like the dress, especially in bright daylight or torchlight, with the colours I described to Martillac; they are on a white background.

I was going to ask you for news of Mme d'Oppède just as you tell me some. It looks to me as if she is additional good company or perhaps the only company. I don't think that jealousy should prevent your enjoying it. M. de Grignan's times are mapped out, and he is not in love in the mornings, any more than M. de Nemours. I think you should recite to him this line of Corneille: *Allez lui rendre hommage, et j'attendrai le sien.**

As for Monsieur d'Aix, I must say that I wouldn't believe Provençaux on the subject. I remember very well how they thrust themselves forward and live only for tittle-tattle and opinions they bandy about to liven things up and find something to do. You must not altogether believe Monsieur d'Aix. You must be guided *a fructibus*. For my part I would not easily believe that a man *who had been a courtier all his life*, who repudiates anointing and baptism, who doesn't bother about the intrigues of consuls, would lose his soul by false oaths. But it is up to you to judge on the spot.

The ceremony of your *brothers* took place on New Year's Day at Versailles. Coulanges is back from it and thanks you a thousand times for your nice answer. I admired all the thoughts that come to you, and how well turned it all is and applicable to what was written to you! I don't do this to all and sundry, for I never re-read their letters, and that is bad. Well, he told me that they began on Friday, as I said to you, with ecclesiastics in fine robes and collars and looking very grand. On Saturday it was all the others. Two Marshals of France had stayed. Maréchal de Bellefonds totally ridiculous because out of modesty and lack of interest in his appearance he had omitted to put ribbons on the bottom of his breeches, so that he looked quite naked. The whole band

* 'Go and pay him homage and I will await his.' Corneille, *La Mort de Pompée*, II, 3.

was magnificent, and M. de La Trousse one of the best. There was some muddle about his wig, which made him wear the side at the back for quite a time, so that his cheek was quite uncovered. He went on pulling, but what was wrong refused to come right; it was a minor disaster. But in the same line M. de Montchevreuil and M. de Villars got caught up in each other so furiously – swords, ribbons, lace, all the tinsel, everything got so mixed up, tangled, involved, all the little hooks were so perfectly hooked up with each other that no human hand could separate them; the more they tried the more muddled they got, like the rings in the arms of Roger.[1] In short the whole ceremony, all the bowings, the whole performance having come to a halt, they had to be torn apart, and the strongest won. But what completely upset the gravity of the ceremony was the negligence of old d'Hocquincourt, for he was dressed so like the Provençaux and Bretons that, his breeches being much more skimpy than his ordinary ones, his shirt wouldn't stay tucked in, however much he begged it to. Conscious of his state he kept on trying to put it right, and always to no avail, so that Madame la Dauphine couldn't hold in her laughter any longer. It really was a great shame. The King's Majesty was on the point of being shaken, and never in the annals of the order had such an adventure been seen. The King said in the evening, 'It is always I who hold poor d'Hocquincourt up, for it was his tailor's fault.' Anyhow it was very funny.

It is certain, my dear, that if I had had my dear son-in-law in that ceremony, I would have been there with my dear daughter. Incidentally there was plenty of room, though everyone thought it would be a crush, and it was just like that carousel. The next day the whole Court was resplendent with blue ribands. All the fine figures and young men wore theirs over their coats, the others underneath. You can take your choice, at all events in the matter of fine figures. You should have let me know who were those who took it upon their consciences to answer for M. de Grignan. I was told that absentees would be informed in writing to take the riband being sent to them with the cross: it is for Monsieur le Chevalier to send it to you. Thus ends the chapter on blue ribands.

Let us say one word more about a certain thought I admit I found silly to the last degree. I cannot understand that the old master of such

1. ... *rings in the arms of Roger*: in Ariosto, *Orlando Furioso*.

intelligence should have approved it and I confess I am delighted that M. de Grignan shares our sentiments. For the Lord's sake don't think I shall ever say a word about this, I would rather die. You don't yet know my little perfections in that respect, yet I could produce good witnesses. But one can't prove that one is discreet, for by proving it one ceases to be so. Anyway, dear one, I thought like you and am vain about it.

I hope the poor Marquis is satisfied with what you give him in your regiment. I think that if it is the first company he will say 'I am satisfied' in his Marquis's tone.

It is true that I like my *little underlinings*, they draw the attention, make you think and produce answers. Sometimes they are epigrams and satires, in fact you can make what you like of them.

The King of England was caught, it is said, trying to escape as a huntsman. He is in Wital[2] – I don't know how to write that word. He has his captain of the guard, guards, nobility in attendance when he rises, many marks of honour, but all under a strict surveillance. The Prince of Orange at Saint-James, which is the other side of the park. Parliament is to meet. May God guide that vessel! The Queen of England will be here on Wednesday; she is coming to Saint-Germain to be nearer to our King and his bounties.

Boufflers, answering my letter about his blue riband, asks me to compliment you both on yours.

Abbé Têtu is still in a very pitiful state. Often opium has no effect on him, and when he sleeps a little it is because of exhaustion and when they have doubled the dose.

I remember you, my dear, to everyone you wish. The widows are all yours on earth and in the third heaven. On New Year's Day I went to wish M. and Mme Croiset a Happy New Year. I spent two hours there and saw Rubantel, who told me excellent news of your boy and his growing reputation, his goodwill and courage at Philippsburg, which has pleased Monsieur le Chevalier. The Chevalier gives invaluable instruction to his nephew. He counts, calculates, keeps accounts on the journey, reports. He is not difficult, he is a good manager. Oh how that quality can save millions!

Do please embrace little Adhémar for love of me. I wish her good

2. Whitehall.

holidays, good friendship and above all the gift of perseverance. Don't let her forget me. I like the sound of your retreat and rest at Sainte-Marie. Those Christmasses are amazing! Good-bye, my dearest love.

M. de Lauzun was three-quarters of an hour with the King. If this goes on you can guess who will want to see him again.[3] I am more yours than I can say. It is freezing fit to split a stone. What is it like with you?

To Madame de Grignan

[Paris, Wednesday 5 January 1689]

Yesterday I took my Marquis with me. We began by calling on M. de La Trousse, who was kind enough to dress up again both as a probationer and as a fully fledged member of the order, as on the day of the ceremony. Those two kinds of garments are very becoming to men with good figures. A frivolous and quite irresponsible thought made me regret that the fine figure of M. de Grignan had not shone at that ceremony. This page costume is very pretty, and I am not surprised that Mme de Clèves fell in love with M. de Nemours with his fine legs. The cloak is a representation of royal majesty. It cost La Trousse eight hundred pistoles, for he bought it. When I had seen this fine performance I took your son to see all the ladies in the neighbourhood. Mme de Vaubecourt and Mme Ollier welcomed him very kindly. Soon he will be going on his own.

La Vie de Saint-Louis led me into reading Mézeray; I wanted to look up the last kings of the second dynasty, and I want to connect Philippe de Valois and King Jean, which is an admirable part of history on which the Abbé de Choisy has written a very readable book. We are trying to knock into your son's head a desire to know a little about what happened before him. It will come, but meanwhile there is plenty of food for thought in considering everything that is going on at present.

You will see from today's news how the King of England has fled from London, apparently with the connivance of the Prince of Orange. Politicians are arguing about whether it is more advantageous for this king to be in France. One says yes because he is then safe and won't

3. Mademoiselle.

be forced to give up his wife and son or be in danger of having his head cut off; another says no because he will then leave the Prince of Orange Regent and revered when that happens naturally and without crime. What is true is that war will soon be declared against us, and perhaps we shall even declare it first. If we could make peace in Italy and Germany we should be free to attend to this Anglo–Dutch war more fully. It is to be hoped so, for it would be too much to have enemies on all sides. Look where my wandering pen is taking me, but you can see that conversation is full of these great events.

I do ask you, my dearest, when you write to M. de Chaulnes, to tell him that you have a share in my son's obligations to him, that you thank him and that the great distance that separates you doesn't lessen your interest in everything concerning your brother. This reason for gratitude is rather a novel one; it is to excuse him from commanding one of the regiments of militia he is raising in Brittany. My son cannot face re-entering the services that way, it fills him with repugnance and he only wants to be forgotten in his own province. The Chevalier agrees with this sentiment, and so do I, I assure you. Don't you feel the same, dear child? I value your sentiments, which are always right, above all concerning your brother. Don't go into details, but say in a general way that whoever gives pleasure to the brother does so to the sister. M. de Maumont has gone to Brittany with some troops, but so subservient to M. de Chaulnes that it is a marvel. These beginnings are mild, we shall have to see the sequel.

Yesterday I found Choiseul with his riband; he is very happy. If you didn't meet five or six every day now you would be very unlucky. Did I tell you that the King has removed the communion from the ceremony? I had wished he would for a long time; I rank the beauty of this action roughly with that of suppressing duels. And just think what it would have been like to mix this holy act with the giggles excited by M. d'Hocquincourt's shirt. Yet several did perform their devotions, but without ostentation or being forced to do so.

We shall now be free to go to the reception of their English Majesties, who will be at Saint-Germain. Madame la Dauphine will have an armchair in front of this Queen, although not a queen herself, because she is deputizing for one.

Dear daughter, I wish you were at everything, I miss you everywhere. I understand all your engagements and all your reasons, but you are so good everywhere that it is not possible to get used to not finding you where you would be so necessary – I often get sentimental over that thought. But it is time to finish this letter which answers nothing and means nothing. Don't waste time answering it. Look after yourself and take care of your chest.

To Madame de Grignan

[Paris, Monday 10 January 1689]

We often think alike, my dear; I even think I wrote from Les Rochers what you write in your last letter about time. It is true: *we consent to its passing*. There is nothing so dear or precious in the days left to me now. I used to feel them thus when you were at the Hôtel de Carnavalet. I have told you so a score of times, I never came home without appreciable joy; I savoured it, got the best out of the hours, was greedy over them, felt like weeping every evening at their flight. In separation this is no longer so, you don't bother about them, you even hurry them along sometimes. You hope, you hasten towards a time you want or aspire to. In fact you are doing a piece of tapestry you want to finish, you are generous with the days, you throw them at whoever wants them. But, my dear one, suddenly I confess that when I think where this squandering and impatience with the hours and days is leading me, I tremble and find I cannot rely on any more of them, and reason shows me what I shall probably find in my way. My dear, these thoughts are for myself alone, and I mean to abandon them with you and try to make them really valid for myself.

The Abbé Têtu is going through a bout of insomnia that makes one fear the worst. Régis and Fédé[1] are not prepared to pronounce on the complete breakdown of his mind. He gets over-excited about the slightest thing; he realizes his own condition and that is painful. He is only kept going with opium. The other day they gave him ambergris by mistake and he nearly died. He tries to find diversions and things to occupy himself. He looks out for distractions. We want to send him to Saint-Germain to have the pleasure of seeing the King and Queen of England and the Prince of Wales installed there. Could

1. *Régis and Fédé*: doctors.

one see anything more noble and likely to take his mind off things?

I can understand all your tears from my own. Mme de Chaulnes, strong as she is, did the same. As for the flight of the King, it seems that that was what the Prince of Orange really wanted. He sent him to Exester,[2] where he wanted to go. He was very closely guarded at the front of the house, but all the back doors were left open. The Prince was unwilling to cause his father-in-law's death. He is in London in the King's place but without taking his title, only seeking to re-establish a religion he thinks right and maintain the laws of the country without spilling a drop of blood. That is exactly the opposite of what we thought of him; these are widely divergent points of view. Meanwhile our King is doing divine things for their English Majesties, for is it not to be in the image of the Almighty to uphold a king who has been banished, betrayed, abandoned as he is? The great soul of our King enjoys playing this noble part. He went to meet the Queen with all his household and a hundred coaches and six. When he saw the carriage of the Prince of Wales he alighted and insisted that the young child, pretty as an angel, so they say, should not do so. He tenderly embraced him, then hurried to meet the Queen, who had stepped down; he bowed to her and spoke for a few minutes, then placed her on his right in his own carriage, presented Monseigneur and Monsieur to her, who were also in the carriage, and took her to Saint-Germain, where she found herself provided like the Queen with all sorts of garments and a rich casket containing six thousand gold louis. The King of England was to arrive the next day; our King awaited him at Saint-Germain. He arrived late because he came from Versailles. Our King went to the end of the guardroom to meet him. The King of England bowed very low, as though he meant to embrace his knees; our King prevented him and embraced him three or four times most cordially. They conversed softly for a quarter of an hour; the King presented Monseigneur, Monsieur, the princes of the blood royal and Cardinal de Bonzi, then he led him to the Queen's room, who had difficulty in holding back her tears. They had a few moments' talk, then the King led them to the Prince of Wales, where they were for a few more minutes, and he left them there, not wishing to be escorted to his coach, saying to the King, 'This is your home; when I come here

2. Presumably meant for Exeter, but in reality Rochester.

you will do the honours to me, and I will do so to you when you come to Versailles.' The next day, yesterday, Madame la Dauphine went there, and all the Court. I don't know how they will have arranged the princesses' chairs; for they had them for the Queen of Spain, and the English Queen Mother[3] was treated like a Daughter of France. I will let you know the details. The King sent ten thousand gold louis to the King of England. The latter looks old and tired, the Queen thin, with eyes that have wept but are beautiful and black, a good complexion if a little pale, big mouth and fine teeth, a good figure and plenty of intelligence, a self-possessed person whom people find pleasant. There, my dear, is enough to last you a long time in public conversation. You will have in addition the Abbé Bigorre's account.

I have told you about the ceremony of the Blue Ribands. But if you have not taken care to return your profession of faith, *auto da fe* and particulars about your way of life to the Secretary of State who sent to you, you won't get either brevet or blue riband. Perhaps you have done so and are teasing me. I hope so.

The poor Chevalier still cannot write or go to Versailles, which we are very sorry about, for there are all sorts of things to be done, but he is not ill. Last Saturday he had supper with Mme de Coulanges, Mme de Vauvineux, M. Duras and your son at the home of M. le Lieutenant Civil, where they drank the health of the *first* and *second* ladies, meaning Mme de La Fayette and you, for you cede priority by length of friendship.

Yesterday Mme de Coulanges gave a very nice supper to the gouty ones, namely the Abbé de Marsillac, the Chevalier de Grignan, M. de Lamoignon (nephritis took the place of gout), his wife and the *Divine Ones*, always a mass of swellings, myself by virtue of the rheumatism I had twelve years ago, Coulanges who deserved it. There was plenty of talk, the little man sang and entertained the Abbé de Marsillac, who admired and felt for his words with tones and mannerisms so very like his father's that we were moved. We talked about you and that visit they advised you not to pay him. It was thought you were much too far away. We drank your health. The Chevalier was not inconvenienced.

Your boy was with Mlles de Castelnau. There is a young sister who

3. Henrietta Maria, widow of Charles I.

is very pretty and charming, and your son found her to his liking and left the older one to Sanzei. He had brought a wind player and they danced until midnight. This group appeals to the Marquis. He found there Saint-Hérem, Jeannin, Choiseul, Ninon; he was among friends and happy as a lark. I don't think the Chevalier is much concerned with marrying him off, any more than M. de Lamoignon, who is in no hurry either to marry his daughter.

We can't talk about the plans of Mirepoix; it is the doing of M. de Montfort. It's like a spell; all heads have changed their way of thinking. Anyway, he is a man strongly called by his destiny. What do you think can be done about it?

I am not blaming you at all for having changed your mind about your commissions – on the contrary. Pauline will be the prettier for it: she who has only one dress has none. I think you will like the one you will receive, unadventurous though it be. The cornet is very pretty, and the red rosettes. Anyway, it will mean that you won't lightly ask me for clothes without thinking twice about it. My poor cornet is only too fortunate to come in for Pauline, my dear, for it wasn't much good and I was ashamed of it myself. I am delighted that Marsillac has stolen it. Pauline writes an admirable letter that gives us all pleasure. It is natural, and you think you can hear her talking. She depicts to perfection her beauty, her adornment, and then that killjoy with the cruel voice who takes her for a servant. Pending my answer, give her a kiss for me; it will be best.

In a quarter where they sometimes ask me I will say how well in you are with the Archbishop. My dear, tell your fault-finders that you thank them for their zeal and that you will name them, since they are so certain of what they retail. How you would send them scattering! You see from this that their pleasure and entertainment is to stir up trouble, cause discord and make themselves necessary. Fie! Give up this provincial, Provençal style, and when you think you have cause for complaint speak about it yourself. Have it out with people and it will soon blow over.

It is terribly cold. I leave you, my dear, and beg you to love me always as no daughter has ever loved her mother, for that is true, and I am amazed I have been destined to have the happiness and good fortune of enjoying this miracle.

I thank dear Pauline for her letter and I am very sure she would please me. So she hasn't found any other relationship to me than 'Madame'? That's serious. Just think of some other word.

M. de Lauzun has not gone back to England. He is lodged at Versailles and is very pleased. He has written to Mademoiselle asking for the honour of seeing her; she is angry. I have achieved another masterpiece – I've been to see Mme de Ricouart, who recently came back very glad to be a widow. You need only give me your acknowledgements to finish, like your novels; do you remember? My own dear, look after your health, that is to say your beauty that I love so much.

To the Comte de Grignan

Good-bye, dear Comte. So you are vexed with me and I with you for not seizing that fine riband. I condemn you to wear it for the first days over your coat as they have done here. I am sorry you haven't enjoyed my neighbour's letters. By the way, Mme de Vins is coming back tomorrow. M. and Mme de Pomponne are back already. You were very glad to have the news of the 15th October. The Chevalier is in despair at having been let down over the thousand écus for *chevaliers*. Alas, you won't yet see the colour of this money! We are sorry about that.

To Madame de Grignan

Good-bye once again, my dear child. Yes, I really do believe that you would throw yourself *across the door to prevent time flying out as it does and bearing away what it bears away*, if that were a way of stopping it, but it can only be held by paper chains as at the Château de La Trousse.

[Paris, Monday 10 January, 10 o'clock at night]

I have been to see Mme du Puy-du-Fou about this marriage. M. de Montausier and Mme de Lavardin came. I remembered you to Mme de Lavardin, she is very fond of you. A moment later a brilliant troop arrived. Mme la Duchesse de La Ferté holding her daughter's hand, very pretty and her little sister in the same colours, Mme la Duchesse d'Aumont, M. de Mirepoix, who made a wonderful contrast. What a lot of noise and compliments on all sides! The Duchesse always wanted M. de Mirepoix, she cast her eye on him and having gathered that the proposition had been accepted, she spoke to the King about it, which settles it and cuts everything short. The King said, 'Madame, your daughter is very young.' 'That is true, Sire, but the matter is urgent because I want M. de Mirepoix, and in ten years' time, when Your Majesty knows his worth and rewards it, he won't want us.' That is well said. Thereupon they wanted to publish the banns before the articles were drawn up; you never saw so many *carts before horses*. Mme d'Olonne has given a fine girdle. Mme la Maréchale de La Ferté is radiant. All the wedding party is delighted. Mme de Mirepoix has written to you, Mme du Puy-du-Fou is swept away in the whirlpool. You can't hear yourself speak. The young man hadn't even set eyes upon his betrothed; he doesn't know what it's all about. My pen won't work, so I say good-night, my dearest.

To Madame de Grignan

[Paris, Friday 14 January 1689]

Here I am, my dear girl, after dinner in the Chevalier's room. He is in his armchair with countless little ailments all over his body. He has slept very well, but this business of staying in, unable to go out, gives him a great deal of annoyance and depression. I am sympathetic and I know the trouble and its consequences better than anyone. It is extremely cold. Our thermometer is down to the bottom degree. Our river is frozen. It is snowing, freezing and re-freezing at the same time. You can't keep your footing in the streets. I don't leave the house or the Chevalier's room. If it didn't take fifteen days to get a reply from you, I would ask you to let me know if I am not upsetting him by being here all day long, but as time presses I ask him direct, and he seems to want me to. This cold adds to his discomforts. He could do without one of these cold spells; it is bad when it is excessive like this.

I have reminded M. de Lamoignon of the plea you addressed to him for M. Bigot; this man will feel your gratitude from afar as well as near to. I like this way of not having mere passing gratitude; I know some people who not only have none at all but put aversion and rudeness in its place. M. Gobelin is still at Saint-Cyr. Mme de Brinon is at Maubuisson, where she will soon get bored. That woman cannot stay in one place. She has made lots of conditions and changed convents many times – her great intelligence doesn't exempt her from this fault. Mme de Maintenon is very taken up with the play she is having produced by her girls. It will be very fine, according to reports.[1]

She has been to see the Queen of England who, because she kept her waiting a moment, told her she was annoyed at having lost this time when she could have seen her and talked to her, and she received her very well. People are pleased with the Queen, she is very intelligent. Seeing the King caressing the Prince of Wales, who is a very beautiful child, she said, 'I envied the good fortune of my son, who does not appreciate his misfortunes, but now I pity him for not appreciating the caresses and kindness of Your Majesty.' Everything she says is right and sensible. Her husband is not the same thing at all; he is brave, but has a commonplace mind and he recounts everything that has happened in England with a lack of sympathy that deprives one of any for him. He is a sociable man and takes part in all the pleasures of Versailles. Madame la Dauphine will not go to see this Queen. She would like to be on the right and have an armchair, and that has never been the case. She will always stay in bed and the Queen will come and see her. Madame will have an armchair on the left side, and the princesses of the blood royal will go only with her, in front of whom they only have stools. Duchesses will be as at Madame la Dauphine's. All that is laid down. The King has learnt that a King of France had only allotted an armchair on the left to a Prince of Wales, and he wishes the King of England to treat the Dauphin in the same way and take precedence over him. He will receive Monsieur with no armchair and no ceremony. The Queen bowed to him and has not failed to tell the King our master what I have told you. It is not certain that M. de Schomberg has yet got the place of the Prince of Orange in Holland.

1. Racine's *Esther*. For an account of the performance by the girls of Saint-Cyr see 21.2.1689.

This is the year for telling lies. The Marquise improves with every post on the news she has sent. Do you call that knowing everything that is going on? I hate what is false.

M. de Lauzun's star is waning again. He has no official lodging nor his former entrées. The romantic and magical aspect of his adventure has been taken away; it has become just plain, as you might say. That is the world and the age we live in.

To Madame de Grignan

[Paris, Monday 21 February 1689]

It is true, my dear daughter, that we are cruelly separated from each other: *aco fa trembla*.* It would be a fine thing if I had added the journey from here to Les Rochers or Rennes, but that won't be just yet. Mme de Chaulnes wants to see various things through, and I am only afraid she will set out too late, given my plan to come back next winter for several reasons, the first of which is that I am certain that M. de Grignan will be obliged to come back for his order, and you could not find a better time to get away from your tumbledown and uninhabitable château and come and pay your court with M. le Chevalier de l'Ordre, who won't be that until that time comes.

I paid mine the other day at Saint-Cyr, and more enjoyably than I would ever have thought. We went on Saturday, Mme de Coulanges, Mme de Bagnols, Abbé Têtu and I. We found our places kept for us. An official told Mme de Coulanges that Mme de Maintenon was keeping her a place next to her; think what an honour that is. 'For yourself, Madame,' he said to me, 'you may choose.' I put myself with Mme de Bagnols in the second row, behind the duchesses. Maréchal de Bellefonds chose to come and put himself on my right, and in front were Mmes d'Auvergne, de Coislin, de Sully. The Marshal and I listened to this tragedy with an attention that was noticed, and certain whispered praises, well placed, which weren't perhaps in the heads of all these ladies. I cannot tell you how exceedingly enjoyable this play is. It is a subject not easy to put on the stage, and will never be imitated, with a relationship between music, poetry, singing and acting so perfect and complete that it leaves nothing to be desired. The girls

* 'It makes you tremble.' (Provençal expression.)

playing kings and other characters seem made for them. Everyone is attentive, with no other care but to see such an enjoyable play through to the end. Everything in it is simple, innocent, sublime and touching. The fidelity to the Bible narrative inspires respect; all the singing suitable to the words, which are taken from the Psalms or the Book of Wisdom and fitted into the subject, is so beautiful that one cannot hold back one's tears. The measure of approval given to the play is that of taste and concentration. I was charmed by it, and so was the Marshal, who left his place to go and tell the King how delighted he was and that he was sitting next to a lady very worthy of seeing *Esther*. The King came over to our seats and, having turned round, he said to me, 'Madame, I am told that you liked it.' Without getting flustered I answered, 'Sire, I am charmed, and what I feel is beyond words.' The King said, 'Racine is very clever.' I said, 'Yes, Sire, he is very clever, but really these young ladies are very clever too; they throw themselves into the subject as though they had never done anything else.' He said, 'Oh yes, that's true,' and passed on, leaving me an object of envy. As I was practically the only newcomer, he was quite glad to see my sincere admiration without noise or fuss. Monsieur le Prince and Madame la Princesse came and said a word to me. Mme de Maintenon just flashed by; she was leaving with the King. I had an answer for everyone, for I was in luck. We came back in the evening by torchlight. I had supper with Mme de Coulanges, to whom the King had also spoken in a quite familiar way, which had made her feel pleasantly happy. I saw the Chevalier in the evening and told him quite straight-forwardly about my little bits of good fortune, not wanting to hide them without knowing why, like certain people I might mention; he was very glad, and that was that. I am sure he didn't think afterwards either that it was silly vanity on my part or bourgeois pretentiousness – ask him yourself. Monsieur de Meaux talked a long time to me about you, and Monsieur le Prince also. I was sorry you weren't there. But how could you be, my dear child? One can't be everywhere at once. You were at your opera at Marseilles: as *Atys* is not only *too happy* but too charming, you cannot possibly have been bored, and I bet this high living is better than in Aix.

But on this same Saturday, after this beautiful *Esther*, the King heard of the death of the young Queen of Spain, after two days of severe vomiting; it smacks of poison. The King said so to Monsieur the next day, that is yesterday. The grief was very keen. Madame cried aloud, and the King left the room in tears.

There is good news from England, they say. Not only has the Prince of Orange not been elected king or protector, but he has been told that he and his troops had better go home; which cuts short a lot of worries. If this news is confirmed our Brittany will be less disturbed and my son will not have the unpleasantness of commanding the nobility of the viscounty of Rennes and the barony of Vitré, who elected him as their leader against his will. Another man might be delighted with this honour, but he is annoyed, not being enamoured of war in these parts, by whatever name it may be called.

Your boy has gone to Versailles to enjoy himself during this Shrovetide, but he came upon the grief about the Queen of Spain, and he would have returned were it not that his uncle is going to join him soon. It is a very sad carnival time, with deep mourning. Yesterday we supped with the *Civils*, the Duchesse du Lude, Mme de Coulanges, Mme de Saint-Germain, the Chevalier de Grignan, Monsieur de Troyes, Corbinelli. We were quite jolly. We talked about you with much affection, esteem, regret at your absence, in fact very kind remembrances. You must come and keep them alive.

Mme de Durfort is dying of hiccups with malignant fever. Mme de La Vieuville also, of a smallpox rash. Good-bye, dear child. Of all those in command in the provinces, M. de Grignan is in the pleasantest position, believe me.

To Moulceau

[Paris, Wednesday 2 March 1689]

What a lot of things to say, Monsieur! What an event in the story of the King is the way he has received the King of England, the presents with which he has loaded him on his departure for Ireland, vessels at Brest where he is at present, frigates, troops, officers, M. le Comte d'Avaux as ambassador extraordinary both for advice and looking after the troops; and money: two millions on departure and later all he asks for! On top of these great things he has given him his arms, helmet, cuirasse, which will bring him luck. He has given him enough to arm ten or twelve thousand men. But it is the little things and comforts that are in abundance; post-chaises perfectly turned out, barouches and horses, saddle-horses, gilt and silver dinner-services, toilet sets, linen, camp beds, richly decorated swords and swords for active service, pistols, everything you can imagine. As he said farewell and embraced him the King said, 'Monsieur, you cannot deny that I am very sorry to see you go. Yet I confess that I hope I may never see you again. But if by ill fortune you were to come back, be persuaded that you will find me just as you see me now.' Nothing could be better said or more right. Never have generosity, magnificence and magnanimity been exercised as they have been by His Majesty.

We hope that the war in Ireland will be a powerful diversion and prevent the Prince of Orange from harassing us with raids, so that all our three hundred thousand standing army and troops so well positioned everywhere will serve to make the King feared and respected, without anyone daring to attack. This is a time for argument and politics; I should like to hear what you have to say about all these great events.

These are the sentiments of a good upholsterer on your wife's questions. But whatever he says about a gold fringe with taffeta, and whatever there is here already, nothing is so pretty and nice and fresh for the summer as to use those fine taffetas for plain furnishing and for tapestry too. I have seen it used by two or three people, and nothing is better. You should turn it all up as he has said, and pleat it. For the other piece of furniture you need damask or brocade.

As for our friend, Monsieur, he will tell you what he is doing himself; I don't know. Since he has been living here I have seen no more of him, and when he is asked why, he answers *I live too near*. This joke is a truth. If sometimes in the morning I find myself passing him on his way to one of the three or four dinners to which he is invited daily, I would not recognize him. I am constrained to wish he were in the Faubourg Saint-Germain so as to renew the friendship we have had for more than thirty years. Isn't it true, Monsieur, that there is no kind of jealousy that can find material in that behaviour? Yours will be very satisfied.

M. de La Trousse has been on a milk diet all through the winter and is much better. He will, it is thought, command a separate corps in Poitou. There are three hundred thousand men ready for action, five or six armies, but nobody is yet quite sure of his position. My daughter's is in Provence, mine will be in Brittany this summer.

The young Marquis has a fine company in his uncle's regiment. And everywhere, Monsieur, I shall keep a real respect for you together with a friendship that should make the *jealous* tremble.

From Corbinelli

I am living in the Hôtel de Carnavalet simply to be revenged on you. But what will surprise you is that I haven't seen her since I've been living with her. I hope you won't believe a word of this because it is an incredible thing and you will put it down to over-subtlety. Public events are important and worth your attention, but as I am given to imputing all events to God, I admire Him alone in everything and only set my eyes on Him. Good-bye, my friend. I am all yours, jealous or tranquil, no matter.

A thousand greetings to Madame your wife; I wish I could do her some greater service. Is Mme d'Aumelas coming? Oh how I disapprove of the lawsuit they want to bring against her!

To Madame de Grignan

[Paris, Friday 25 March, Annunciation Day, 1689]

We have not had your letters, my dear, but all the same we begin to write to you. You look as if you have set a good example today. This is a great holy day and seems to me the foundation of Easter, and in a word the holy day of Christianity and the day of the incarnation of Our Lord; the blessed Virgin plays a big part in it, but not the leading one. In fact M. Nicole, M. Le Tourneux and all our preachers have said all they know on the subject.

I went next to Mme de Vins; we talked a lot about you, of your brothers and M. du Plessis. She would like him to pledge himself to serve her, and would willingly give him half a year and wait until the New Year. He seems to me to be paying out a thread that amuses him and that he thinks will lead him to some tutorship which is the object of his desires. With this in view he will not commit himself, but she is asking him not to commit himself to anyone else, and if what he hopes becomes a certainty to let her know so that she can look elsewhere. He is too happy, he is wanted everywhere! He is charmed and overwhelmed by your offers, which he has seen. He wanted to write to you again at once, although he has done so already; indeed nothing could be more obliging and show so well the esteem you have for him.

Your son has written me a most affectionate letter. He very much mourned his good uncle the Archbishop, whose successor will soon be here, it is thought. He will appeal against the court judgement if he likes; as for us, we have won that of the *Grand Conseil* at sword point. Monsieur le Chevalier has seen M. Talon; he will speak of the appeal at the fourth stage. M. de Lamoignon assures us he will do us no harm; it would be very difficult for him to do us any in this tribunal. M. Bigot has won his case and knows exactly who has petitioned for him.

Monsieur le Chevalier is sending you two hundred louis by this post, which it seemed you didn't want, for M. de Grignan protested so much that he had not gone for the four hundred thousand francs. The Chevalier has handled this affair so well that you will make some money out of it; there is no end to the debt you owe him. I admire you, my dear, you think of everything; you have already sent the Easter quarter's rent. We are agitating for repairs to a place where the rain comes in, and for the courtyard repairs; those people are real rogues.

I am having an argument with Mme de Chaulnes; I don't want to leave until after Easter. My dear one, how sorry I am to leave you again! I do feel this separation: *La raison dit Bretagne, et l'amitié Paris.**
Sometimes you have to give in to that tyrant reason. You know how to do it better than anyone; I must imitate you.

Listen to this, my dear. Do you know M. de Béthune, the *extravagant shepherd* of Fontainebleau, alias *Cassepot*? Do you know what he looks like? Tall, skinny, wild-looking, dried up, in fact a real wraith? Such as he was, he lodged at the Hôtel de Lyonne with the Duke, the Duchesse d'Estrées, Mme de Vaubrun and Mlle de Vaubrun. The last-named went two months ago to Sainte-Marie in the Faubourg Saint-Germain; it was thought that it was for her sister's sake that she became

* 'Reason says Brittany, but affection Paris.' (Adaptation of Boileau: '*La raison dit Virgile, et la rime Quinault.*' *Satire*, II.)

a nun so that she would have all the money. Do you know what this *Cassepot* was up to at the Hôtel de Lyonne? Love, my dear, making love to Mlle de Vaubrun. Just as I'm telling you, she loved him. Benserade would say, as he did about Mme de Ventadour who loved her husband, 'All the better if she loves him, she can still love another.' So this young girl of seventeen has made love to this *Don Quixote*, and yesterday he went and smashed down the grille of the convent, found Mlle de Vaubrun, who was expecting him, seized her, carried her off, put her into a carriage, took her to M. de Gêvres's home, went through a marriage on the hilt of a sword, slept with her, and in the morning at dawn they both disappeared and have not yet been found. In this case you can indeed say: *Agnès et le corps mort s'en sont allés ensemble.** The Duc d'Estrées is crying that the laws of hospitality have been violated, Mme de Vaubrun wants to have his head cut off. M. de Gêvres says he didn't know it was Mlle de Vaubrun. All the Béthunes are making some show of wanting to prevent a lawsuit being brought against their family. I don't know yet what they are saying at Versailles. There you have, my dear, the Gospel for the day. You know what it's like, they talked of nothing else. What do you say about love? I despise it when it plays with such horrible people.

I am impatient for Dulaurens to be with my Marquis, my dear little *pussycat*. I shall be thrilled that there are two eyes with no other job in the world than to watch over him continually.

Good-night, my own dear. I'm off to see Monsieur le Chevalier. If our letters come I shall write some more, if not we shall make up our packets. I'm off to think about your grey material. I embrace you tenderly and mean to take away with me, if you please, dear, the hope of seeing you next winter. Good-night Comte, good-night dear Pauline. And *Martille?*[1] I will write to him on Monday.

To Madame de Grignan

[Les Rochers, 29 June 1689]

I cannot tell you, my dear child, how much I pity Monsieur le Chevalier; there are few examples of such a misfortune. His health has

* 'Agnès and the dead body have gone off together.' Molière, *L'Ecole des femmes*, V, 5.

1. Martillac.

been in such a bad state for some time that he cannot count on past ills, diet or time of year. I appreciate this state both on his behalf, for one cannot know him without profound affection and admiration, and on your child's, who thereby loses everything one can possibly lose. All that can be seen at a glance, and to go into detail might wound his modesty. I am full of these truths and keep my eyes on God, who instead is giving this Marquis a man like M. de Montégut, who is wisdom itself, and all the other members of this regiment who are doing wonders for the little Captain to please the Chevalier. Is it not a kind of consolation not to be found in other regiments less attached to their Colonel? The Marquis wrote me such a nice letter that I was really touched. He never ceases congratulating himself on having M. de Montégut. He teases me and compliments me about the fine piece I wrote on Monsieur d'Arles. You are very funny to have sent it on to him. He says he has given up poetry, that they scarcely have time to breathe, always up in the air, never two days in peace. They have a very vigilant man to deal with.

Let me have plenty of news of the Chevalier. I pin hopes on the change of climate, the properties of the waters and still more on the joy and consolation of being with you and his family. I think he is a beneficent stream, and with more justice than you credit me for; it seems to me that he will give a happy turn and good order to everything. It is true that the Earldom of Avignon is a gift of Providence it was not easy to foresee. Let us turn away from our gloomy thoughts – you have too many yourself without getting repercussions in my letters. You must look after your health, the loss of which would be an even greater evil; mine is still quite perfect.

This opening medicine of the Capuchins, in which there is no senna, tastes to me like a glass of lemonade, and that is what it really is. I took some so as not to have to bother about it any more, because I hadn't had medicine for a long time, but I didn't notice any effects. You do this remedy too much honour. My son goes out in the morning in spite of it. It is a remedy that takes away the very superfluous superfluity, that doesn't go looking for complications or waking sleeping dogs. We lead such a regular life that it is hardly possible to be ill. We get up at eight, very often I go out and enjoy the fresh air of the woods until the bell for Mass at nine. After Mass, we dress, pass the time of day with each other, go back and pick orange blossom, then have dinner.

Until five o'clock work or reading, and since my son is no longer with us, I read to save his wife's weak chest. At five I leave her and go off to these lovely groves. A manservant follows me, I have books, I change destinations and vary the routes of my walks. A religious book and one on history, turn and turn about for the sake of a change. A little meditating on God and His Providence, possessing one's soul, thinking of the future. Finally at about eight I hear a bell; it is for supper. Sometimes I am at some distance, and I pick up the Marquise amid her nice flower-beds. We are company for each other. We have supper at dusk, and the servants do the same. I go back with her to *La Place Coulanges*, in the middle of the orange trees. I look enviously at the *holy terror* through the fine iron gate you don't know. I would like to be there, but there is no pretext left. I like this life a thousand times better than at Rennes. Isn't this solitude very suitable for a person who has to think about herself and who is or wants to be a Christian? Well, anyhow, my dear child, you are the only thing I prefer to the melancholy, quiet rest I enjoy here, for I must say that I envisage with too keen a pleasure that, God willing, I shall be able to spend a few more days with you. I must be very sure of your affection to have let my pen wander on in the narrative of such a dull life. *Quand c'est pour Jupiter qu'on change ...* * This passage is very pretty; your mind is keen and free. You are adorable, my dear daughter, and your courage, strength and worth beyond those of others; you are well beloved, too, more than others.

Good-bye, my most beloved. I hope you will give me news of Pauline and the Chevalier. I embrace the Comte, whom one *loves too much*.

From Mme de Sévigné's daughter-in-law

Really, dear sister, I know just what to say; yes, certainly *one does love him too much*.[1] I daren't say that I also love his son very much; the confusion would be too great. I do want, however, to beg him to stop

---

* 'When it is for Jupiter that you change ...' [i.e. there is no shame in changing]. Quinault, *Isis*, I, 4.

1. Family joke. Charles's wife was supposed to be madly in love with Grignan, whom she had not yet seen.

calling me Aunt; I am so small and delicate that I am only his cousin at best.

Mme de Sévigné's health is not at all like mine; she is tall and strong; I look after her in a way that would make you jealous. But I confess that it is without any constraint. I let her roam in the woods with herself and her books; she rushes there naturally, like the weasel into the toad's jaws. As for me, with the same tastes and the same freedom I stay in the garden *al dispetto* of consideration for her which we remove from the list of virtues as soon as it can be named by its name and is not of our own choosing. You delight me, dear sister, by telling me that Mme de Sévigné is fond of me; my taste is good enough to appreciate the value of her affection and to love her also with all my heart.

We have had a share in your triumphs and glories, but I would not like M. de Sévigné to see it all, for it would spoil him for the quiet life from which he is only dragged by a wretched provincial whirlwind which will cost us five hundred pistoles. By way of consolation let me embrace you with all my heart. I dare not say M. de Grignan, for I have not yet trampled all my honour underfoot.

I wanted to add that I approve completely of what my daughter-in-law has written; but, dear child, I have just had your letter of 18th which was held up at Vitré, although no doubt it arrived with that of 16th. This letter informs me of the arrival of the Chevalier looking unwell, not holding up at all and with a bad chest. Do you know what I did on reading that letter? I wept like all of you, for I cannot bear the idea and take an interest as though I were really one of his family. I do hope that the air and rest will restore him to a better state. Your nursing is usually successful. I trust so with all my heart and beg you to tell him so. Tell me what room you have put him in so that I can mentally pay him visits.

How I pity Pauline and Mme de Rochebonne for having been at Aubenas while you were at Avignon. What a horrible difference! Don't divide your gratitude for the victory of the Grand Conseil. In reality the Chevalier and the consideration people have for him and your friends did the whole thing; you are too kind to want to give me the joy of having played my part. I wish similar success to Monsieur d'Arles. I embrace and passionately love my dear Comtesse.

To Madame de Grignan

At last I have had that letter of 1st September, my dear. It had gone to Rennes, a journey my letters do sometimes take. They put in one bag what should go in the other, and you don't know who is to blame. Anyway, here it is, I should have been very sorry to lose it, for it is a link in a conversation that tells me all I was missing. A quick word about the visit of our good Duc de Chaulnes, the magnificent and most friendly reception you gave him; a household in the grand manner, good food, two tables as he has in Brittany, served lavishly, numerous company, and the cold wind didn't interfere. It would have deafened you, nobody would have heard anyone speak. There were enough of you without that. I think Flame knows well how to serve you, with no upsets and carried out in style. I can visualize it all, my dear, with inexpressible pleasure. I wanted you to be seen in your glory, at any rate your country glory, for that at Aix is even grander, and I wanted him to eat something different from our chicken or omelette with bacon. He now knows what you can do, and you are well set up for doing whatever you like in Paris. He has seen the thin and the fat, the mutton pie and the pigeon one.

Coulanges has played his part as clown very well, too; he hasn't yet come down to earth. I fear the change for him, for gaiety is a great part of his merit. I think that down there he was full of joy, taking interest in everything going on and transported by the perfections of Pauline. You always accuse him of only being pleasant with dukes and peers, but I have known him very amusing with us, and you told me about the supper-parties five years ago, while I was here, that had amused you very much. M. de Chaulnes has written; here is his letter. You will see that he is delighted with you all and the way you can do the honours of your home. He made you laugh about *genius*. *Mine* was not on view at Grignan; we have other things more agreeable to do than discuss that. You knew what he would have said and you paid too much honour to remembrance of me. You mentioned me several times and drank my health. Coulanges climbed on to his chair. That trick strikes me as very perilous for a little man as round as a ball and clumsy at that. I am very glad he didn't go head over heels to pledge my health. I very much want to have a letter from him. I think the dinner you conjured up with Flame's magic wand in that *Noah's Ark* you describe so amusingly, must have been charming and spell-binding. The music was quite novel, it must have brought back memories of the menagerie at Versailles. Anyhow, my dear, you are most generous, as you say, to give such a warm reception to an ambassador who is going to do you so much harm. I am sure he is very upset about it.

Mme de Chaulnes writes that there will be great difficulties at the conclave and then over this cruel affair of the franchises, and I say all the better: *Rome sera du moins un peu plus tard rendue.** The Earldom and that lovely Avignon will wait while the Holy Spirit chooses a Pope and negotiations are going on. It is well said, my child, it was the day when you were at the Louvre ball, all blazing with jewels; the next day they all had to be given back. But what remained to you was better, and you were more beautiful that following day than your income will be in its present state. On that I say, as you do in your funeral orations, *don't let us talk about that*. Certainly it didn't show at Grignan when you received this particular Excellency. I don't know how it can be done and how one can still run so well with no legs; it is a miracle that please God will last for ever. Mme la Duchesse de Chaulnes has sent me the letter you wrote to her. I have never seen anyone know how to express so precisely everything that has to be said as you do; everything is in its right place and absolutely suitable. What can I say? I enter in every way into all you have done so perfectly; self-esteem, affection, gratitude are all satisfied. I suppose your brothers-in-law did not go until after helping you do the honours of your house. I say nothing about the deputation; it was all too slow and too long. We'll talk about it another time.

Your dear child is well and has been everywhere with M. de Boufflers, sword in hand. My dear, that boy, *God keep him*! I shall never change that refrain.

Mainz has surrendered, this news surprised me. People were so happy about this siege that I still made light of M. de Lorraine. They say that the Marquis d'Huxelles comes out of it with the respect of

* 'At least Rome will have surrendered a little later.' (Adaptation of: '*Rome eût été du moins un peu plus tard sujette.*' Corneille, *Horace*, III, 6.)

friends and enemies alike. I tremble lest the brother of the Doyen may be in the number of the dead or wounded. None of those brave brothers will make old bones. He is persuaded of that by the nonchalant way he listened to what M. Prat told him. He is used to hearing such news. I am worried about poor Martillac. What can you do with no legs in a town taken by assault? What din, what confusion, what an inferno; it worried me, I don't know why. I pity M. de La Trousse. When we saw him carrying out alterations to La Trousse we said rightly, 'The worst thing that can happen to him is to enjoy the expense he is incurring.' We spoke rightly and all too truthfully.

You want to know how we live, my child? Alas, like this. We get up at eight. Mass at nine. The weather decides whether one goes for a walk or not, often each goes his own way. A neighbour looks in, we discuss the news. After dinner we work, my daughter-in-law at all sorts of things and I at two strips of tapestry which Mme de Kerman gave me at Chaulnes. At five we separate and walk alone or in company. We meet at some beauty spot. We have a book, say a prayer, think of our dear daughter, build castles in Spain or Provence, sometimes gay sometimes sad. My son reads us some very good books, one on devotion, others on history and that amuses and occupies us. We discuss what we have read. My son is indefatigable, reads aloud five hours straight off if need be. Receiving and answering letters takes up a large part of our lives, particularly for me. We have had company, we shall have more. We don't wish for any, but when people are there we are very happy. My son has some workmen in. He has had his big avenues *done up*, as they say here.[1] They really are fine. He is having his new parterre sanded. So you see, my dear, it is strange how, with this empty and rather dreary life, the days fly by and get lost, and God knows what else escapes us at the same time. *Oh don't let's talk about it*. But I do think about it, and so one must. Supper is at eight. Sévigné reads after supper, but amusing books for fear of going to sleep. They go off at ten. I don't go to bed much before midnight. That is more or less the rule of our convent. Over the door is written: *Sacred liberty, or do what you please*. I prefer this life a hundred times to that at Rennes; it will be time enough to go and spend Lent there for food for body and soul.

1. Freshly raked.

Du Plessis has written that his *chimera* had only shown the tip of her nose, that she has not yet come out, but that he is married to somebody quite perfect, exactly to his taste: with wit, beauty, of good family, who puts him in the position of needing nothing more. You make me doubt it. But he still seems to listen to Mme de Vins. Anyhow, here are his own words, *I love this wife much more than the late one*. That befits the grief he had at losing her: do you remember?

To Madame de Grignan

[Les Rochers, Sunday 15 January 1690]

You are right, I can't get used to this year's date, and yet it is well under way and you will see that however we spend it, it will as you say soon be over and we shall soon get to the bottom of our bag of money.

You really do spoil me, and so do my friends in Paris. Scarcely does the sun jump up like a flea than you are asking me when you can expect me at Grignan, and my friends here beg me to settle the hour of my departure so as to hasten their joy on my behalf. I am too flattered by these attentions, above all by yours, which are incomparable. So I shall say, my dear Comtesse, and mean it, that from now until September I cannot entertain any thought of leaving these parts; it is the time when I send my little payments to Paris, and so far only a small part of this has been done. It is the time when the Abbé Charrier deals with my ground rent, a matter of 10,000 francs. We will discuss it some other time, but we must be content to put away any hope of moving a step before the time I have said. Finally, my dear child, I am not saying that you are my object, my aim in life, you know that perfectly well and that you are part of my heart in such a way that I should be very afraid that M. Nicole might find much to circumcise.[1] But there, such is my disposition.

You say the sweetest thing in the world when you wish never to see the end of the years of happiness you wish me. We are far from coinciding in our wishes, for I told you a truth that is very right and proper, which God will perhaps grant, namely to follow the natural order of divine Providence. That is what consoles me for all the weary

1. The reference is to circumcision of the heart.

journey of old age, and this sentiment is reasonable, whereas yours is too out of the ordinary and attractive.

I shall be sorry for you when you no longer have M. de La Garde and the Chevalier with you; they are such perfectly good company. But they have their reasons, and that of getting a pension renewed for a man not yet dead seems most important to me. You will have your boy, who will fit in beautifully at Grignan; he should be very welcome there for many reasons and you will be very glad to embrace him. He has written me a nice letter to wish me a happy New Year and asks me to love him always. He seems miserable at Kaiserslautern; he says that nothing prevents his going to Paris, but that he is waiting for orders from Provence, and that is the spring that actuates him. I think you keep him too inactive. His letter is dated 2nd; I thought he was in Paris. Make him go there and hurry on to you after a brief appearance. It looks to me as though, if you found a good match for him, His Majesty might well grant this young man the succession to your very good position. You will find that his character and Pauline's are not in the least alike, yet certain qualities of the heart must exist in both. But temperament is another matter. I am so glad that his sentiments meet with your approval. I wish he were a little more inclined towards the sciences and reading, but that may develop. As for Pauline, that devourer of books, I would rather she swallowed bad ones than not like reading at all. Novels, plays, Voiture, Sarasin are all soon exhausted. Has she tried Lucian? Is she within reach of the *Petites Lettres*? After that there is history; if it is necessary to pinch her nose to make her swallow I am sorry for her. As for the fine books of devotion, if she doesn't like them it is her loss, for we know all too well that even without any religious feeling you can find them delightful. With regard to the moralists, as she wouldn't put them to such good use as you, I wouldn't want her to poke her little nose into them, neither into Montaigne nor Charron nor others of that kind; it is early days for them. Real morality, at her age, is what is learned from good conversation, fables and examples; I think that is enough. If you give her a little of your time for talk it is really what would be the most useful. I don't know whether all I'm saying is worth your reading; I am very far from agreeing with myself.

You ask me whether I am still *a devout little thing not worth much.* Yes, exactly that, my dear child, that is what I am and no more, to my great regret. Oh, the only thing good about me is that I do understand my religion and what it is about. I shall not take the false for the true. I know what is good and what only looks good. I hope not to make any mistake about it and that God, who has given me right thinking, will go on doing so. Past graces make me hope for more to come, and so I live in confidence mingled, nevertheless, with a great deal of fear. But I do criticize you, my dear Comtesse, for calling Corbinelli the *devil's mystic*. Your brother nearly died of laughing and I scolded him as you do. How do you mean, *devil's mystic*? A man who never thinks of anything but destroying his own power, who is constantly in touch with the devil's enemies, who are the Saints of the Church? A man who counts his own miserable body as nought, who suffers poverty like a Christian (you will say like a philosopher), who never ceases celebrating the perfections and existence of God, who never judges his neighbour but always excuses him, who spends his life in charity and the service of others, who never seeks delights and pleasures but is entirely governed by the will of God! And you call that the *devil's mystic*! You can't deny that all that is a true portrait of our friend. Yet there is in that term a vein of humour that makes you laugh at first and could catch the simple-minded. But I am resisting, as you see, and I defend the faithful admirer of Saint Theresa, of my grandmother and the blessed John of the Cross.

A propos of Corbinelli, he wrote me a very nice letter the other day, in which he gave an account of a conversation and a dinner party at M. de Lamoignon's. The actors were the masters of the house, Monsieur de Troyes, Monsieur de Toulon, Père Bourdaloue and his companion,[2] Despréaux and Corbinelli. The conversation turned on the works of the Ancients and Moderns. Despréaux defended the Ancients, with the exception of one Modern who, in his view, surpassed old and new alike. Père Bourdaloue's companion, who fancied himself as an expert and had attached himself to Despréaux and Corbinelli, asked him what this book was that he singled out in his mind. He wouldn't name it. Corbinelli said, 'Monsieur, please do tell me, so that I can read it all night.' Despréaux answered laughingly, 'Ah, Monsieur, you have read it more than once, I am sure.' The Jesuit persisted and, with a supercilious look, a *cotal riso amaro*, urged

2. Jesuits were never allowed out alone.

Despréaux to name this marvellous author. Despréaux said, 'Father, don't press me.' The Father went on pressing. In the end Despréaux seized him by the arm, squeezed it hard and said, 'Father, you insist. Very well, it's Pascal, by God!' 'Pascal,' said the reverend Father, red in the face with amazement, 'Pascal is as good as the false can be.' 'The false! the false!' said Despréaux, 'I'd have you know that he is as true as he is inimitable, he has been translated into three languages.' The reverend Father answered, 'That doesn't make him any truer.' Thereupon Despréaux lost his temper and, shouting like a madman, 'What, Father, will you deny that one of your people has had printed in one of his books that a Christian is not obliged to love God? Will you dare to say that that is not true?' 'Monsieur,' furiously answered the Father, 'we must make a distinction.' 'Distinction,' said Despréaux, 'distinction, for God's sake! Distinction, distinction whether we are obliged to love God!' And taking Corbinelli by the arm he fled to the other end of the room, then running back like a mad thing he would not go near the Father, but went and rejoined the rest of the company, who had stayed in the dining-room. Here ends the story; the curtain falls. Corbinelli promises to tell me the rest, but I am sure you will find this scene as amusing as I did, and so I am writing it down, and I think that if you read it in your lovely voice you will find it rather good.

My dear, I am vexed with you for being anxious about me for a single moment when you don't get my letters; you forget the vagaries of the post. You must get used to them, and if I were ill, which I am not by any means, I would let you have at least a few lines, or my son or somebody would. Anyway you would have news of me, but we haven't got to that yet.

I am told that various duchesses and grand dames were furious at Versailles because they were not at the Twelfth Night supper – now that really was an affliction! You know the rest of the news as well as I do. I have sent Bigorre's letter to Québriac, who sends you many thanks, he is very satisfied with your *Court of Love*. I think Pauline is very clever to be able to play chess; if she knew how far that game is above my head I should fear her scorn.

Oh yes, I do remember and I shall never forget that journey. Alas, is it possible that is twenty-one years ago? I just don't understand it. It seems like last year to me, but I can guess from the brevity of that length of time to me what the years to come will seem like.

314

From Charles de Sévigné

I am very much of your opinion, my lovely little sister, about the *devil's mystic*. I was struck by that way of speaking and wandered round and round the thought, and whatever I said didn't please me. Thank you for teaching me to explain in so few words and so correctly what I had in my mind for so long. But what I admire most in that *mystic* is that his peace of mind in that condition is an effect of his piety; he would scruple to quit that state because it is in the order of Providence and it would be impious in a mere mortal to seek to go against what has been ordained. Don't conclude from this that he never goes to Mass; that would wound the delicacy of his conscience.[3]

Since you have at last allowed Pauline to read the *Metamorphoses*, I advise you to stop worrying about bad books she might be given. Don't all the nice stories appeal to her taste? There are a thousand little books which amuse and also greatly improve the mind. Wouldn't she read with pleasure certain parts of Roman history? Has she read the *History of the Triumvirate*? Are Constantine and Theodosius exhausted? Oh how I pity her keen and active mind if you don't give it something to work on! As she is, like her uncle, coarse-grained enough to be unable to dally with the subtleties of metaphysics, I pity her, but don't expect me to blame her or look down on her; I have my reasons for not doing so. Good-bye, my sweet little sister.

To Coulanges

[Grignan, Thursday 26 July 1691]

So M. de Louvois, the great minister, the eminent man who held such a great position, whose personality, as M. Nicole says, was of such immensity, who was the centre of so many things, M. de Louvois is dead! How much business, how many plans and projects, how many secrets and interests to disentangle, wars begun, intrigues and chess-moves to make and carry through! 'Oh Lord, give me a little time, I do so want to foil the Duke of Savoy, checkmate the Prince of Orange!'

---

3. It would appear from this that Corbinelli was something of a Quietist.

'No, no, you won't have a single moment, not one!' Can one be reasonable about this strange happening? No indeed, one must reflect upon it in private. This is the second minister to die since you have been in Rome. Nothing could be more different than their deaths, but nothing more similar than their fortunes, their attachments and the hundred thousand million chains by which they were both tied to this earth.

And amid these grand matters which must carry one up to God, you find yourself troubled over your religion with regard to what is going on in Rome and in the conclave! My poor cousin, you are making a mistake. I have heard that a man of very great intelligence drew a quite opposite conclusion from what he saw in that great city, and deduced that the Christian religion must be quite holy and miraculous to survive unaided amid so many disorders and profanations. Do as that man did, draw the same conclusions and remember that this same city was formerly stained with the blood of an infinite number of martyrs, that in the first centuries all the intrigues of the conclave ended by choosing from among the priests the one who appeared to have the greatest zeal and the strength to bear martyrdom, that there were thirty-seven Popes who suffered martyrdom one after another, and the certainty of that death did not make them flinch or refuse a position which entailed death – and what a death! You only have to read this History. And some people make out that a religion surviving by a continual miracle both in establishment and duration is a mere figment of men's imagination! Men do not think in this way. Read St Augustine in *The Truth of Religion*, read Abbadie, very different from that great saint, but very worthy to be compared with him when he speaks of the Christian faith (ask the Abbé de Polignac whether he values this book). Gather together all these ideas and don't come to such frivolous conclusions, believe that whatever trickery goes on in the conclave it is always the Holy Spirit which creates the Pope. God makes all; He is master of all. And this is how we ought to think (I have read this in some good book): 'What ill can befall a person who knows that God makes everything, and who loves everything that God makes?' I leave you with that, my dear cousin. Adieu.

To Madame de Guitaut

[Paris, Wednesday 3 June 1693]

I have left you in your silence, Madame, tactfully respecting your good judgement and just knowing your news. You could not break that silence, my dear Madame, at a moment that affected me more deeply. You were well aware of all the worth of Mme de La Fayette, either from your own knowledge or from me or your friends. On that you could not overestimate. She was worthy to be one of your friends, and I was only too happy to be loved by her for a very considerable time. We never had the slightest cloud in our friendship. Long habit had never accustomed me to her worth, and the taste was always keen and new. I did all sorts of things for her simply out of love, without the obligation friendship entails. I was sure also that I was her most tender consolation, and it was the same for forty years; that is an extraordinary time, but it is the foundation of our true relationship. For the past two years her infirmities had been very serious. I always defended her, for people said she was absurd to refuse to go out. She was mortally depressed – how absurd also! Isn't she the most fortunate woman in the world? She admitted that, too, but I said to these people who were so hasty in their judgements, 'Mme de La Fayette was not absurd,' and I stuck to that. Alas, Madame, the poor woman is now all too justified; it needed her death to prove that she was right both to stay at home and to be depressed. She had one kidney quite useless and with a stone in it, and the other *pullulant*;[1] you can hardly stir abroad in that condition. She had two polypuses in her heart and the point of the heart wasted; wasn't that enough to give her those depressions she complained about? Her bowels were hard and distended with wind, and a colic was always giving her trouble. That was the condition of this poor woman who used to say, 'One day they will find out . . .' and they have found it all out. So, Madame, she was right during her lifetime and right after her death, and never was she without that wonderful reason which was her outstanding quality. Her death was caused by the largest of these foreign bodies in her heart, which interrupted the circulation and at the same time paralysed all the nerves, so that she

1. *Pullulant.* Mme de S. means *purulent*.

was unconscious all through the four days of her illness. Mme Perrier, an admirable person, stayed by her day and night with a charity for which I shall love her all my life; she will tell you that all this happened as I have told you, and that for our consolation God bestowed on her a very special grace which marked a real predestination, namely that she had confessed on 21 May with a meticulousness and feeling that could only have come from Him, and she received Our Lord in the same way. So, dear Madame, we look upon this communion, which she normally took at Whitsun, as a mercy of God, who wished to console us for her not being capable of receiving the last rites. I felt on this occasion an inner resource of religion which would have redoubled my grief had I not been upheld by the hope that God has had mercy on her. Dear Madame, I could not help telling you all this. You will excuse me because of the feeling you know I have for you, which has led me to open my heart on a subject so near to it. I should have taken advantage of you still more if you had been here. After that I must change my tone to answer your letter.

I am very sorry that you have found your affairs in the state you say. I am surprised and would never have thought it, and I understand your bursting head over the concentration you have needed to disentangle this muddle. I wish you could find a way of not pushing any further an exhaustion that is more serious than you think. So, my dear Madame, get yourself taken care of and don't make light of what I am saying.

It is true that the natural antipathy of Boucard and d'Hébert is astonishing and has displeased me; it makes me think I am lucky to have leased out my little bit of land.

As for our chapel, with no more beating about the bush I urge you, Madame, to speak about it to M. Tribolet, who is a very nice man, and also, if he were available, to M. Poussy, and tell him from me that I know he is not serving our chapel as he ought to now that the income is greater, *and what I wish he would do*. I could, through him who as curé has the right to concern himself with this affair, manage either to make him do his duty or get our curé to put somebody else there who would do it much better. This little benefice is not worthy of the opinion M. Poussy has of him; hence I think it would not be difficult to persuade him to get rid of it. Just think it over quietly, dear Madame; this business won't give you a headache.

As for those dues I have to collect from Courcelles, it is an unpardonable negligence on Boucard's part, and he has committed others more serious. I don't know how a man of this dilatoriness and indifference to my interests can criticize, as he does, a man who has nothing comparable for which he can be blamed, and I shall write to him about it. I have seen enough of M. de Montal in Paris for him to think he has mentioned this lawsuit to me. Is it devotion to the interests of a person to abuse his confidence in this way? I am going to try to rekindle some feeling in Boucard about all these things, and I shall tell him to confer with M. Tribolet, who has written to me several times and I think very intelligently. If all this comes back to you, you will be kind and charitable enough to give orders.

I thank you a thousand times for your charming letter, which makes up for the time that has passed. The only thing I might wish for is that you should not always write in flourishes as you do; why don't you write like me and as they did in our fathers' time? You don't mention when you will be coming back.

I have just written to Boucard a rigmarole about M. de Montal and these dues owed me by this Mme Druy, which will prevent his suspecting anything, and I have asked him to speak to you about this business and about M. Poussy; it will all come back to you. And I am writing to Hébert to let me know how many Masses he says at Bourbilly, so that he can show that he wasn't the one who dropped me a hint – in fact I am being very subtle. I know that Boucard's wife is not *so exact* as he is, and this annoys me. I am asking them for the money for the grain Hébert sent them to sell.

My daughter sends you many, many humble compliments, and I, dear Madame, am indeed wholly devoted to you.

La M. de Sévigné

I recommend promptness, for July approaches, and the people waiting for my money are very thirsty. Stir up Tribolet, that will hurry up the conclusion.

To Coulanges*

[Grignan, Thursday 29 March 1696]

All things passing, I weep and bewail the death of Blanchefort, such a nice fellow, quite perfection, whom one held up as an example to all our young people. An established reputation, valour recognized and worthy of his name, a temperament admirable for himself (ill-temper is a torment), good for his friends, good for his family; responsive to the love of his mother and grandmother, loving and honouring them, recognizing their worth and enjoying showing them his gratitude and returning all their kindness; good sense and a handsome face, not at all intoxicated with his youth like all the young men who seem to be unconquerably restless – and this fine young man disappears in a moment, like a flower blown away by the wind, with no war, no cause, no infection. My dear cousin, where can suitable words be found to express what one thinks of the grief of those two mothers and to make them realize what we are thinking here? We are not proposing to write to them, but if sometime you find the right moment to mention my daughter and me and Messieurs de Grignan, those are our sentiments about their irreparable loss. Mme de Vins has lost everyone, I admit, but when the heart has already chosen between two sons one has eyes for only one. I can't talk about anything else.

I bow to the sacred and modest burial place of Mme de Guise, whose renunciation of that of kings merits an eternal crown. I think that M. de Saint-Géran is exceedingly fortunate, and so are you, to have his wife to console; say to him on our behalf whatever you think suitable. And for Mme de Miramion, that mother of the Church, it will be a public loss.

Good-bye, my dear cousin. I can't change my tone. You have had your jubilee. The delightful journey to Saint-Martin has followed close on the sackcloth and ashes you mentioned. The delights M. and Mme de Marsan are at present enjoying deserve your seeing them sometimes and putting them into your basket. And I deserve to be in the one in which you put people who love you, but I fear you have no basket for these.

* This is her last letter. She died on 17 April 1696.